# "For the People"

## By: Robert O. Rowland

### A recipe for freedom.

### A Handbook for all true Americans.

Copyright 2000 by Robert O. Rowland

Published By:
Rowland Books Unlimited Inc.
P.O. Box 189
40 S. Walnut St.
Chillicothe, Oh 45601

**This book is dedicated to the members and supporters of the N.R.A, and to all true-blooded Americans.**

# THE TEN COMMANDMENTS

1. I am the Lord thy God, which have brought thee out of the land of Egypt, out of the house of bondage. Thou shalt not have no other Gods before me. Thou shalt not make unto grave image, or any likeness of any thing that is in heaven above, or that is in the earth beneath, or that is in the water under earth; Thou shalt not bow down thyself to them, nor serve them.

2. Thou shalt not take the name of the Lord thy God in vain.

3. Remember the Sabbath day, to keep it holy.

4. Honor thy father and thy mother.

5. Thou shalt not kill.

6. Thou shalt not commit adultery.

7. Thou shalt not steal.

8. Thou shalt not bear false witness against thy neighbor.

9. Thou shalt not covet they neighbor's possessions.

10. Thou shall not covet they neighbor's wife."

# THE BILL OF RIGHTS

## Amendment I

Congress shall make no law respecting an establishment of religion, or prohibiting the free exercise thereof; or abridging the freedom of speech, or of the press; or the right of the people peaceably to assemble, and to petition the government for a redress of grievances.

## Amendment II

A well-regulated Militia, being necessary to the security of a free state, the right of the people to keep and bear Arms, shall not be infringed.

## Amendment III

No soldier shall, in time of peace be quartered in any house, without the Consent of the Owner, nor in time of war, but in a manner prescribed by law.

## Amendment IV

The rights of the people to be secure in their persons, houses, papers, and effects, against unreasonable searches and seizures, shall not be violated, and no warrants shall issue, but upon probable cause, supported by oath or affirmation, and particularly describing the place to be searched, and the persons or things to be seized.

## Amendment V

No person shall be held to answer for a capital, or otherwise infamous crime, unless on a presentment or indictment of a Grand Jury, except in cases arising in the land or naval forces, or in the Militia, when in actual service in time of War or public danger; nor shall any person be subject for the same offense to be twice put in jeopardy of life or limb; nor shall be compelled in any criminal case to be a witness against himself, nor be deprived of life, liberty, or property, without due process of law; nor shall private property be taken for public use, without just compensation.

## Amendment VI

In all criminal prosecutions, the accused shall enjoy the right to a speedy and public trial, by an impartial jury of the State and district wherein the crime shall have been committed, which district shall have been previously ascertained by law, and to be informed of the nature and causes of the accusation; to be confronted with the witnesses against him; to have compulsory process for obtaining witnesses in his favor, and to have the Assistance of Counsel for his defense.

## Amendment VII

In Suits at common law, where the value in controversy shall exceed twenty dollars, the right of trial by jury shall be preserved, and no fact tried by a jury shall be otherwise re-examined in any Court of the United States, than according to the rules of common law.

## Amendment VIII

Excessive bail shall not be required, nor excessive fines imposed, nor cruel and unusual punishments inflicted.

## Amendment IX

The enumeration in the Constitution, of certain rights, shall not be construed to deny or disparage others retained by the people.

## Amendment X

The powers not delegated to the United States by the Constitution, nor prohibited by it to the States, are reserved to the States respectively, or to the people.

Look for the truth contained in these two lists of ten throughout this book. By the time you are done reading Chapter 3, you will understand why I put these in the front of the book.

# Table of Contents

A Note From the Author     12

A Writer's Words     17

Introduction     21

<u>Chapter 1</u>:     **The Proliferation of Big Government**     32

*Big Government: Fact or Fiction*     33

*The Beginnings of Big Government*     40

*Over-Regulation*     43

*Case Studies of Big Government*     47

*Who's Watching Big Government*     53

*A Conflict of Interest*     55

*The Governmental Blame Game*     58

*Bill Clinton and His End to Big Government*     59

*The Future of Big Government*     61

*The Path of Socialism: A journey from freedom*     64

<u>Chapter 2</u>:     **The Abuse of Power: Politicians and Government Out of Control**     76

*Heads Up: An essay by Doug Fiedor*     78

*The Unelected Representatives and the Policy of Protectionism*     85

*The Origins of the DEA*     86

*The Abuses of Big Government*     89

*Governmental Waste*     97

*Perpetuating the System of Misappropriation*     103

*Pork Barrel Projects*     105

**Chapter 3:**    **The Loss of a Principled Society: The Myth of the Separation of Church and State**     108

*A Nation Under God*     109

*The Truth About the Constitution*     112

*Adversarial Neighbors*     119

*The Corruption of Our Leadership*     126

*Bill Clinton: Taking the Cake of Corruption*     131

*Morality and Youth*     139

*Never Too Late*     146

*The Bill of Rights & The Ten Commandments*     147

**Chapter 4:**    **The Deterioration of the Constitution: Case Studies in the Erosion of American Freedom**     158

**Case Study #1: Firearms: The Insurance Policy of Freedom**

*America Guns and Liberty*     162

*A Struggle for the Right to Defend Liberty*     166

*The Credibility of Our Government*      171

*The Abuses of the BATF*      178

*The 2$^{nd}$ Amendment: A National Treasure*      189


**Case Study #2: The EPA and the Destruction of the Right to Own Property**

*Wetlands- The Big Issue*      202

*The Increase in Government*      213

*The Greenhouse Effect*      216

*Eco-Scam and the New World Socialist Order*      219

*Criticism: The Backlash Begins*      240

*Fighting Back: Freedom Lovers*      246

*Un-American Politicians*      250

*A Recipe for Fascism*      272


**Chapter 5:**      **Restoring Freedom and Preserving The Union**      274


*The Road to Fascism*      275

*A Recipe for Freedom:*

     Eradicate Conflict of Interest      280

     Stop Governmental Dependence      286

     End Socialist Tendencies      290

Protect the Constitution                                  295

Solidarity of the People                                  299

The Return to Local Control                               301

Statesman not Politicians                                 307

**Conclusion:**   *The Constitution-*                     310
                  *A Foundation of Freedom*

**Appendix A:**   **Congressional Mailing List**          319

# A Note From the Author

## A Call For Freedom Lovers, Not Fighters

Years ago, after the election of Richard Nixon, I began to realize that our government had become a government **for** the government and **by** the government. I saw that one vote could not reverse these trends, but by calling attention to the problems, maybe a solution could be found. I decided to serve my fellow Americans with a sort of summons . . . to show them where the problems lie, shake off our political apathy, and try to work together to save the government of our forefathers.

The realization of this dream, that is, the manuscript you hold in your hand, is a symbol of the many things that I believe in. For years I had tried to put my deep love for freedom into words, but I lacked the ability to do so. I could not find the words to sum up the true feeling of freedom in its purest form.

Of course, I knew the standard catch phrases, or the patriotic words and songs that we were all taught in our youth. Sadly enough, none of these could ever properly explain my deep-rooted feelings for the right of a man to own a piece of land and make a living off of it.

It seemed like history gave the best stories to describe freedom. Stories about pioneers finding a track of land and working it to produce the fruits of life. America, in my mind was the vision of a place where a man could find a home. It was a place where you could set your own path, your own rules, and no one could tell you how to worship, what to own, or where to live.

Any words I came up with to define this freedom lacked the strength to convey to a reader the utmost respect and admiration I held for those who secured my freedom, and yours. And no words could describe my distaste I have for the corruption that has led to the widespread distrust we have for our own government.

This is why the realization of this book is both a triumph and a tragedy. Yes, I have finally found the words to express my feelings about freedom. However, it comes in a time when I see that freedom fading fast.

I realized, years ago, that this country began down a path that was taking us in the wrong direction. I began to see the freedoms won in the past, lost in the blink of the eye. Sadly, I was finally able to put into words a description of freedom, only after it was slowly being eroded away.

This book is my amends for not telling people how precious freedom was, before now. I found that I had to write this book, finish this book and publish this book in time, so that we may one day turn back the tide of governmental regulation and intrusion into our freedom. I firmly believe that the smaller the government, the more freedom there is. Day by day I have witnessed all of the citizens of the United States, slowly hand away our autonomy to the government, believing that they will help ensure our freedom into the future. Little does everyone know, that each new aspect of our lives that comes under the control of government, strikes a blow at the autonomy that is necessary for freedom to flourish.

Sadly enough, we are surrounded today in the media with stories of fanatics, arming themselves to the teeth and destroying federal buildings. Although I in some ways sympathize with those who have become so terrified of government intrusion that they turn to isolationism and violence, I do not like the fact that anyone who speaks out against the expansion of government is typified as a fanatic.

Most of the time when we hear individuals that speak out against our current government, we hear only the loudest, and most radical. Common, everyday citizens who express concerns do not get the same media attention. After all, how many of us would want to watch a news program that talked to Bob and Jane about politics, as opposed to a special edition, up-front interview of Lunatic Larry and his band of armed rebels who plan on blowing up every building in the city of Chicago if the ATF is not disbanded today.

This is a very disappointing phenomenon. There is a trend slowly developing in America, where any person who speaks strongly against governmental practices is viewed in the same category of these aforementioned zealots. I am not going to deny that individuals do exist who take some of the same feelings that I personally have too far, but this should not mean that any person who speaks out strongly against the government is someone who is out to hurt other people.

Take for example a great freedom fighter of our time, Milton Friedman. You probably have not heard of him, but those who follow the cause of freedom may have seen some of his work from time to time. Mr. Friedman is not a militia clan leader who dresses up in fatigues and drills in preparation for a battle against Black Army CIA Helicopters. In fact, he is a Nobel Prize winning economist who has begun a train of thought that has evolved into a group of followers who are called "The Friedmans". As reported by William H. Peterson, a scholar with the Heritage Foundation in Washington, this group is comprised of:

> "... anti-statists... [whose] guiding values are outlined in their memoirs: "the promotion of human freedom, opposition to rent control and general wage and price controls, support for educational choice, privatizing radio and television channels, an all-volunteer army, limitation of government spending, legalization of all drugs, privatizing Social Security, free trade and the de-regulation of industry and private life to the fullest extent possible."

This philosophy is one based on a singular notion, that freedom is superior to all other things. Now, many of us may not agree with all of these views, I certainly take issue with some of the aforementioned. But, the truth of the matter is that men like Mr. Friedman are indeed out there. Men and women whose goal is to question the government on their shortcomings. Individuals who peer through the glass surrounding our constitution and question the size of the federal government as it currently is. Those who stand up for freedom, but get back page news articles written about them. The media chooses to cover violence, gore, and sensationalistic viewpoints, rather than the individuals who are fighting for all of our rights.

I wish we could see more about groups like the Friedmans (even the name denotes a connection to freedom). They try to remind people that for every governmental action to control one thing, there are negative, or possibly unwanted side effects. Therefore, the only good way to ensure that governmental action does not foul everything up is to severely limit it. Let me explain.

A very popular trend in recent modern thinking, is a concept called "unintended consequences". Simply put, this concept refers to the fact that for every action, there are phenomena that occur which were never planned for. Let's look at an example in regards to government. The government currently subsidizes farming in order to limit the amount of food production and to be sure that the most suitable land for certain crops is utilized to its fullest potential. These are not bad ideas, but by utilizing the government, instead of trusting the experts, i.e. farmers, the following unintended consequences have developed.

First of all, we have farmers in the U.S. being paid not to farm. Many of these individuals are not allowed to farm their own land, or agree not to farm it, so the government pays them to do nothing. Second, food prices will rise because the supply is controlled. Third, we, each year, have tons of foodstuffs rotting away because the government under-subsidized, or over-subsidized certain markets. This occurs while people are starving in other countries. Finally, and most importantly, there are government officials, members of the un-elected representation, who march around and tell what each and everyone one of us can do with our land. There are some places where the regulations are such that they can tell you whether or not you can grow a certain crop on your land. In my opinion, this is the destruction of our right to own personal property, and thus, a fundamental violation of the Constitution.

These are important facts to point out. Very few Americans even know about the concept of unintended consequences and its association with governmental intrusion. Every time the government takes some action, instead of trusting the people, there are limitations placed on our freedom. Most of us would agree that some of those are necessary, for example, laws about speeding, but there has to be an end to the limitless numbers of laws and regulations that govern our existence. Most of us do not even know how many laws govern our lives, and everyone of us are most likely in violation of some regulation or law right now. How can this be? The problem is not us, it is the government.

Yet, it is not just the government, it is the simple fact that individuals like Milton Friedman are not placed on the 6 o'clock news to talk to us about freedom. One does not have to be a raving lunatic with his finger on a trigger to love freedom and the Constitution. The true freedom fighters, ones who love this country, the people, and respect the rights of others, need to be heard. To speak out against the government does not make one un-American, in fact, it is a defining characteristic of a true American.

That is the exact reason why I wrote this book. I only wish I had not waited so long. It is true that we never know how great we have it until the splendor of the past is washed away and we stand under the boot of tyranny wishing we had possessed the foresight to see such a negative conclusion.

I am not forecasting doom, I am warning all Americans to be cautious of those who seek to only further their own agendas. Government runs on our tax dollars, therefore they should have to prove everyday that they are needed. A system that is self-perpetuating can never be trusted to give accurate reports on its own efficacy. Therefore, it is no surprise that those in the government want men and women like me to be villainized in the media and made to look like ranting and raving lunatics.

This is why this book is a call for freedom lovers, not fighters. We live in a republic, where democratic principles are endorsed. We are the people, and together we can insure that our government remains one that is indeed, "Of the people, by the people and **FOR THE PEOPLE**.

# A Writer's Words

When I was a young boy, I was always told that everyone has opinions, but some people should just keep their mouths shut. As I got older and went on through college and into a career I began to see the logic of this argument. I mean, there had to be over a million people in this country who seemed to not have a clue what words were coming out of their mouth. The ignorance that surrounded me in college and the workplace was astonishing and I began to struggle with my unwavering love for freedom of speech. It was true that while in college I gained a tremendous respect for the Constitution and I celebrated the first amendment as one of the most important. However, it began to make more logical sense to myself to just silence many people because their opinions were so moronic, that I found them unworthy of my time. Furthermore, I lost faith in the American people to filter out the rubbish and listen to those who spoke truth, rather than lies.

Many opinions that I opposed were not just simply annoying, they were dangerous to the status quo. Mind you, I felt that the United States was indeed a free nation and that those who threatened that freedom (the status quo) were a threat. Many opinions foster rampant racism, sexism and other forms of discrimination that end up hurting those around us. I firmly believed that if one citizen of this country lost their freedom to discriminatory practices, then we all lost a little bit of our freedom. I had learned that philosophies such as Nazism started with little more than an opinion and a collection of ideas. The end result was fascism and the annihilation of entire generations.

The childhood cry of "sticks and stones may break my bones but words will never hurt me" may help rationalize schoolyard tomfoolery, but it does not hold true in the realm of world politics. Words start wars, enact oppressive policies and lull the masses into idleness.

Learning all of the woes and worries that accompanied a society filled up with free speech compelled me to reach this logical conclusion: Freedom of speech should be limited. I started to believe that only those who had demonstrated responsibility should be able to speak out on certain topics, or be given the avenue to do so. I felt that those with ardently racist ideas, or ideologies that called for the demise of millions of people, should just shut-up or be forced to take a seat and let those who fully understand government run the show. Of course, I never once believed that my opinion should be subject to this judgment; after all, I was right.

Over the years though, I began to gain wisdom, rather than logic and knowledge, and it is now that I realize the importance of free speech. Although I still feel that the majority of people out there would be better served with a wired jaw rather than a megaphone. However, I soon realized that freedom was a high priced commodity and that many times we allow logic to overpower wisdom. With wisdom we learn the value of free speech, although many times the logic of the dialog produced escapes our understanding.

In opposition to tyranny, many people of the past have spoken out on issues that others, of the time, would scoff at. Most of the time, history proved them wrong, but there are the celebrated few who became the trailblazers of the future. Some of these trailblazers we refer to as Founding Fathers.

I am concerned about a world in which a person refrains from speaking their mind out of fear of governmental or social reprisal. Instead, I must live with the inevitable trade off that freedom brings: A world full of multiple ideologies, some of which are accepted and endorsed despite their obvious flaws.

Freedom of speech is indeed the foundation upon which all other freedom is built. Maybe that is why our Founding Fathers, in their wisdom, placed it on the top of the list. Sometimes I like to think that as the Bill of Rights was being written, everyone immediately cried out for the freedom of speech, and it was placed on the top of the chalkboard where the foundations of our society began as an experiment.

As I grow in wisdom and knowledge, I have been faced with accepting the fact that open discussion of opinions and facts is far healthier than a subversive underground opposition to conventional wisdom.

Having to listen to the seemingly moronic opinions of others is not the only price of freedom. High crime rates, teenage pregnancy and poverty are all unintended consequences of freedom. In a society where the rights of the accused are paramount to the interests of government, crime is an inevitable conclusion. With age, I learned that abhorrent as it is, crime is a necessity in a free society. For it is true that the more fearful we become of the criminal elements, the more we put our trust in government and police control. There has never been a society that existed with high levels of freedom and high levels of governmental control and police powers.

With freedom, comes choice, and with choice comes poverty. I am the first to admit that there are numerous factors that lead to poverty, however it is undeniable that a large portion of those who are poor (bearing children who are, of course, unable to be held accountable for the actions of their parents) are that way because they have chosen a life of idleness. As much as it turns my stomach to see a lazy individual sit back and allow their children to starve while they smoke a crack rock in the baby's room, I have to accept the fact that it will happen somewhere in our society. This is the price of freedom.

Maybe it is time that we all begin to accept the price of freedom. Maybe we should all ante up, and chip in with our individual wisdom and logic and realize that freedom is the greatest gift our Founding Fathers bestowed upon us.

The price of freedom is eternal vigilance. We must watch closely those who seek power and wield it to their advantage. We must always keep a clear eye on those who try to lie and manipulate their way into power. We must keep watch for those who get lost in a sea of bureaucracy and use the shield of their office to shy away from accountability. It is not necessary in this society to accomplish this important task with weapons or riots. Rather, we must wield the sword of freedom and democracy and exercise the rights that others have fought to preserve. Our vigilance must be resident at the voting booths, the polling centers and in the pens of the people who can write, call and visit their governmental representative. We must never let them forget that they are our representatives.

A teacher of mine once asked me, "Do you know who started the rumor: 'You can't beat city hall?'" His reply to my shrugging shoulders was "City Hall". This statement applies to all governmental leaders and representatives. There is no doubt that the pope himself started the notion of papal infallibility; or that the kings of the past created the notion of "chosen by the gods". Those in power have always been willing to sell out the masses to preserve their piece of the proverbial pie. No one is immune to this temptation, although some do reject it.

Thus, we must remain vigilant at our posts as citizens of this great nation.

When I was asked to assist in the writing of this book I was presented with the ideas of one man, many of them I did not agree with. However, it was his desire to preserve freedom that was so in line with the beliefs that I had begun to realize. The ideas and motivations that led Bob Rowland on a crusade to speak his mind represented a dedication to the notion of vigilance that few of us are willing to take part in.

The ideas that shaped this book came from a man whose eagle eye was staring in the face of every faction of government, peacefully reminding them that he was still there. His eye was the eye of freedom looking into the souls of our leaders, and asking the question of whether or not they will succumb to the temptation of tyranny. Whether or not I agreed with all, some or none of his beliefs, I had to admit one thing: this man volunteered to pick up the slack for the rest of us, and make sure that he watched others to ensure that freedom would be there for my children and yours.

Therefore, say what you will. Call it gibberish, call it rambling, call it tripe, call it visionary, call it whatever you wish. I call it the symbol of eternal vigilance that protects freedom, makes tyrannical leaders quiver where they stand and guarantees the hopes and dreams of tomorrow.

B.W.

# INTRODUCTION

"It is rather for us to be here dedicated to the great task remaining before us- that from these honored dead we take increased devotion to that cause for which they gave the last full measure of devotion- that we here highly resolve that these dead shall not have died in vain- that this nation under god shall have a new birth of freedom and that government of the people, by the people, for the people, shall not perish from the earth."

These words sum up America, and what it stands for. The blood that has been shed by our forefathers to insure our liberty forms a river of hope for future generations that they may not have to lose their lives in the preservation of liberty. It is for this reason that we must consider exactly what the words above represent. Most importantly, we must ask ourselves, "Is our government today one that is of the people, by the people, and for the people?"

Those who comprise our government are definitely citizens of our country, and therefore the first part of the above question may be considered answered. We are a government comprised "of the people". The next two parts of the question are not as clear. First of all, we must question whether or not our government is created "by the people". It is arguable that although we do not live in a pure democracy, elected officials are still derived from publicly held elections which espouse the philosophy of one citizen, one vote. Yet, elected officials actually comprise only a very small percentage of the total number of government workers. Most of our government is comprised of appointed and hired individuals who are part of a vast bureaucratic network that runs most of the executive functions of our political system. Is this truly what our forefathers had in mind when they created this country? Is this what Abraham Lincoln imagined as he looked over the graves and battlefields of Gettysburg where over 20,000 men had fallen to preserve our great nation? Do we, as citizens of the United States truly want a government that has become so large, and out of control, that there is not one single person, or even a small group of individuals, that know how the entire system works?

The fact is, the United States no longer has a government that is elected by the people. The few individuals that we do elect have very little impact upon the daily operations of our country. This task is left in the hands of bureaucratic agents who only see the needs of a nation through the eyes of policies and procedures. Most of us, in our lifetime, will be remarkably effected by government, yet never once have a single governmental action directly imposed upon us by an individual who we approved of. This is not a government of the people.

There are many examples of how this lack of a government of the people has plagued our country for too long. A few cases will be outlined in this book, including how certain branches of the government whose employees, whom I call the Unelected Representatives of America, work solely to perpetuate their own particular agencies existence without ever accomplishing one major task to fulfill the true need of the people. They simply create an artificial economy that sucks up our tax dollars and redistributes them to individuals who do nothing but hinder our individual freedom.

These ideas relate directly to the last point made by Abraham Lincoln in the Gettysburg Address. How can we possibly have a government 'for the people' when the individuals in charge of its operation do not have the citizens best interests in mind? I believe that our current government, which has become bloated with taxpayer money, has grown to such a size that it has begun to infringe itself upon our personal liberties.

Personal liberty is one of the most important principles upon which our country was founded.

> "We hold these truths to be self-evident, that all Men are created equal, that they are endowed by their creator with certain unalienable rights, that among these are Life, Liberty, and the Pursuit of Happiness."

When the United States was founded, it represented one of the greatest political experiments in the history of the world. Our Founding Fathers incorporated the political philosophies of countless academics, and created a system of government that guaranteed each citizen with protections against the intrusion of the state. In our Declaration of Independence to the King of England, the symbol of the tyrannical state that oppressed us, we stated emphatically that Life and Liberty were what made men truly free. Furthermore, by fighting the Revolutionary War, and many wars after, we further stated that life in the absence of liberty, was meaningless.

Millions of our young men and women have laid down their lives throughout history to protect our liberty, and thus our lives and our right to the pursuit of happiness. Now, as our freedoms are slowly being eroded away in a slippery slope towards government oppression, Americans sit idly by and the words of patriots fall upon deaf ears. From the graves of our forefathers we can hear the songs of liberty, if we could just listen through the bustle of a governmental system that became too complex.

Our government has become a self-perpetuating system, which is not right. Government is there to preserve the rights of the people. Therefore, it should only intrude itself upon our lives when a clear and present danger threatens the livelihood of individual citizens or the state. Even then, the government should move to solve a problem and then get out of the way, instead of lingering around for generations and making matters worse.

If we only would have followed the plans of our forefathers, this country could have been as close to a utopian society as ever possible. No society will ever be perfect, but the fact remains that the smaller a government is, the closer it is to perfection.

American citizens have become apathetic in the face of today's governmental titan. Election days, a chance for Americans to exercise one of the most vital sources of liberty, have become an embarrassment to us all. The number of voters who turn out for national elections represents only a small percentage of the total voting population. Additionally, the percentage of voters who turn out for local elections is laughable. Amazingly enough though, every citizen claims the right to complain about the negative effects government has on our lives.

This phenomenon is not really surprising when you think about it. As stated before, just how many day-to-day interactions do we have with our elected officials? How many of us have read the paper and sighed at just how little Congress accomplishes in a year, with all the vacations, junkets, political back-scratching, log-rolling and lobbying going on. The apathy of American voters stems directly from the imposing size of the national government and the fact that hundreds of agencies are comprised of non-elected officials.

We watch the nightly news and observe countries newly freed from the bonds of a dictatorial ruler flooding to the polls in order to get a taste of democracy. They are eager to voice their opinions, and exercise their newfound freedoms. Americans squander this precious freedom as we are quick to forget the great sacrifices that must be made to obtain liberty. Freedom is being taken for granted.

One would be hard-pressed to find an American who does not have an opinion regarding government today. Most of these opinions would be critical in nature. Everyone complains about high taxes, an over-abundance of laws, and elected officials that care nothing about the needs of the people. What people do not realize is that there is no one else to blame but ourselves. It is our apathy that has led us to stand by calmly and witness the erosion of liberty, as the rights guaranteed by the Constitution are slowly taken away one by one. Together we have turned the living document created by our forefathers into nothing more than an idealistic essay printed on a piece of parchment. If there is not an open opposition to the status quo, our representatives have no reason to push for change. They realize that they can get away with doing nothing, because the American people will do little about it. This is indeed a tragedy.

These years of voter neglect have led to a bloated government with hundreds upon thousands of non-essential programs that pop up whenever a politician needs a sound bite to make it look like he or she is accomplishing something. These new programs disperse resources to already existing government agencies, or create new ones, filled with people whose primary motivation is to keep their job. Therefore, the individuals in charge of these agencies develop and implement programs in such a way that they never truly solve any of the problems that plague our country. For, if the problem were solved, their jobs would no longer be necessary. The Unelected Representatives that staff these agencies attempt to make their jobs seem like the most important jobs around. Therefore, they use their vast resources, paid for by American tax dollars, to lobby Congress and pass new laws that give their particular office more power and influence over the disbursement of government funds. Slowly, these agencies have become the entire government, utilizing Congress as a pawn in a global game of chess played in such a way that none of the opposing side's pieces are seized. This power, money, and job security has been extended to these agencies without one single vote from the American people.

When this point is pondered, a very frightening realization is brought to mind. We live in a pseudo-dictatorship. For, when you are ruled by people who have immense power over you, without your consent, in the absence of a direct democratic process to control their behavior, a dictatorship exists.

Many of us can identify at least one branch of the government that we feel exercises their power in an improper manner. The Environmental Protection Agency (EPA) is a perfect example of a governmental agency that solves few problems and creates many. Later in this book, I will explain how the EPA has become one of the major dismantling forces of American Liberty and how it is an agency that has stuck a wedge into the American way of life, severing our ties to the very principles our country was founded upon. Yet, even if you agreed with me, we would be hard-pressed to find a way to stop the EPA by ourselves. Although our tax dollars pay their salaries, and they truly work for us, we could never enter a local EPA office and have any control over what they would do. Sure, we could write our congressperson, but do they really have control over the EPA? Does the president concern himself about the day-to-day operations of the EPA? Who is truly running the show here? There is simply a long line of bureaucratic leaders who I guarantee, if asked to do something about a problem, would send the request on down the line, stating that they can do nothing about it. We are in a dictatorship, with no identifiable source of control, which simply put, says that our government has become so complex, that it no longer serves the people.

Now, there are some government organizations that are very essential. Some form of government is vital to the orderly operation of our society. This is best exemplified by the Highway Department, and federal funds granted to the various states to keep up our national highways and roads. Good infrastructure is vital to the maintenance of a strong economy, which benefits all Americans. These are the agencies that should receive our monies. In no way do I advocate the elimination of all government, but there is no need to continually pump our hard earned money into agencies that actually work to limit our freedoms.

We must awaken from our collective political slumber and realize that public affairs are directly correlated with our personal interests. Americans, lulled into apathy by a luxurious culture and media generated consciousness, have sat idly by as the liberties guaranteed to us by the Constitution have slowly been whittled away. It is strange that in a time when the aforementioned incompetence of government is becoming more apparent, we all choose to take no action. The voices of opposition are few and far between. Furthermore, the voices that we see in the media are usually those of a radical few who preach the destruction of the government through violent opposition. These radical voices paint a demonic picture of any person who chooses to oppose government expansion. Everyday citizens are afraid of being cast into this classification of people if they speak out about the gross injustices that plague our society. It has become necessary for reasonable, tax paying, and freedom loving citizens to come forward and stand up for the same principles many men and women have died for in the past.

Despite the obvious failures pointed out before, in this book I do not advocate allowing America to slip into anarchy, where no government exists. Rather, we as a whole should work to reduce the size of our government and regulate its power so that it becomes a protector of individual liberty rather than an aggressive force that tears at the ties that bind us.

There is no easy answer to this dilemma, but the first step is the gathering of information and the organizing of support. Americans must become vocal, and express their distaste with the current government system in the public sphere. No longer is it acceptable to only voice our dissatisfaction over beers in a bar, or at the dinner table. As more people begin to speak out, silent members of our society who also oppose the destruction of liberty will begin to see that it is not only the radical individuals who are calling for a change.

After all of the negative changes that have occurred, we must resolve ourselves to build the country that our forefathers set out to create. This will not be an easy task. This is because the very reason why we must make the change, an enormous, over-powering juggernaut of a government, is the same reason why it will be difficult. The most important thing we must do is call for our public officials to actually read the Constitution and abide by it as strictly as possible. The Constitution was written in very vague terms so as to make it a "living document" that could always be applied to the new changes in human society. But, when it comes to the guarantees of liberty, as designated in the Bill of Rights, few can call the wording of these rights vague. It is written that, "Congress shall pass NO LAW abridging the freedom of speech". This does not mean some laws, or a few laws, or even one law. There is no other way to interpret this amendment. The guarantees of religion, speech, firearm ownership, due process and protection from governmental intrusion are absolute and public officials must be forced to adhere to them. The citizens of the United States, whose tax dollars have paid the salaries of those who have slowly dismantled our liberties, should compel those in power to use those very same resources to restore our rights. There must be an end to warrantless searches, no-knock rules, gun regulations, governmental intrusion in religious practices and the censorship of free expression.

Governmental regulatory agencies should all be audited closely, utilizing strict guidelines to ensure that U.S. tax dollars are being spent properly. Any agency whose existence or actions do not benefit the greater majority of citizens should be eliminated outright. Future government spending to all agencies should be more closely monitored to ensure that money is not filtered into meaningless administrations that do nothing more than create an artificial economy. Finally, any agency that is deemed necessary by this audit, should be reviewed often, by an impartial panel of citizens, to be sure that: a) there is still an actual problem in existence that necessitates the existence of the particular agency, and b) that the current operating procedures of that agency are designed in the best possible way to alleviate the problems they were created to solve. Once the problem has been solved, the agencies are no longer necessary, and should be dismantled, or vastly reduced to nothing more than skeleton staffs that can make sure the problem does not re-surface.

Government has become self-perpetuating, which it should never be. Each employee in a government office strives to make it look like his or her job, and the agency they work for, is the most vital for societal functioning. This type of mentality breeds wasteful spending and places people in power that are only motivated by self-interest. I am sure if the employees of the Department of Agriculture were polled, very few of them would actually know what the purpose of the Department of Agriculture is. Granted, they would be able to tell you about their particular job, department, or the project they are currently working on, but not even the Director probably knows why the entire Department exists in the first place.

I have no doubt that many of the original executive departments of the federal government were created to solve certain problems. My concern arises when after those problems were solved the agencies were not dismantled. In fact, as time went on, these agencies, in an attempt to save their jobs and creditability, had to find new ways to justify their existence.

Any of you who have worked in government around budget time know the drill. There are times when governmental agencies have to find ways to spend (waste) money. The reason being, if they don't use that money, they will not have it appropriated to them the next year. We cannot trust these unelected representatives in our government to make decisions that benefit us all. They will continue to find ways to perpetuate the influence and longevity of their job in an attempt to maintain employment.

These are just some of the issues that I will address in this book. I believe that the federal government has expanded way beyond its intended zone of containment as set forth by our Founding Fathers. I also believe that we are headed down the path of socialism that will inevitably lead to a totalitarian government and an annihilation of the Constitution. Discussion on this issue will be contained in chapter one of this book.

In chapter two, I will explain how the government has abused its power. I will discuss how the government has overtaken our school system, thrown out God, and forced parents to send their children to learn curriculum they do not personally approve of. I will show how the government, in the past and currently, has overstepped its boundaries and enacted laws that have abridged the rights guaranteed to us by the Constitution. Most notably among these are drug laws, that have led to forfeiture rulings that restrict the freedom of property, and the modern tobacco debate which is leading to the destruction of many farmer's way of life. This chapter will also delve into the abuses of the unelected representatives in our government, that is, the leaders and employees of governmental regulatory agencies whose self-perpetuating practices have led to the erosion of freedom and the loss of citizen control in government.

In chapter three, I will examine the loss of principles in our society. Our politicians, the elected leaders, have become symbols of low morality. I ask the question, why have our leaders begun to represent the most negative sides of our society? Most notably, we have a president, Bill Clinton, who routinely lies to the people, involves us in foreign wars with no discernible gain and enacts policies and rallies public support for measures that serve to weaken the constitutional freedoms guaranteed in the Constitution. Furthermore, we have removed God and the moral lifestyle his word calls for from the public sphere. Misguided, atheistic people have misinterpreted the Constitution. Because of this, our society has lost its way on the path of morality and the only way we can find our way back is by following the time tested rules of God.

Chapter four, possibly the most important, analyzes how big government has gotten out of control in two pivotally important constitutional issues: gun ownership and property ownership. I will prove throughout this book that fascism begins when you take away guns and then take away property rights. In this chapter, I will analyze case studies of how the EPA, one of the most detrimental groups of unelected representatives, have used lies and falsehoods to erode property rights throughout our country. In addition, the EPA's beliefs, heavily favored by Bill Clinton and his lead minion Al Gore, have begun to expand to the rest of the world. The cry of "One World Order" frightens me when it contains subversive governmental activities that encourage the degradation of property rights. Next, in this chapter, I will discuss how assaults against the $2^{nd}$ amendment threaten the insurance policy of freedom our founding fathers placed second on the list of most important rights. Each step taken to limit the freedom of decent, law-abiding Americans to own weapons and be part of a non-governmental well-regulated militia, is a step towards Totalitarianism either in the form of fascism or communism.

Chapter five delves into some of my ideas on how we as a society can get back to a micro-level form of governmental control. Despite claims of the end of big government, our federal government continues to increase in size and complexity each year. It has therefore become necessary to take some action to reduce that government and the unelected representation that walk the halls of Washington bureaucracies. I want to instill the reader with three major virtues that I think must be emphasized if we intend to turn this country off the path of self-destruction it is currently heading on. These virtues are:

1. A return to the principles of God

2. The return of personal responsibility and self-reliance

3. The protection of "Life, Liberty and the Pursuit of Happiness" that includes protecting property rights as well as personal freedoms.

I hope you will enjoy this book and take it to heart, that coming in the next few years we, as citizens of this great nation, have some important decisions to make. Do we follow Bill Clinton and Al Gore's bridge to the 21$^{st}$ Century, that apparently intends to bridge our rights; or will we endorse a future of freedom and call for the end to big government and reinforce the principles upon which this country was originally founded?

# CHAPTER 1

## The Proliferation of Big Government:

## The First Step on the Path of Socialism

# Big Government: Fact or Fiction

I guess the first step in convincing you of the crisis in America is by proving that the government is indeed getting too big for its britches. Well, this is not a very difficult task at all. Simply look around the room you are currently in. Almost everything around you has some sort of government regulation associated with its existence. Everything you purchase, you have paid tax on; and furthermore, every cent you earn, unless you are committing a crime, has to be reported to the federal government.

Be cautious not to misunderstand my motivations for writing this book. I am not calling for the overthrow of our government, nor am I saying that capitalism and democracy don't work. In reality, I am saying that we are moving away from capitalism and democracy. The government in one-way or another employs 1 out of every 7 people. All of our lives have become intertwined with a large federal system. This was surely not the intention of our founding fathers.

Few of us realize just how large the federal government is, so let me shed some light on the subject. On July 9, 1996 (approximately 3 years before I wrote this book) the U.S. House of Representatives met to discuss the cost of government. It was noted that the total cost of government is $3,380,000,000,000 each and every year. That's almost 3.5 trillion dollars! On the average, it costs each individual citizen $13,520 dollars to keep our federal government functioning. Of those 3.4 trillion dollars, 730 billion dollars are spent in Federal Regulatory costs. In other words, almost 25% of the money spent by big government is utilized to create new regulations that tell you how to live. That's over $3,000 a year per person in this country. I ask the question, how can you possibly expect to fight "city hall" when they are annually spending approximately $3,000 dollars to regulate your personal life each year, at the federal level alone?

The truly frightening fact is that our government continues to grow. I believe, the 90's have, for the most part, been a great decade. The United States economy has experienced sustained growth throughout the decade. In addition, all I heard about in the media was a downsizing of our armed forces. The world is relatively peaceful, except for the wars that Bill Clinton involves us in to take our attention off his extra-marital affairs. So, I ask you, if everything is going so well, why does our government continue to get bigger and more expensive?

In 1989, the total cost of government as a percent of the Net National Product was 48.2%. In 1996, that percentage had increased to 50.4%. Therefore, over half of the money that comes into the United States is used to run the federal government. That is money not feeding our children, putting clothes on their back, educating them and preparing them for college. This is your money, but I am sure very few of us realize where any of this money goes. In Chapter 2, I will show where a lot of this money goes, out the window and into the pockets of those who do not need it.

At a Congressional hearing in 1996 it was read into record that:

"Whereas the cost of Government in general and excessive regulations in particular have placed a tremendous drain on the economy in recent years by reducing worker productivity, increasing prices to consumers, and increasing unemployment; Whereas if the average American worker were to spend all of his or her gross earning on nothing else besides meeting his or her share of the total cost of Government for the current year, that total cost would not be met until July 3$^{rd}$ (of each fiscal year)"

The implications of this statement are frightening. It means that you and I, on the average, work over 6 months of the year just to pay for the operation of the federal government. I really do not believe this is what our founding fathers intended when they created a Union of States with a weak centralized government and strong state rights.

In a time when corporations are streamlining operations and cutting the fat, the federal government continues on its path of societal self-destruction. This big government has expanded itself such to the point that Americans have become reliant on the federal government for jobs, subsidies and entitlements. Are we going to end up like other Socialist countries that have unemployment rates in the 20% range and individuals who milk their lives off the hard work of others?

Already, federal income tax receipts from individual taxes have increased more than thirteen times the number they were in 1960. The federal government has become a stifling juggernaut that harms the small businesses throughout the United States. I believe that America was founded on the notion that any man could start his own business and make his own way. Regrettably, that goal is hindered by the fact that there is a 400 billion dollar a year burden on businesses in this country from government over-regulation.

The federal government should only be providing essential services, yet it continues to grow with the years. In 1985, there were 1,013 federal programs, in 1996 there were 11,390. Each time a new program is developed, a new organization must be created, or expanded to regulate and control that program. In 1996 there were 53 federal regulatory and executive agencies. I personally don't know any single American who could name all of them, or explain why they are necessary. Despite that fact, they continue to multiply like rabbits and spread like a plague across this free nation.

This negative reality is compounded by the fact that the government is extremely inefficient and wasteful. Supposedly, the federal government serves as the watchdog of this country's industries and services, but who is in charge of over-seeing the problems with government? Sure, there are Oversight Committees in the Senate, but the true watchdog of the government is the American people. Regrettably, however, the American people do not understand the complex system that has become our federal government (how could anyone) and therefore have become disenfranchised, allowing federal bureaucrats to waste our hard earned money.

This situation has led to tremendous waste. For example, it is stated in government records that:

> "It is estimated that about 10 percent of every health care dollar in this country is lost due to fraud and abuse. Using that assumption, it is estimated that combined total losses for Medicare and Medicaid due to fraud amount to approximately $2.6 billion, or $89 million dollars each day."

In my opinion, this is intolerable. If you were a CEO of a major corporation and your business manager was losing 89 million dollars a day, would you not fire that individual? Most of us would take action immediately to stop this. It is true that the government tries to stop this type of fraud but they attempt to do it the wrong way. Inevitably, legislators enact more regulations, increase the amount of paperwork, thereby increasing the number of bureaucrats needed to handle the situation. Finally, it ends up that the government has just grown bigger and the fraud and abuse have continued on. The point being, government is not the answer, yet many politicians in Washington today simply believe that more bureaucracy, increased government spending, and stricter regulations will lead to a more secure, better America. They are wrong.

Bless the Republicans for making some attempts to reduce government, but even they are caught up in a system of pork-barrel projects and a government so large that no one can chip away to the core of the corruption and over-extension. I firmly believe the Republicans could have made more headway if they wouldn't have had Bill "Big Government" Clinton in office, along with his sidekick Al Gore. For example, the Republicans pushed the line item veto through Congress in order to allow the president to trim some of the fat off of bills in order to reduce government spending. Bill only used them to advance his own political agenda of socializing this country and inevitably the line item veto power had to be removed.

The Republicans throughout the 90's have attempted to cut the spending all around. However, the Democrats have consistently stopped any cuts that even resemble Human

Services. Even when Republican members of Congress were attempting to call for reductions in big government, this was the response from Representative Moran (D):

> "The difference in our two parties has been in our priorities. We have attempted to protect spending on important areas such as education, health care and the environment, while others have pursued spending cuts without considering their human costs. Had we agreed to carefully consider every bill that spends money, we probably would not be considering this resolution today, because it is a waste of taxpayer dollars. The printing of this resolution and the printing of this debate in the Congressional Record is a waste of spending."

I could not believe what I had just read when I first saw this statement. First of all, Republicans were calling for cuts in the federal government across the board. They believe, like myself, that the money saved in cutting down the federal government would be better used in the hands of the individual taxpayers and their local and state governments. The Republicans never claimed to abandon education, health care or the environment. Instead, they simply said that local and state governments could better use that money. In the end, the Democrats wanted to maintain appropriations for the U.S. Department of Education. This is a big building in Washington DC, where no kids go, except maybe for tours. None of those bureaucrats in the Department of Education do anything to teach your children. So, the Republicans are saying, "Let's get the federal government out of there, and give that money back to the people so they can put it into their local schools." Yet, the Democrats, believing that no one can handle any problem better than government, insist on maintaining a large bureaucracy in Washington that does nothing each year to educate our children.

Secondly, the Democrats were so quick to blame, in that aforementioned quote in 1996, the Republicans for not carefully considering all of the expenditures of the past. If I recollect, it was the Democrats who had an overwhelming control of

Congress throughout the eighties and the early nineties. Now, that they see the mess they created, the Democrats want to blame Republicans for not carefully considering appropriations. This is absurd. On top of that, the Democrats actually believe that talking about reducing big government is a "waste of taxpayer money". How can this be? The finger pointing of the Democrats, led by the finest swindler of them all, Bill Clinton, is doing nothing to break down the juggernaut of big government.

The Republicans have called for reductions in the budget of the EPA who routinely overuse their power and rob the people of the true benefit of their own land. The Republicans have tried to cut federal spending in the areas of welfare and health care. The intention was not to hurt people by taking money away, but to give that money BACK to the people so they could use it better in their local communities without having to lose over half of it to government bureaucracy. As Representative Delay (R) from Texas stated:

> "I think it (the resolution to reduce big government) gets to the crux of the matter... the American family today started on July 4 working for itself... They (Democrats) know that. They are trying to cover it up. For 40 years they have built the federal government to such a huge size and taken money from the American family that now we work until July $3^{rd}$ for the federal government... No one is talking about their bad regulations. What we are talking about is rushing into regulations, rushing to judgment without cost-benefit analysis and taking a common sense approach to regulations."

Nonetheless, despite all of these warnings, big government continues to expand. July $4^{th}$ has become a day of celebration not only for our independence from Britain, but also for the independence from our government. The average U.S. family donates half of its income to the government. In a day and age where two parents must work to support their family, one of those parents is working only to pay the federal government. In a day and age where criticism of day care and single parent families are paramount, why is it that our own government removes both parents from the household just so they can maintain the status quo.

A large portion of this governmental juggernaut is comprised of 131,000 individuals, the highest level in U.S. history, which are employed in "rule-making" sectors of the U.S. federal government. Rules are put out on a daily basis, and quite frankly, nobody knows all the rules that apply to any one particular item. It is true though, that in the State of Massachusetts, all of the legal red tape and bureaucratic nonsense may stop a life-saving drug from being marketed for up to fifteen years. Now, I am always in support of being cautious, but how can our biotechnological and medical companies compete with foreign markets, such as Japan and Germany, if they have such regulations holding them back?

Between 1994 and 1996, President Clinton and his minions issued 4,300 new rules. These rules regulated things from small businesses to the environment. In the end, all it spelled out was more control over our daily lives. Even the Republicans' "Contract With America" was an utter failure, and not just because of the Democrats. The fact remains, as the Washington Post reported on March 1, 1995:

> "Make no mistake: the Contract With America is big government—and a big government from Washington... In defense and national security affairs, the contract does not call for significant cuts, while in the domestic policy arena it would maintain a large federal policy-making, administrative and funding role in crime policy, environmental management and many other areas."

This article goes on to point out that despite the good intention of House Republicans, the reality is that if the funding, whether in block grants to states or direct appropriations to federal agencies, is from the federal government, the system is still going to continue to expand. House Republicans are trying to change a system that has gone drastically wrong, from the inside. Regrettably, this is almost impossible. Their efforts will only cut spending in certain areas, while the government will continue to grow in size and complexity. All I have to say is that at least the Republicans are trying, when, on the other hand, you have the Democrats lining up to spend your tax dollars.

The president boasted on May 17, 1997 that the new budget deal had contained the biggest expansion in federal education spending since Lyndon Johnson occupied the Oval Office. It had not been long before this statement that the GOP leaders had given speeches about getting "Uncle Sam" off the back of local communities and allowing them to determine how there children should be educated. I am hard-pressed to believe that the money Clinton will ask for in this new program will actually benefit individual children. It will most likely end up creating an entirely new section of the U.S. Department of Education that will request re-appropriation each year for the next couple of decades. In the end, that money could have simply gone back to the communities that had sent it to Washington to be disbursed directly to the children. It is truly a sad day when our leaders are actually boasting that they have increased federal spending in certain areas the most in 30 years!

## The Beginnings of Big Government

Many have argued for some time now, just when big government started. Some say it began with F.D.R.'s 'New Deal', whereas others believe it did not start until Lyndon Johnson's time and the beginning of the Progressive Era. Despite this debate, there is no denying that government spending really did take off during the "New Deal" era. As a percentage of GDP, government spending reached its peak in 1944 at 45%, although a lot of this was the result of the World War. Nonetheless, F.D.R. did begin to increase social welfare spending that encourages many to call him the first president of big government.

I believe that we need to examine the issue much more closely to truly understand how deeply the federal government has become ingrained into our way of life. Historian Jeffrey Roger Hummel writes in his book, *Emancipating Slaves, Enslaving Free Men: A History of the American Civil War*, that the Civil War set the precedent for the future spending of big government.

It was the Civil War that brought taxes to a new height. Pre-Civil War, the federal government only collected taxes through tariffs. Additionally, revenue for the federal government was raised through land sales. However, during the Civil War, Lincoln began to tax real estate, sales and licensing. In addition, he ushered in the era of income tax on incomes more than a certain amount. Lincoln began the Internal Revenue Service and doubled the already existing tariffs.

In addition to taxes, the Civil War brought on large spending programs and big government agencies. Each of which were precursors to their modern counterparts. In 1866 the government began its first Veteran's pension, which grew from 2% of all federal spending to 29% in 1884. The Civil War era also ushered in the Department of Agriculture, the Government Printing Office, the Bureau of Engraving and Printing, and the National Academy of Sciences. Furthermore, against popular belief, Jimmy Carter did not found the first Department of Education in 1980, it was founded in 1867.

The number of government workers during this time period also rose dramatically, despite the demobilization following the war. Still, the largest change in government operations during this time period was the intrusion of the federal government in monetary issues. Prior to the Civil War, U.S. currency consisted of little more than bank notes supported by a gold standard. During the war, Lincoln created the U.S. Dollar and set up nationally chartered banks. In the end, he had to create the Secret Service in order to investigate counterfeiters.

Regardless of what we personally believe about the Civil War, the fact remains that the Lincoln era may have been the start of big government. History tells us that the Civil War was not fought over slavery (slavery would have inevitably ended even if the South would have successfully ceded from the Union), rather it was fought over the idea that a strong centralized federal government was usurping the power of the separate states. This fact, in the opinion of the South, was reason enough to fight a bloody 5-year conflict. Despite the positive gain of maintaining the Union, one of the unintended consequences might have been the laying of the foundations of big government that resulted in the current plague about our system.

The motivation for all of this is not to discredit past leaders, only to point out that the issue of big government is largely entrenched in our society. Deviation from its path of continuous growth will not be easy, because it was not just started in the past 8 years with Clinton (although he's helped it quite a bit), nor was it just in the last 40 years. The growth of government has been a disturbing trend for over 100 years, first noticed by the Southern States when they attempted to free themselves from what they saw as an oppressive central government.

# Over-Regulation: The Inevitable Conclusion of Big Government

Big government has led to little more than extra spending and over-regulation. There are so many rules and regulations being implemented that the reality of it all is mind-boggling. As Ronald Reagan pointed out in the 1980's, and the Republicans continue to say today, federal regulations only lead to stifled businesses and stumped growth. True, we need some regulations, but things are getting pretty ridiculous.

Take for example the effect over-regulation had on New England banks back in 1992. It was reported by the Boston Globe that Boston Fed president Richard F. Syron claimed that

> "... ill advised (regulatory) policies have sucked billions of dollars out of the pool of available loans in New England. The result has been the death of banks and the bankruptcy of businesses that could not find credit. The recession in New England was not caused by this, but it's clear it was exacerbated by it."

It appears that as the recession of the late 80's and early 90's was in full swing, federal regulators began to tell local banks just how they could manage their money. These banks were forced to cut off loans to individuals the local banks deemed investment worthy, but federal guidelines had deemed too risky in the tumultuous time. In order to shield the FDIC from another major S & L failure, government regulators from the FDIC and the Office for the Comptroller of the Currency made banks hold massive amounts of capital in reserve and did not allow them to invest it in the local communities.

Regrettably, at that time, the local bank owners knew very well that the industries in the New England states needed the money that was being held back in reserve. In the end, the federal government took control away from the local banks and forced them to put many small businesses out of commission.

This caused increased unemployment, lower consumer spending rates and inevitably extended the recession. The problem here is that someone in Washington who did not know the people who needed the money was calling the shots. Individual banks simply could not give out money that they knew they would get a return on because a number cruncher behind a desk said no.

This is not the only example of rampant federal regulations and the damages they cause. In 1995 during a Small Business Committee Hearing in the Senate, government agencies, such as the IRS, OSHA, EPA and FDA came under heavy fire from small business experts and owners. These individuals claimed that by obeying every little law and regulation that governed their business, they were losing valuable time and money that could have been re-invested in the company to make it more successful. Some of the problems reported by small businesses at these hearings were:

- Non-bank financial institutions have a better advantage over traditional banks because federal regulators do not govern them as tightly. Their overhead is cheaper and they are not required to file as much paperwork. It was reported in the Commercial Appeal that: "First Tennessee Bank spends $10 million a year on regulatory compliance. Without such expenses, other financial businesses can offer products at a lower cost than banks can. Examples of regulations that cause problems for banks include rules such as those that leave the lender liable for environmental problems on foreclosed property."

- Arleen Goodwin, chairman of the delegation from Tennessee, reported that she had closed her KOA campground after 20 years because the paperwork had gotten to the point where she felt like she was working for the government. In order to handle all of the red tape, she had been forced to hire a business manager and build a new office.

- Ron Pickard, chairman of Sofamor Danek Group Inc., raised more allegations of too much red tape in the FDA. The pre-market approval average has climbed 6 months in the past 6 years and it now takes an average of nine months to bring a new product to the market. The expenses incurred during this long wait are passed on to the consumer who then may not be able to afford life-saving equipment or medications.

- David Hagedorn, general manager of Frank A. Cvonkling Co., reported that OSHA regulations were so numerous and restrictive that each time he is visited by an inspector, he is in violation. For example, he reported that his company was fined $700 because the horn on a forklift was not operational.

- John Lindamood, a farm manager in Tiptonville, TN, said that the EPA requires farm workers who work around chemicals to wear protective clothes at all times. He says that wearing protective clothes in the summer months for 12 hours is not practical, and all of his employees and others like him who violate this rule on a daily basis, subject themselves to possible prosecution. Furthermore, Ruth Shoaf said that wetlands and anti-erosion rules also hamstring agri-business people. She claims that since these people make their living off the land, they are the best ones to know and determine what is best for the environment. She, along with other agribusiness leaders believe that environmental and labor laws are so stringent that the small profit margins of agribusiness are damaged if one attempts to comply with all the bureaucratic nonsense.

These are just a few examples of the damaging consequences of over-regulation by the federal government. Over-regulation is the inevitable consequence of big government constantly expanding and being forced to justify its existence.

# Case Studies of Big Government

Later in this book, I will examine more closely two regulatory agencies of Big Government that have been major players in the erosion of civil liberties and the destruction of the American Dream. These are the Bureau of Alcohol, Tobacco and Firearms and the Environmental Protection Agency. Nonetheless, at this time, I wanted to give you some examples of Big Government and how we, as American citizens, have welcomed increased regulation and control when it might not be the best option.

## Federal Deposit Insurance Corporation

Most of us have heard of this entity of the federal government and, therefore, many of us have been able to sleep better at night. Basically, the FDIC was created in 1933 by Franklin D. Roosevelt to increase consumer confidence in the U.S. banking system. Many historians have suggested though that even F.D.R. had his reservations about this system.

However, in the July 1996 issue of the Memphis Business Journal it was reported that:

> "In subsequent decades (after the creation of the FDIC), however, no bank depositor has lost any money insured by the FDIC, and no tax revenues have been used to repay them. The sense of security this provides is widely appreciated and bank consumers almost universally support deposit insurance. It has become something of a sacred cow."

In reality, many banking analysts have begun to question the sanctity of this federal institution. Allegations have been made that the FDIC does little more than destabilize national and global banking. Individuals such as Thomas Garrett, president, CEO and Chairman of the Board of National Commerce

Bankcorp have referred to the FDIC as "an irrational system" that was created in a time when banking was done differently. According to individuals like Mr. Garrett, the FDIC is no longer necessary and has become little more than a pacifier of the people, that at times, disrupts world banking.

You see, when F.D.R. created the FDIC, he did so in a torrid stream of bills signed into law in a matter of a single day. It was all part of his New Deal program designed to lift the country out of the Great Depression. At that time, banks were collapsing left and right and people had little or no confidence in the security of any bank. Many of these banks failed because of the tough economic conditions of the time, but most failed because of a loss of consumer confidence. The FDIC was formed in order to increase consumer confidence, which it succeeded in doing, and the number of banks closing in the next three decades was considerably lower. However, one should be cautious to give full credit to the FDIC, because the three to four decades that followed the Great Depression were also ones laden with strong economic growth.

The problems arose in the 1970's when the economy began to take a downturn. Here we began to see an increase in bank closings and many analysts blame the FDIC for this. It seems that many banks counted on the FDIC to back them up when they made poor management decisions. As Adam Feibelman writes:

> "Hence the moral hazard (of the FDIC): A number of troubled institutions, particularly S&Ls, in the 1980s took huge last minute risks (calculated on the premise of federal insurance) to attract badly needed funds. Such institutions offered higher interest on deposits, attracting money from all over the country and, in some cases, made risky investments with that money to dig themselves out of trouble."

Thus, the original wisdom behind the FDIC (to insure a single depositor up to 5,000 dollars) was used to encourage millionaires to divide up their money among different banks, each insured up to $ 100,000. In the end, when all the dust settled, many banks had to close, and the American taxpayer was stuck with the bill that came with the S & L failure.

This did not go unnoticed by many, and in 1991 critics and financial experts began to call for the end to Federal Deposit Insurance, or at least some serious changes in its regulations. However, while facing the bettering economy, this priority was placed at the bottom of the list, and still today, the FDIC has been left to regulate itself. The call for a privatized deposit insurance company has gone unnoticed and our banking system is easy prey for another S & L crisis. Proof positive that a regulatory system, designed to save the people money, ends up costing us all a lot more. Furthermore, it is also a perfect example of how new federal program perpetuate themselves even after the crisis is over. FDR enacted the FDIC to get us out of the depression. Thus, when the depression was over, why wasn't the FDIC dismantled? Even in the face of criticism from banking experts, this federal program continues on and makes the U.S. economy susceptible to another tragedy. I guess the politicians don't care because they think the American taxpayer will just keep on paying the costs of big government.

## Housing and Urban Development

The Department of Housing and Urban Development was designed in order to insure that Americans would have a roof over their head. Its budget annually is very large and many of us, especially those who have rented property, have heard of HUD subsidized properties. Many of us feel that HUD, in many cases, supports unemployment and welfare, along with the laziness that accompanies them. But, nonetheless, I used to take heart in the knowledge that Big Brother would always have a place for me to rest my head if for some reason I lost my job for an extended time. I believed this until I learned a few facts.

It appears that in 1997, a consulting firm by the name of Ernst and Young had a major financial advisory contract with HUD. Fearing the fact that they would not be renewed in their contract, they made a $132,000 donation to the Clinton campaign, and presto, they had a $20 million dollar contract extension. This, despite the fact that almost every single career contracting officer within HUD had objected to the deal.

That was bad enough, but it is not the only problem with HUD. It turns out that their own Inspector General has cited the department for wasting hundreds of millions of dollars of your tax money. The Department of Housing and Urban Development has made a habit of the little deals mentioned earlier. Our tax dollars are ending up in the pockets of major corporations like Lockheed Martin, Price Waterhouse, Chase Manhattan and 35 others. All these companies had to do was make generous donations to the current administration and they had contracts, many of them with no benefits to the welfare of the American people, renewed.

The Inspector General found that this occurred because no one was placed in charge of checking the bills that came in each month and verifying they were accomplishing some departmental goal. The report found that about 4,800 contracts had not been audited in the last year. 129 of these contracts had costs of over 900 million, and they were never audited before their completion. In other words, the money has already been spent and no one knows where it went. The contracts in HUD awaiting audit are backlogged back to 1989. When questioned about this by the Washington Times, reporters learned that HUD has apparently turned over all management and oversight duties to the contract managers. That's kind of like asking your own child to count the cookie jar and make sure they did not take one when you were not looking.

This irresponsible management of public funds is indicative of big government. All too often, checks are being written for large sums of money, and no one knows if anything is being accomplished by appropriating these funds.

## U.S Forest Service

The deeper I dug into the juggernaut of our government, the more negative things I uncovered. I personally love the outdoors, I love land. Nothing made me happier than to think that there was land being cleaned up and preserved for all of its beauty. Land of course, which was owned by the government, not by you or me. The Forest Service, I always thought, kept parks nice and pretty, prevented and fought forest fires, and found lost people when they got sidetracked on the local trails. I was never particularly bothered about paying federal taxes for that, despite the fact that local communities could probably have accomplished the same goals with less bureaucracy and money. I learned, however, that whatever the federal government touches turns to dust, and it regrettably holds true for the Forest Service as well.

It was discovered by the *Christian Science Monitor* in 1997 that the Forest Service was utilizing funds set aside to "maintain" roads in order to destroy roads. That's funny to me, because I always felt maintenance was defined as "keeping up, or protecting." But, nonetheless, Forest Service engineer Skip Coughlan reported in 1997 that in the next year the Forest Service planned to build 400 miles of new road while destroying 1,500 miles of old road.

You see, it seems that the roads that exist are too functional. That's right, too functional. Apparently, people are using these roads too much to visit National Parks and they are therefore disturbing the parks primary clients, or residents, like bears, birds and such. In a time when the infrastructure of our country is quickly depleting, your federal tax dollars are being utilized to tear down roads.

Regrettably, it does not end with roads. Environmentalists have also convinced the Federal Energy Regulatory Commission to recommend that we start tearing down already existing dams. For example, in 1997 the commission recommended that the Edwards Dam on the Kennebec River be removed. It seems that although these dams provide much needed power for the local citizenry (of course tearing them down will cost more money to build alternate power facilities), they also impede the progress of salmon swimming up stream. Therefore, it was determined that wasting tax dollars and destroying that which was already built was prudent. Would it not have been easier to simply build an alternate path for the salmon?

I believe the sentiment expressed in the next quote, best sums up how the U.S Forest Service feels about your interests and your hard-earned tax dollars:

> "Human happiness, and certainly human fecundity, are not as important as a wild and healthy planet. I know social scientists that remind me that people are part of nature, but it isn't true. Somewhere along the line—at about a billion years ago, maybe half that— we quit the contract and became a cancer. We have become a plague upon ourselves and upon the earth. Until such times as Homo Sapiens should decide to rejoin nature, some of us can only hope for the right virus to come along"

David M. Graber
National Park Service

Take those words to heart and then remember, we are paying his salary! It's almost enough to make me want to cry. Please note as well, humans have only been around for approximately 30,000 years, this man is also ignorant of the natural world he so boldly protects.

# Who's Watching Big Government?

One of my biggest concerns lies in who is watching the federal government. True, there are House Oversight Committees, but are they not part of the federal system themselves? In my research for this book, I sought to answer this question as best I could. What I learned was even more troubling, almost enough to make me wish I would have just lived in ignorance.

Despite protests from almost every federal regulatory agency, Congress approved the Inspector General Act and created the first Inspector Generals in the United States. These were people whose job was to insure that federal regulatory and executive agencies were following the rules, laws and regulations governing their actions and budgetary appropriations. In general, these people were hired to keep an eye on big government. That is why the aforementioned protests from almost all federal agencies were not a surprise. Somebody was raining on their little parade of self-regulation.

I learned that the number of Inspector Generals had grown today to 60, which undoubtedly represents the dramatic increase in the number of regulatory agencies and personnel. Their job is simply to uncover the waste, fraud and abuse of the people we entrust our tax dollars to each year. The discretion of the Inspector Generals is extremely broad, and they can only be fired by the President, thereby giving them a theoretically strong position to truly analyze the government.

I soon learned however that anything that is spawned from the federal government is subject to the corrupting reality of big government. In 1998, The Washington Post reported that Treasury Department Inspector General Valerie Lau had been involved in a multitude of unethical activities that subverted her ability to successfully watch the federal government.

As it turns out, an extremely slow bureaucratic process that allowed her to get away with her unethical activity for some time protected Lau. To put it simply, there was no one watching the watchdogs. In the end of my research, I had to conclude that the only true watchdog of the federal government was the American people. Although I do not wish to insult the individual integrity of all of the Inspector Generals, I find it hard to believe that anyone who works within the system, and does not have to answer to somebody independent of that system, can ever truly and objectively evaluate the members of that system.

In the end, I am sad to say, that there is no one watching the federal government as long as we trust the government to monitor itself.

# A Conflict of Interest

For too long we, as the rightful rulers of this country, have allowed big government to call the shots and regulate itself. Even the Inspector Generals placed in charge of overseeing this monstrosity are being corrupted by the system. Agencies like the EPA, BATF, U.S. Forest Service, HUD and countless others have been playing a game with our tax dollars. Their job each year is not to serve the populace, but to ensure their own survival. How can we possibly trust an agency to self-regulate when, if they do find out that they are doing a poor job, all those people in that agency will be fired? Therein lies the conflict of interest.

Too many regulatory and executive agencies in our federal government are allowed to get away with regulating themselves. Look at the story of the FDIC. Congress, despite the problems in the 1980's, allowed the FDIC to not only continue operating, but they requested that the FDIC come up with its own form of regulation. Let me ask you this, if you were faced with the possibility of privatizing the industry that employed you, fed your family and put clothes on your back, would you make an unbiased decision that served the interests of the public first? I don't think so.

The truth is that big government continues to expand because we trust those inside the system to watch the system and regulate themselves. Different agencies and bureaus have always devised ways to increase their departmental prestige. A good example of this will be contained in the next chapter when I talk about the origins of the DEA. Right now however, to further drive this point home, let's examine the Food and Drug Administration.

Already in this book I have cited examples of how the FDA is incredibly slow in granting permits to utilize new medical technologies. This is not a problem in just one region, it is nation-wide and many experts have begun to criticize them for it.

The Warfield's Business Record for Baltimore Maryland reported in 1996 that the FDA had become a broken down bureaucracy that needed repaired. Actually, it needs a complete overhaul. One example given involved a Maryland medical device firm that had lost millions of dollars because it had to wait over two years to receive approval from the FDA. The delay was due to a minor change in its manufacturing facility that the company could not get the FDA to rule on. In addition, the Warfield's Business Record reported that a small biotechnology firm went out of business when it was forced by the FDA to build a $50 million dollar manufacturing plant that met FDA specifications. That would not have been so bad, if the FDA had not rejected the drug they were going to manufacture in this facility after the facility was built.

These are just a few of the allegations that have surfaced around the country about the FDA, and it has become widely known today that the FDA is badly in need of improvements. However, when these concerns were raised to Congress, the issue was deferred back to the FDA for consideration and agency-induced change. It appears as if the FDA was attempting, with all of its might, to fight off the Congressional inquiry. The Warfield's Business Record reported that:

> "The agency (FDA) says it's reforming administratively, pointing to more than a dozen changes it has announced in the past nine months, including a pilot program to allow third party review of a medical device. Critics, however, say the agency has been kicking and screaming the whole way. That so-called flurry reform, they add, is really a calculated move to head off a congressional overhaul of the agency."

I believe this is extremely frightening. The agency has forgotten that they are servants to the people. The FDA and the administrators in charge of its operation do not have the interests of the American people in mind. Instead, they have their own personal and agency goals in the forefront. You can bet that a lot of money has changed hands in that debate over the years, and the only winner is the FDA.

I find it very concerning, and you should too, that many of the people who make their livings off our tax dollars have forgotten whom they work for: the American people. The FDA is not alone, almost every agency is like this. There is not a single one of them that will admit they are unnecessary and give up their money, jobs and cushy offices so that the people can get more for their tax dollars. This has got to change. The Inspector Generals have failed, Congress has failed, the President, at least currently, is a lost cause. Who can we turn to but ourselves?

# The Governmental Blame Game

Who is to blame for this ever expanding, overgrown federal government? True, Democrats have definitely taken the cake when it comes to governmental spending, but no one can deny that Republicans have done their fair share of running up the tab on U.S. taxpayer's credit cards. So, in the end, who is truly to blame?

I believe that each individual citizen has to share some of the blame. Americans have collectively become apathetic. We each look to the government in order to solve our problems, despite the fact that none of us trust government. Look at the issue of Health-Care reform. The Christian Science Monitor reported in 1994 that over 83% of Americans were calling for health care reform, however Everett Carl Ladd of the Roper Center for Public Opinion Research stated, "Despite a widespread desire for health-care reform, there was a great public aversion to a government-controlled plan."

Despite American mistrust of big government, the citizenry elected a President in 1992 who had promised to reform health care and give us all government subsidized insurance. This shocks me. Despite our mistrust, and knowledge that the federal government would most likely screw up health care reform, we elected a socialist president who almost succeeded in ruining one of the finest health care systems in the world.

Most Americans (74%) do not trust the government and 76% believe that government serves the interests of the rich. However, whenever anything goes wrong in our country, we immediately turn to the government and ask them to come up with some type of program or some law to control our lives even more.

Case in point- childcare. Already mentioned in this chapter was the fact that one parent, in a two-parent family, must work full-time to pay for the operation of the federal government each year. Therefore, there is no doubt that the size of the federal government is, in part, to blame for the lack of parental supervision in the homes. Now, the issue of child-care has come up, and many people have begun to turn to the government for assistance. So, Bill Clinton responded to the people. In 1998 the Dallas Morning News announced that President Clinton had suggested to Congress that they pass a 21.7 billion dollar spending package aimed at improving and expanding childcare around the United States. I find this startling: the federal government's overspending and over-regulation are two of the major causal factors for the need for child care (by forcing both parents out of the home to work). Despite this, Bill Clinton suggests throwing more money at the problem, which will, in turn, make taxes even higher. Instead of spending more money, Bill Clinton could have designed a plan to reduce the size of government and cut taxes. This would have freed up more money for parents to seek out more reputable childcare agencies, or simply quit one of the night jobs they are working to keep the federal government going.

At the current rate of growth, the government will undoubtedly keep expanding, taxes will rise, and people will become more and more disenfranchised with the system. Who's to blame? The leaders of our country are definitely at the top of the list, but more importantly, we must blame ourselves.

## Bill Clinton and His End to Big Government

Bill, being the politician that he is, caught on to the polls and realized near his second term that the people where getting really fed up with an expanding government that controlled their daily lives. In his speeches, he began to include facts on how he had reduced the federal workforce by 250,000 and that the era of big government was over. He had the audacity to make these claims in the face of the facts mentioned earlier in this book on how government was actually increasing.

The truth is, the federal government has in no way begun to shrink. Sure, Clinton did reduce federal employment rolls by 250,000 but most of those individuals were part of the military downsizing that was begun by President Bush after the Cold War and the Gulf War. To add insult to injury, right after Clinton was making his campaign promises of small government in late 1996, Congress adjourned and with the approval of our dear president, increased the annual budgets of federal departments and agencies by 15 billion. The Washington Post reported on October 20, 1996 that Clinton, congressional Democrats and GOP moderates teamed up to prevent all but modest tinkering with a vast range of government functions and innovations dating back to the 1960's.

Clinton has all but sealed the fate of the "minimalist government" proposed by President Reagan back in the 80's. Minimalist government was:

> "A spare and stingy creature, which offered evenhanded public justice, but no more. Its vision of the good society rested on the strength and productive potential of free men in free markets. It sought to encourage the unfettered production of capitalist wealth and the expansion of private welfare that automatically attends it."

This philosophy is in direct conflict with the current practices of our government. Each year, our leaders seek to maximize the size of government. A false sense of security is created when hypocrites speak of a small, unobtrusive government, and then foster the expansion of the current system.

Sadly, the hopes of a minimalist government are quickly fading when outright liars like Bill Clinton continue to squander American tax dollars and increase federal regulations that stifle the free man and destroy the free market.

# The Future of Big Government

I hope each day when I turn on the TV that Bill Clinton will perform a Metamorphosis right out of Kafka's classic story. I pray that he will have some bastion of goodness in him and that he will truly be the leader who takes us into the 21$^{st}$ century with a smaller federal government. But, regrettably, his State of the Union address in January of 1999 did little to ease my mind. In fact, it only made matters worse.

There is cause for concern when one listens carefully to Bill Clinton's State of the Union speech. To some of you who may not have heard, I must be the bearer of bad tidings. The bad news is that Bill Clinton wants to federalize every aspect of American life. The bad news is that if the President accomplishes all of his goals, our local and state governments will no longer be necessary. We will be able to hand over all power to the Feds. In addition, we will probably have little need for churches, families, charities or other societal institutions as well. After all, the federal government will surely take care of us. Where is the good news, and good future that Clinton is promising? We're still waiting.

The giant maelstrom forming in Washington was forged from our federal tax dollars, trillions of them, flowing into and back out of Washington. Bill apparently believes that if you have a problem—a headache, sore throat, naughty child, bad carburetor, depression or you just simply need a vacation—he will find a government program just for you.

In the first few minutes of his speech, he attempted to take false credit for the small effort made by the GOP led Congress to get rid of big government. I would like to say that no one fell for this little trick, but the 65% of Americans who approved of him shortly after his speech downs my hopes. If his lies and deceit would have ceased at this point I possibly would have gotten a little sleep that night, but alas, Bill had no intention of stopping. Instead he unveiled his new "One World Order" that consisted of socializing America just like many countries in

Europe had done. He began to list government expansions not seen since Lyndon Johnson's era.

Bill made sure, throughout his speech, that he promised plenty of our money to the people who got him to the top-federal workers, day-care providers (we already talked about what a great idea that was), environmentalists, trial lawyers and so on, until he had disbursed almost all of your first 13 paychecks. He had to list something for everyone, unless you were someone like myself, sitting at home, begging the government to just leave you the hell alone and get out of your life.

Despite his big promises to save Social Security and reduce big government, Bill granted over 100 billion dollars (spending it all in just one hour) to: higher veterans pay, increased military wages, federal land purchases (gifts for his boys in the EPA), new bike paths, carpool lanes, mass transportation, farms, homelessness, school construction, child care, drug testing, Americorps and last, but certainly not least, global warming research. He rattled off more and more spending so fast that I doubt Raymond from the "Rain Man" could have kept up. This whole time, I was cowering with each blow, while Congress, some GOP moderates too, were given him round after round of applause. Some of it actually seemed sincere.

Despite my constant pleading to the TV, he did not stop there. He continued to suggest, not in real dollar terms, more programs that could end up costing us twice as much as the aforementioned. He promised an increased minimum wage (to help more small businesses go out of business); supported the Justice Department's suing of the tobacco companies for Medicare reimbursement (blaming a company for the individual choices of Americans); asked for expanded family leave (once again killing small businesses); and requested that our trading partners adopt our over-regulated standards so they too can stifle their countries trade. Then, just when I thought it could not get any worse, he suggested that the government should invest the Social Security Trust fund into the stock market. Mind you, this is not privatization, but the exact opposite. Bill Clinton would like it if the federal government owned large shares of privately traded companies!

He said all this, after opening up with his garbage about the end of big government. I could not believe it. His vision was so abhorrent that I nearly fell out of my chair. What surprised me even more were two major facts: 1) The American people are eating this up, and loving his vision of the "New World Order", and 2) Some Republicans are apparently jumping on board with this nonsense. Bill Clinton fully intends to continue on with big government, and, if this type of leadership continues, we might as well just hand over everything right now to the Feds.

# The Path of Socialism: A Journey from Freedom

One of the major reasons why I am writing this book is because I see some disturbing trends in our society. As mentioned already, there is the trend towards the erosion of personal rights and the Constitution. This whole Chapter has explained that the United States federal government is over-sized and continuing to expand at a rate that may soon be overwhelming. Furthermore, there is major trend in our governmental leadership that is calling for increased socialistic reforms. This, in my opinion, is the first step to totalitarianism and the elimination of freedom.. In other words, the destruction of the American Dream.

Big government is the first step in this path. Each time citizens of this great nation hand another part of their life over to the control of the government; we take a step towards socialism and totalitarianism. Our country was originally founded with a weak centralized federal government. Our founding fathers realized that the more control citizens give to a ruling government, the less control they have over their personal lives.

Thus, a situation arises where, one day, Americans wake up and realize that the government controls every part of their lives and that they can no longer have the freedom they once treasured.

There is no reason to believe that the United States is still not vulnerable to socialist rule. There are four major prerequisites, identified throughout history, that usually occur before a totalitarian regime takes power. Each of these prerequisites could easily occur in the United States. First of all, there must be millions (a large percentage of the population) of people, especially those in a middle class, who quickly become unemployed, or remain only marginally employed, during an economic recession. Anyone reading this can remember something happening like this in the late 1970s. The great "Rust Out" put a lot of people, especially in the industrial north, out of work and unable to find good jobs. Today, something like that is not an impossibility. Our service based economy opens us up for tremendous unemployment if the consumer confidence levels drop to the point that retail sales plummet. Therefore, any country, including ours, is not far away from having the middle, or working class, quickly placed on the unemployment roles.

Secondly, a country is more susceptible to socialism and the inevitable totalitarianism if there is a weakened confidence in political democracy and the institutions that represent it. This, regrettably, has already happened in the United States. Throughout this chapter, I have proven that the government has gotten so big, that it no longer cares about the needs of the individual citizen. People have little or no confidence in our politicians, who are regrettably typified by people like Bill Clinton. These are people of low morals with no sense of responsibility. The agencies that represent our government have become self-serving and out of control, allowing them to freely oppress the people with their rampant regulations.

The third characteristic is when the economy turns into a monopolized capitalistic system where the rich get richer and poor get poorer. Thankfully, I still believe that the United States is a place where hard work and dedication will indeed bring you success. However, the back scratching and logrolling that goes on in Washington has begun to favor the rich, who can afford lobbyists, over the common citizen. This must come to an end, or we may face the consequences.

The final characteristic is a loss of religion. Many countries that have already turned to socialism only accomplished this goal by suppressing religion. Too many American citizens, and too many leaders, have turned away from God and the principles of the Ten Commandments. This loss of religion makes us much more susceptible to the godless ways of the communists and other totalitarian governments.

The United States is dangerously close to meeting all of these criteria. Furthermore, with a socialist President in office and another socialist, Al Gore, with a good chance of being elected, the danger of losing our freedom is ever present. The combination of big government, a loss of principles, and a corrupt political system will allow the vultures of socialism to lay prey the American people.

I feel the best way to exemplify this phenomenon is to look at history. The statement, "Those who do not learn from the mistakes of the past are destined to repeat them" may be over-used at times but the wisdom contained in its words still remains. Therefore, I would like to briefly examine the history of a country that went from a Monarchy (like the original 13 colonies), to a Constitutional Monarchy, to a PseudoParliamentary System, to Socialism, to Communism, to Totalitarianism, to Ruin. That country was Russia.

In the early 1900's the people of Russia began to reject the Tsarist rule they had experienced for centuries. The rest of the modern world was heading towards more democratic forms of government that included a representative government chosen by the people. With the onset of Capitalism, an industrial based economy, and increased access to information (i.e. printed books and communication lines), the citizens of many countries began to criticize Dictatorial and Monochratic rule. This era, including the late 1800's, was a time of tremendous worldwide upheaval where governments were changing like the seasons and citizen support for aristocratic and dictatorial leaders was diminishing quickly.

This situation is not unlike today's world where third-world dictators and even larger nations are undergoing tumultuous change. Whenever there is rapid change, coupled with multiple competing ideologies, there is great danger. In the United States, most of us would agree, with little debate, that times are changing so quickly that many people are feeling disenfranchised and discontent with the current social climate. Therefore, just like Russia in the early 1900's, the United States is experiencing incredible change and some of it, as I will point out throughout this book, is detrimental to freedom and a proper social order.

Because of this outcry, Russia in the 1900's changed from an autocratic multinational empire to a constitutional monarchy. This period of political change was referred to as the Duma Monarchy. Hoping to curb the peoples desire for governmental change, the Tsarist government attempted to create a Council (i.e. legislature) that was little more than a puppet form of government under the control of the Monarchy. This action was motivated, in some part, by the failed revolution of 1905. The creation of a new form of government was also accompanied by the "October Manifesto". This document set up the basic rights bestowed to citizens of a free nation and guaranteed Civil Rights. It also created the founding principles upon which a theoretically representative legislature could be formed. These actions were taken in the hopes of appeasing the people and thwarting any future rebellions. However, as history had demonstrated before, these nominal efforts to subdue dissension only ended up wetting the lips of freedom.

This system, just like the Monarchy of the past, quickly became corrupted. The process by which individuals were elected and power was granted favored the wealthy influences in Russian society. The peasants, or commoners, were still kept in the same state of powerlessness they had been in before the revolution of 1905. This made the people extremely discontent with the form of government that existed. After all, the October Manifesto and the new puppet government had been created under the guise of increased freedom and democracy. The increased proliferation of printed material and other forms of widespread public information delivery systems allowed a large number of people to hear the ideals of freedom. From this information, people began to see that their lives could improve, if they only supported their government. Upon realizing that the government was nothing more than the work horse of the wealthy landowners and aristocrats, public support for the government diminished quickly.

I cannot help but draw a similarity from this scenario to that of the modern United States. As mentioned earlier in this section, Americans have slowly given more and more control over the minutest detail of our everyday lives to the federal government. At the same time, the sea of bureaucracy created by big government has resulted in most Americans losing touch with their representatives and elected officials.

The way I see it today, the two most powerful forces in Washington are lobbyists and something I call the unelected-representation. I personally find this fact extremely frightening, especially because the most powerful influence in Washington should be the common everyday citizen.

Therefore, we currently have a system of government that routinely restricts the access of every day working-class citizens, who do not have the money to fight the system, and gain influence in legislative and executive actions. Large lobbying firms pump millions of dollars into the pockets of our elected officials and scoff at the needs and desires of the common, hard-working American. Then, the members of the unelected-representative government, the leaders and workers of government regulatory and administrative agencies, enforce rules that individual citizens had no say in the creation of.

In the end, the United States is quickly losing a form of government that is "by the people and for the people". The real trick is that as the bureaucratic nonsense becomes more and more complex, we, the citizens of this great nation, turn to the very people who made the system so complex and ask them to run it for us. In other words, the people in charge, lobbyists and unelected representatives, have created a self-perpetuating system that no longer includes the citizenry. Meanwhile, those whom we have entrusted with the care of government, have swindled us into believing in this system that is no longer protecting our freedom.

This is very similar to how Russia must have been in the early 1900's. Freed from a Monarchy and presented with a fake form of representative government, the people received a taste of what real freedom might feel like. However, they soon realized that the freedom they longed for so much was being hidden away by the rich, who only wanted to perpetuate their own wealth.

The political change from a Monarchy to a Constitutional Monarchy was too fake and the people were able to see through it. Therefore, when they turned to their "representatives" they soon learned that those they had supposedly elected to positions of power were nothing more than the puppets of the Monarchy. As a result, the people became more disgruntled and unhappy.

The newly discovered ideology of freedom fostered an out of control press that criticized the government and the

Monarchy. Geoffrey Hosking wrote in his book, Russia, People and Empire that:

> "In this sense, Russia became abruptly part of the twentieth-century world, with all its problems over sensationalism, press freedom and press responsibility... The considerable degree of de facto press freedom undoubtedly helped both to discredit the authorities (including the Emperor himself) in the eyes of the population and to intensify political conflict springing from socioeconomic and ethnic motives"

In response to this, the government began to shift towards a parliamentary system similar to the Germans at the time. The Monarchy quickly lost power, and positive changes were beginning to take place. Regrettably, changes take a long time and the people had lost faith in the new government because it had started out as an elaborate attempt to deceive the people into believing that they were gaining freedom.

The government took efforts to preserve individual's rights that included the protection of private property from government seizure. However, communistic ideals had begun to spread, and many landowners began to voluntarily take part in communal farms and property ownership. Any efforts the new parliamentary government attempted to take were unsuccessful because the people were distrusting of a system that seemed to have interests, other than their own, in mind.

In Russia, Socialist groups exploded on the scene despite attempts by the government to diminish their popularity. One of the competing ideologies of the time that played a part in the rise of Socialistic tendencies, were groups of academics that adhered to a philosophy referred to as the "Intelligentsia Tradition". Preying upon the discontentment of the workers, socialist groups, supported by the members of the Intelligentsia, spouted doctrines of workers rights and freedom. However, these were all carefully crafted lies and misconceptions used to deceive the people and pull them away from the positive changes representative democracy was making in their nation.

Even though Socialism, and its partner, Communism, was gaining popularity in Russia, there were still individuals who spoke out against a socialist form of government. Led by a man named Petr Struve, former Marxists who realized the folly of the philosophy of Socialism cautioned the people in a collection of articles called the Vekki. The criticisms were poignant, and, coming from former believers of this particular ideology, the credibility was high. For example, Bogdan Kistiakovskii had wrote the following statement about socialist groups and parties:

> "... left wing activists had proved incapable of observing elementary civil liberties: 'In our meetings freedom of speech was enjoyed only by speakers acceptable to the majority... The legal consciousness of our intelligentsia is at a stage of development corresponding to the forms of police state."

The godlessness of the Socialists was well summed up by Sergel Bulgakov when he wrote:

> "... it's social repentance not... in the sight of God but in the sight of "people" or the "proletariat". This had become a form of idol-worship, the divination of human beings."

Struve wrote himself, that:

> "The intelligentsia's dedication to the people did not impose any obligations on the people and did not expect from them any attempt at self-improvement. The preaching of Populism and even more of Marxism was transformed in historical actuality into debauchery and demoralization"

Marx called religion the "opiate of the masses" and socialists sought to destroy and deface it. Marx believed that religion had allowed the people to succumb to Capitalism, and therefore give up their value as the workers in society. However, it can be proven in early Russia that Socialism was the "opiate of the masses", not religion. Religion had encouraged the people to continue working with the government to create a free society. Nonetheless, in the end, the people began to support the ideology that was nothing more than idol worship and debauchery .

At this time, before we conclude the tragic history of a country corrupted by self-love, godlessness and socialism, I find it prudent to examine those earlier quotes and compare them to today's America.

In response to the first quote by Kistiakovskii, I must ask: how many times have we heard liberals trying to limit the free speech of moral, godly men and women who are trying to spread the word of God? For that matter, how many times have we been prevented from teaching our children good morals because it offends the socialist liberal? In reality, the liberals, who call for gun control and the suppression of religion are the ones who cannot comprehend civil liberties today. That first quote I mentioned is so similar to the current state of our society that it's downright eerie. However, the truly frightening facts are revealed when I continue with the analysis.

The godlessness of socialism is demonstrated by the second quote by Bulgakov. Socialists, in the past and still today, preach about worshipping ourselves rather than the lord and master. How can any form of government that does not recognize humans as the servants of God ever survive the test of time?

Furthermore, in the United States today we are faced with teeming prison populations, burgeoning welfare roles, teenage pregnancy and a total lack of personal responsibility. This is the same thing that was said in the Vekki about the socialists, like Bill Clinton, who were trying to drag down Russia in the early 1900's. All around us, we see a lack of personal responsibility: murderers blaming their parents, the lazy blaming society for unemployment (in a time of incredible employment opportunities, I might add), liberals blaming gun manufacturers rather than criminals for crimes, etc....

Many of us in America are fighting this Socialist movement, and have been for decades. But, in Russia, the people were truly entranced by this doctrine and their country turned into the fascist communist state it was for almost all of the 20th century. The United States is on this same pathway to self-destruction and totalitarianism. When we reject God, our personal responsibility, and accept big government and the cult of self-love and aggrandization, we step closer to fascism and away from the freedom provided to us by our founding fathers.

Socialism did not just quickly sweep through the Russian people. It took time, a lot of disgruntled citizenry, and swindlers and shysters, like Bill Clinton of today, to slowly lull the people into sacrificing their freedom. In Russia, years of public debate, major social change, and a world war led to the acceptance of Socialism. However, Socialism was nothing more than a pretty package surrounding a social bomb that exploded into the hearts and souls of the Russian people.

In the early months of 1917, a new government overthrew the Tsarists' rule once and for all. This new government was comprised of both the "reds" and the "whites" Few people know that this early Soviet government was a dual-system that attempted to foster understanding and growth between two ideologically different forms of leadership.

Another chance was given to the Russian people to form a government that established the principles of freedom. This new government quickly dismantled the police force, abolished the death penalty, and returned the land to the peasants. However, most citizens of Russia viewed this new government as nothing more than an extension of the old. The view of a centralized government as corrupt, hedonistic and self-serving led the people to embrace local governments that encouraged the communistic principles. Divided, a nation fell and became easy prey for the vultures of communism.

While the moderate socialists and capitalists argued over more rudimentary notions, the radical leftists began to undermine the new governments authority. The indecisiveness of this new government, wrought with debate over mundane issues, opened the door for the more radical wings to capture the allegiance of the people.

This hesitant new government delayed too long in forming the Constituent Assembly as promised, and this move proved fatal. Immersed in a World War, with a nation divided, the Bolsheviks successfully waged the October Revolution and Russia was headed down the path of totalitarianism.

Despite the obvious failings of Socialism, as pointed out by the scholars of the Vekki, the Soviet people rallied to support this new government. In the end, the communist Soviet government gave them what they wanted. There were promises of strong local governments and a successful economy based on the communal sharing of the means of production. The Soviets quickly withdrew from the World War, ending the long disputed expenditure of lives and resources for no discernible goal. Geoffrey Hosking wrote of this time period:

> "The Bolsheviks thus came to power by promising the people through "soviet power" what they wanted but had been unable to obtain from the Provisional Government: peace, land, bread, workers' control in the factories, self-determination for the nationalities. More than that, the Bolsheviks seemed to be fulfilling a dream which peasants and workers had harbored for centuries: control over the land and their own lives."

The great tragedy of this was that it was all a facade. In fact, the best chance the people of Russia had to accomplish freedom was wasted when the Provisional Government was overthrown. Years of corruption had made the people impatient and they were willing to buy the snake juice that the traveling salesman, in this case, Lenin, had offered. It was impossible for the Bolsheviks to follow through on those promises as Hoskings goes on to say:

> "...But those very conditions also made it impossible for the people to retain the benefits they had gained. The Bolsheviks, in order to consolidate their power, inevitably had to deprive the people of the rewards of their fleeting victory. They promised the people peace, but plunged them into a new and terrible civil war. They promised them bread, but instead generated hunger on a scale not seen in three

centuries. They promised them land, but deprived them by force of the fruits of that land. They promised workers' control, but then aggravated the economic breakdown, causing mass unemployment and almost destroying the working class. They promised soviet power but established a single-party dictatorship, closing down the Constituent Assembly that might have been a counter-weight to it. The societies proved to be organizations too labile and chaotic to administer twentieth century state, especially in such adverse conditions, and fell easily into the hands of the most determined and self-confident political party."

After this massive revolution, some people continued to resist the new regime. Although these individuals saw the true reality of communism, it was regrettably too late to take any decisive actions. Small attempts to alter the course towards totalitarianism were thwarted by the new soviet government. The possible detrimental effects that freedom of speech posed to the new government compelled them to outlaw freedom of the press and of religion. Faced with minor revolts throughout the country, Lenin seized the opportunity to entice all leaders to consolidate power in the one party system, the communist party. Concluding that the people were not quite ready for a Marxist system, that is a system free of governmental control, Lenin ushered in a new Soviet Union that exemplified the notions of Totalitarianism.

The rest of history is well known to us all. Years of Cold War and millions of lives lost, both in the systematic genocide in Russia and in the multiple wars that were fought throughout the world between the free world and the communists. Starting with moderate Socialist ideals, and coupled with a corrupt centralized government, communism reared its ugly head and destroyed the foundations of the freedom a new nation was creating.

True, the United States is not a new nation, but today we can see the signs of socialism. Many people in the United States are beginning to become disenfranchised with the large federal government that has become corrupt and self-serving. In the midst of this, socialists like Clinton are taking the government in the wrong direction, making the people more reliant on big government, and forcing people to slowly give up their rights to property, gun ownership and freedom of religion. Hidden under new agendas, the evil face of communism still has its negative appearance.

The promises of so-called moderate socialists like Clinton that adherence to socialistic tendencies will not be damaging scares me to death. Everything the government gets their hands on, they seem to mess up, and the last thing I want to do is give them more power. Just like in Russia, the lies of moderate socialists only opened the door for more radical leftists to seize control.

If you do not believe that this is a possibility in America, then you should think twice. Only through vigilance and careful watch dogging of our politicians can we insure that the communistic trends that we see in our society are stopped. We, as Americans, are lucky that our fore-fathers set down a good foundation, for they have given us a little time to reconsider the course our country is headed on. We should take this gift with gratitude and seize the opportunity to reverse these socialistic trends, reduce big government, and return this country to its original form. As you read throughout the rest of this book, remember the story of Russia. Remember the Secret Police that Stalin used to execute millions. Remember the removal of God from their societal institutions, including schools, and the ritual persecution of those who remained faithful to our Lord. Remember the demise of a free press, the eradication of free speech and the eventual economic ruin of a people and country. Remember the fact that the damages are just starting to be repaired a decade after the end of communism. Most importantly, remember that anything is possible and that it could happen here if we continue to trust snake-oil peddlers like Comrade Clinton.

# <u>Chapter 2</u>

## The Abuse of Power:

## Politicians and Government Out of Control

Hopefully, I have convinced you that the government has indeed gotten too large and that something must be done. However, I am sure there are those among you who still feel that the government is trustworthy and that a big government cannot be all that bad. After all, there is a large number of individuals in this country who have become government junkies, addicted to a big and growing government. Many of us find employment in big government, and find comfort in the stability that it offers. This comfort and addiction is what makes this situation so dangerous. Freedom is not an easy path, and without careful consideration we may start to lose that freedom.

This chapter has been set aside to begin to show you how big government has corrupted so many people. The abuses of big government over the next two chapters will be laid out. Believe me, when I first uncovered this information my eyes began to widen. I had known for sometime that we, as a country, were headed down the wrong path, but I never imagined that it had gotten as bad as it is.

While researching the information for this book, I came across the writings of other people who made excellent points. Upon reading the selection that follows in this book, I found myself wanting to say everything the author was stating. I believe, that before you hear more of my opinions and facts, you should listen to someone else whom I had never heard of before my research. I simply want to emphasize the point that the abuses of governmental power are no longer isolated events that gain widespread media attention. Each day, those we have entrusted with the power over our lives fail to live up to the guidelines of freedom set up by our forefathers. The media does not cover, and could not cover all of these stories, and it is individuals dedicated to warning all of us, like myself, that deserve credit. Therefore, with the permission of the author, I have included his entire essay in the beginning of this chapter. I thank Mr. Fiedor for this addition to my book.

# Heads Up
# A Weekly View From the
# Foothills of Appalachia

February 7, 1999

By: Doug Fiedor

## THE $40-BIILLION RIP-OFF

If you ever wondered how the far-left got so much money to set up protests and advocacy groups, you're going to love a recent report titled "Phony Philanthropy: How Government Grants are Subverting the Missions of Nonprofit Organizations," by Citizens Against Government Waste. This report shows how the big government supporting socialist groups use your money to force you to behave the way they think best.

"Many taxpayers don't know how to look objectively at the effectiveness of nonprofit organizations and who is pulling their financial strings. ... When trying to discover an organization's funding sources, the best place to start is the Internal Revenue Service (IRS) Form 990. This form is a financial snapshot of an organization. The IRS requires most nonprofit to submit a Form 990, which is equivalent to an individuals Form 1040 tax return. The 990 includes useful information such as total revenue within a one-year period, government funding, investments in securities, salaries of the highest paid officials, and net assets (or ftmd balance), which represent the wealth of an organization. Organizations are required to allow anyone from the public to view their 990 during regular work hours either at their principal office or any regional office that has more than three employees. In 1996,

President Clinton signed into law the Taxpayers Bill of Rights. This new law requires organizations to also provide a copy of their 990 to anyone who asks for it in person or in writing."

Back in 1975, the Commission on Private Philanthropy and Public Needs reported that the government contributed about $23 billion to nonprofit organizations and private sources contributed $25 billion. Now we see that, as government contributions grew, nonprofits increasingly became hybrids -- part private, part public institutions, ever more dependent on government funding and bureaucratic control. That is, "Nonprofit organizations that accept federal funding subject themselves to political processes, pressures and priorities." The bottom line is: over 40,000 organizations receive over $39 billion in federal grant funds directly -- that averages out to $340 per taxpayer per year. And, he who pays the -fiddler calls the tune. No big surprise there.

Nor is there any surprise that the far-left socialist organizations are using taxpayer funds to help bureaucrats control the behavior of the American people. As a matter of fact, there is a very active revolving door between these far-left organizations and the federal regulatory bureaucracy. For instance, have you ever wondered where all these totally silly EPA "scientific reports" come from? Well lookee here:

In 1995 and 1996, 105 groups got $4-billion in grants from the EPA alone. Twenty-three of the groups received more than half their funding from the EPA. The grants ranged from $1,000 to the African American Development Association in Oakland to $21 million for the American Association of Retired Persons. Other EPA grants went to the American Lung Association, the Consumer Federation of America, the Environmental Defense Fund and the League of Women Voters Education Fund. Also reported was that the National Caucus and Center on Black Aged, the Rural Community Assistance Program and the National Senior Citizens Education and Resource Center each got 99 percent of their funding in 1995 and 1996 from the federal government.

As the report concluded,

"The sheer volume of grants awarded by the EPA is staggering by itself. But what is more disturbing is that the process is being repeated every year in other federal agencies, costing taxpayers billions of dollars, with little accountability for how the money is being spent."

The Alliance to Save Energy, a business organization designed to "promote the efficient and clean use of energy" received a million-dollar grant from EPA. The American Association of Retired Persons received $79,430,000 in federal funding -- $20,937,108 from EPA. The American Farmland Trust, a group designed to "stop urban sprawl" received $980,273 in government funding. The American Lung Association (a physicians group) received $649,000 in free taxpayer money. The Center for Clean Air Policy got a $1,057,739 EPA grant to "persuade Congress to address the problems of acid rain and ground level ozone pollution in an intelligent way." The World Resources Institute, which is "dedicated to helping governments and private organizations of all types cope with environmental resource, and development challenges of global significance," got $4,180,702. The Bicycle Federation of America got $525,722 in free money to "create walkable and bicycle-friendly communities." The Center for Marine Conservation received $661,181 of our money to support "full funding for President Clintons Clean Water Action Plan and for strengthening the Clean Water Act." The Clean Sites group received a $1,231,270 grant to help "governments, private companies and communities find and implement efficient, effective, and collaborative solutions to environmental contamination problems." The Ecumenical Ministries of Oregon got $1,944,419 to "teach citizens how to avoid and detect lead paint in houses." And the National Senior Citizens Education and Resource Center ripped off a whopping $36,216,787 to help other liberal advocates lobby in favor of big government solutions.

Really! What we have here is Taxpayer Funded Advocacy. And at least three quarters of it is big government, bureaucratic controlled, un-American, un-Constitutional socialist advocacy.

## WHITE HOUSE BUDGET LIES

If ever we needed another law, it would be to punish politicians who do not tell the truth, the whole truth and nothing but the truth. Last week the lies were so ridiculous it was almost comical.

No, not the impeachment trial. That was a major debacle from its inception. This time they were "spinning" the socialist party line for spending trillions of our tax dollars. Obviously, no one at the White House has anything resembling accounting experience. Either that, or they are intentionally lying.

The most flagrant lie around Washington these days is that the federal budget is in balance and that there is a multibillion-dollar surplus. We know that is a lie because the national debt keeps growing at a rate of $316-million per day. In other words, they are spending money belonging to our grandchildren and great- grandchildren.

The national debt is $5.6trillon -- or $20,648.95 for each man, woman and child in the country. The Social Security debt is $10-trillion -- or $36,832 for each American citizen. Which means, due to mismanagement in government, each of us owe more than $57,000 total.

The cold hard fact is that they increased Social Security taxes a few years ago, but did not use the money for Social Security. Instead, they add it to the general fund and spend it all to grow government. Yet, they keep saying that Social Security is going broke. Well, sure it is! They stole all the money to hire more government workers who do not pay the Social Security tax. The February 2nd Washington Times editorial identified most of the problems with Clinton's federal budget proposal:

Before President Clinton's second term, you could count on two fingers the number of times the federal government extracted tax revenues above 20 percent of the nations total economic output since George Washington first took the oath of office. Both times occurred during World War II. Before that, annual federal tax receipts averaged well below 10 percent of economic output. In fiscal 1998, however, taxes exceeded 20 percent of gross domestic product. President Clinton seems to enjoy this state of affairs so much that his fiscal 2000 budget, which he released yesterday, forecasts taxes over 20 percent of GDP as far as the eye can see -- or at least for the next 10 years.

Yeah, and he included a five-year net tax increase of $45.8 billion to help grow government. In fact, a Cato Institute report identified nearly $150 billion in new spending during the next five years.

President Clinton announced a $1.766 trillion budget for fiscal 2000, which he claims includes a surplus for the third consecutive year. And, just as an afterthought, Clinton announced that he will earmark 62 percent of the federal budget surplus over the next 15 years for Social Security and another 15 percent for Medicare.

So, there's the big lie that the hard working taxpayers of the United States are supposed to believe: Social Security is broke and Clinton is going to fix it.

Social Security was supposed to be an insurance fund. That is, we were all supposed to contribute a little each year and draw from it after retirement, if needed. In the beginning, they actually put aside the money collected in the fund. But, somewhere along the line the big government-growing politicians decided they needed it to run government. Today, there is no Social Security fund because there is no Social Security money to put in a fund. Had all the FICA taxes collected been properly deposited in an investment fund, Social Security would today be one of the world's largest investment funds -- $ 10 trillion rich. Instead, it is broke, just like the rest of the federal government.

As can be expected, many Democrats jumped on the Clinton bandwagon and defended the budget. One big government-supporting socialist even called it "bold, innovative and fiscally responsible."

"I think this will be a popular budget among Democrats, and once people know more about it, it will be a popular budget in America," said Rep. John M. Spratt, Jr. (D-SC), the ranking Democrat on the Budget Committee.

We think it will be popular among Democrats, too. After all it's the Democrats who got us in this fiscal mess -- with an assist from liberal Republicans.

Republicans with a little economic sense called Clintons budget proposal "fiction," "fraud" and "honestly phony". A few Republicans issued a critique calling Clinton's Social Security plan "pure fiction at best, fraud at worst." That's an understatement.

However, if we can get Republicans to make a few constructive changes, perhaps there would be an honest budget surplus. For instance, All FICA tax should be kept away from the eager tax and spend crowd and deposited in marketable Treasury bonds. The overall federal workforce should be cut by at least ten-percent. The federal government should only offer one medical insurance plan, the same one for all federal employees, as well as Medicare and Medicaid recipients. And, that national debt must be abolished.

---

I believe that this essay sums up some of the abuses we typically see in government. Furthermore, as government has gotten larger, the potential abuses have become more costly.

Remember the story about the $500 hammer purchased by the Department of Defense? When word got out that the federal government had spent that much for something you could pick up for a few bucks at the local hardware store, a lot of people were shocked at the staggering waste of big government. However the story of the $500 hammer is easy to accept, compared to the one about the $500,000 fly.

That's the amount the U.S. Fish & Wildlife Service forced a San Bernardino, California, hospital to spend to protect the famed Delhi Sands flower-loving fly, the only fly on the Endangered Species list.

Not only did the builders of the hospital have to move the hospital 350 feet from its planned location - they had to set aside 2 acres of dune land for fly habitat, costing around $4 million. Since there were only eight flies that needed federal protection that means the builders had to spend $500,000 per fly. Where is common sense in all of this? There is none. There is no common sense allowed in the realm of big government.

Each time a part of the government, either acting as an individual or part of an organization, abuses its power, the citizens of the United States lose a little bit more of their freedom. Regrettably, many Americans have turned their heads to this madness and have given up hope. Many people have put all of their trust in the government. This is a great tragedy.

In the case of the half-million dollar fly, the Clinton administration is halting millions of dollars worth of construction in the area, including schools, sewers and flood-control projects, until San Bernardino County comes up with $220 million in land acquisition funds to protect the flies. Woe to the housewife who swats one of these flies. If they're caught doing it, they could face fines upwards of $25,000 and possible jail time.

I must reiterate an earlier point. I am not trying to say that everyone in government is evil, nor am I advocating the overthrow of government. I simply am asking you to read these examples of big governmental abuse and draw the inevitable conclusion. Our founding fathers set up a weak federal government in order to protect all of us from the abusive nature of a centralized power structure. Therefore, the only way to keep government, and those who wield its powers, in check is to limit its size. If we do not, we should all expect the following abuses to continue growing in size and frequency.

# The Unelected Representatives and the Policy of Protectionism

You probably can recall my references to the unelected representatives that flow through the halls of federal bureaucracy. To recap, I firmly believe that current and historical events prove that many agencies in our federal government perform acts of self-preservation that reek of conflict of interest.

Regrettably, few of the individuals charged with enforcing the rules and regulations of the massive federal government are hired and fired by you and me (the voters). In fact, the vast majority of people who maintain power over our daily lives are nothing more than federal employees who are paid from our tax dollars.

As the size of government grew, so did the bureaucracy necessary to operate it on a daily basis. As each new department was created, the individuals charged with its operation (unelected individuals) attempted to justify their budgets each year to the congressional appropriators. No matter what, it became necessary to prove that your particular agency was vital to the operation of the United States. Therefore, individuals in those positions of power would do anything, and say anything to keep their job secure. It was undeniable that if an agency, commissioned to solve a certain problem, returned to the President reporting success in the eradication of that problem, they would all be thanked, let go, and sent home.

Thus, as a result, individuals who are employed with certain agencies have a sole purpose in life: to justify, each year, the existence of their agency and the current spending levels. It is, therefore, imprudent for anyone in any of those agencies to actually attempt to accomplish any goals each year. If they succeed in accomplishing their goals, then their agency will no longer be necessary and their budget will be cut, jobs will be lost and the prominence of individuals in that agency will plummet. It is impossible for individuals, placed in this situation of determining their own fate, to make prudent decisions when their services are either: a) no longer needed, or b) unable to accomplish the goal they were instructed to do.

Furthermore, as mentioned before, the individuals entrusted by our government to oversee these agencies and make sure they are making prudent decisions are part of that corrupted system as well. If an Inspector General finds out that a particular agency is handling affairs all wrong and that agency is therefore no longer necessary or prudent to continue operating, then that I.G. will be out of a job. They too cannot be expected to make decisions that benefit the taxpayers and not themselves.

These unelected representatives have grown exponentially in numbers throughout the years because of this Policy of Protectionism. In fact, some agencies were born because of their ability to increase the prominence and respect of their agency, despite information that proved their methods were not as effective as others. Case in point, the D.E.A., which, in the past, was referred to as the Bureau of Narcotics and Dangerous Drugs.

## The Origins of the D.E.A.: A Case Study in the Policy of Protectionism and the Conflict of Interest that Federalism Creates

Drugs are indeed a plague upon our society. They encourage people to give into hedonistic lifestyles that lead only to the path of self-destruction. Despite this, the creation of one of the largest federal law enforcement organizations was not accomplished because it was in the best interest of the American people. In fact, the primary motivation of the individuals who started the Federal Bureau of Narcotics and Dangerous Drugs was not the safety of the people, rather the prominence of the governmental agency they represented- The U.S. Treasury Department.

Against popular beliefs, drugs have not always been illegal in the United States. In fact, the first drug law in the U.S. was the Harrison Act of 1914. The law was designed to limit the trade of heroin and other opiates throughout the United States. This law, in effect, made it illegal for anyone to purchase opiates without a doctor's prescription. Therefore, the control of opiate distribution rested solely in the hands of trained medical professionals, not the federal government.

Early regulation proved to be very ineffective. Some doctors irresponsibly chose to dispense many prescriptions for the drugs even if the person had no ailments. Local law enforcement officials saw to it that these doctors were prosecuted and thus, the doctors willing to distribute the drugs without care were quickly weeded out. However, it was still possible to receive a prescription for the drug from legitimate doctors, and many professionals, supported by the AMA, continued to dispense the drugs in a treatment orientated manner. In other words, to help patients get off drugs.

The doctors' treatments were successful and opiate drug use among the U.S. population began to reduce for the first time after the Civil War. Continued efforts by law enforcement to stamp out any and all distribution of opiates were dealt a blow in 1925 when Dr. Linder, a respected physician, won a day in the Supreme Court. Dr. Linder was accused of illegally selling four opiate-based pills to an addict in order to help her curb her cravings and reduce the deleterious side effects of withdrawal. The Supreme Court ruled that his actions were well intentioned and designed to properly treat his patient.

Meanwhile, the U.S Department of Treasury was looking for a way to increase their prominence in the nation. Most of the good law enforcement duties were relegated to the F.B.I., and the U.S. Treasury was commonly kicked to the curb when it came to the real-action of law enforcement. In this case however, the Harrison Act fell under the jurisdiction of the U.S. Department of the Treasury. Therefore, the Department of Treasury saw opportunity and seized the moment by creating the Federal Bureau of Narcotics and Dangerous Drugs (FBN) in 1930.

The FBN knew that as long as doctors could keep on prescribing opiates, there would always be a legitimate way for individuals to obtain opiates. Therefore, the Supreme Court had ruled that they had little jurisdiction over drug enforcement unless they caught someone dealing in opiates without a prescription. The leaders of the FBN decided to ignore the high courts ruling in the Linder case and they began to arrest doctors and publicly smear them for prescribing opiates, whether or not the doctors were acting in the best interest of their patients. The FBN was attempting to force all legitimate sources of opiates out of business, which would then make them the sole enforcer of drug laws in the United States.

Despite protests by the AMA, few doctors were willing to risk their careers in order to distribute opiates, even if they thought their patients needed it. Soon the AMA, under intense political pressure from lobbyists of the Treasury Department, capitulated and instructed all doctors to stop issuing prescriptions.

The end result was that the drug trade was pushed into the underground. Individuals seeking treatment had nowhere to turn and drug use began to rise again. The FBN, shortly thereafter becoming the DEA, had succeeded in pushing the drug trade into the underground where the Harrison Act gave them power to arrest the individuals responsible. Furthermore, the eradication of any legitimate treatment centers increased the numbers of addicted individuals, causing a problem of almost endemic proportions.

The modern DEA has a multibillion-dollar budget each year, despite the fact that drug use continues to stay at the same levels. Acting with only regards for their own department, the U.S Treasury subjected thousands of Americans to drug abuse and threw thousands more in prison. All of this could have been avoided if the medical practitioners had been allowed to do what they were trained for.

Don't get me wrong, there still would have been people who chose the life of drugs and crime, but the fact that a federal agency intentionally worsened the problem to increase their own bureaucratic stature is despicable. It is a perfect example of the policy of protectionism and the conflict of interest federal agencies create when they try to justify their existence or the prominence of their particular department.

# The Legacy Lives On: The Abuses of Big Government

## Government and Forfeiture

I will be the first one to say that our country should not tolerate drug use. Therefore, the aforementioned story was designed solely to illustrate how an agency of the federal government can be self-serving. The fact remains however, that each time we give more power to the federal government, we give up a little more freedom. Take for example forfeiture laws. These have generated a tremendous amount controversy over the past 30 years.

The government realized that they could strike a blow against organized crime if they could prove that certain possessions and other forms of wealth were obtained through illegal actions and monies. If this connection was identified they would be legally entitled to seize these assets. Undeniable is the fact that organized crime would be more damaged by a loss in revenue from civil forfeiture than an uncertain loss of principle actors resulting from criminal prosecution. It was a good idea utilized to break down some of the criminal empires that had built up across our country. Regrettably, some law enforcement officials became overzealous, and began seizing people's property for less serious offenses. This has led to a very serious problem. Not always is it the criminals' property that is being subjected to governmental seizure,

Furthermore, forfeiture is a civil matter, and the violation of a law by an individual citizen is a criminal matter. Citizens accused of violating a penal code are entitled to constitutional protections. One of these protections is the assumption of innocence and the necessity of proving guilt beyond a reasonable doubt. On the other hand, in a civil case, especially dealing with forfeited property, the individual accused of the commission of an unlawful act is not afforded the same constitutional protections. Whereas, in a criminal trial he must be found guilty to almost a 99% assurance rate, in a civil matter it is only necessary to be thought of as 51% guilty. This is called the preponderance of evidence.

Theoretically, a person could be found innocent of a criminal matter, but still be held liable in a civil court. Case in point, the O.J. Simpson trial. O.J. was found not guilty in a criminal court where it was necessary to find him guilty beyond a reasonable doubt. However, when a jury only had to preponder the evidence, they found O.J. liable in the civil court and awarded the family of Ron Goldman monetary damages.

In a civil trial, the burden of proof rests on the accused. If one ponders this issue, you will realize the difficulty in requiring individual citizens to prove their intentions and innocence when no overt criminal act was witnessed.

How does this apply to the abuses of government? Well, simply put, it means that the government can accuse you of a crime, seize your property and never have to truly prove you were guilty. Governmental agencies get to keep your property and sell it off in order to help raise money for their own operations. There have been plenty of examples of governmental abuse of these forfeiture laws. Some of which I would like to share with you.

Case in point, Mr. Hosep Bajakajain. Mr. Bajakajain has already won two major court battles, but his lawyers fear that he will not be able to win a third one. That's very unfortunate they say, because if he does not it will reinforce one of the most unjust features of the American Judicial System: the forfeiture laws.

Mr. Bajakajian is a Syrian immigrant who owns two service stations in Hollywood. In 1994 he was traveling from Los Angeles to his native land. He was carrying more than $350,000 in cash; money with which he would repay friends and relatives who helped him get started in the United States. A picture of the American dream.

Failing to understand correct procedures, Mr. Bajakajain did not file the required currency reports, and dogs detected the cash in his luggage. For this lapse in procedure, he was arrested. In addition, given the provisions of forfeiture statutes, authorities seized all of his money. His crime was forgetting to file paperwork. There was no other proof of any wrongdoing, besides being sniffed by a dog.

As mentioned already, civil forfeiture laws are designed to separate criminals from illegally obtained wealth. Applied in the civil court, the state files against the property, which is therefore not afforded the same rights as a citizen. Despite the fact that property belongs to the individual citizen. Therefore, the burden of proof lies with the individual being charged, not with the state. In other words, they don't have to prove you were doing anything wrong, you have to prove that you weren't involved in any wrongdoing. Also, most people cannot afford to sue the government to retrieve forfeited property. Governmental rules stipulate that when filing suit against the government, a citizen must post a $5,000 bond to pay for the government's defense against the rightful property owner. Suits against the government in these cases routinely run around $20,000.

Because the money was proven to be lawfully obtained, the judge in the case fined Mr. Bajakajain $5,000 for failing to file the proper paperwork and allowed the government to keep an additional $15,000. However, power-hungry prosecutors, motivated by the desire to capture all $350,000 for governmental use, appealed the decision. They lost again at the 9th U.S. Circuit Court of Appeals, where the judges cited the 8th amendments ban on cruel and unusual punishment that included a ban on excessive fines. Unsatisfied, prosecutors pushed harder.

In the end, the Supreme Court heard the case and ordered Mr. Bajakajian to pay an additional $100,000 in fines. His lawyer's fees ate up the rest of the money. As Roger Pilon of the Cato Institute stated,

> "This is one of the more egregious examples of the forfeiture laws at work. It brings us face to face with the bizarre doctrine that allows the government to seize property on the theory that the property is involved in the crime. It is utterly illogical and archaic. "

In this case, it was unjust, and overzealous, unelected representatives, violating his constitutional rights to protect his property from illegal government seizure, deprived a man of his properly obtained money. There should not be loopholes in the Constitution's protection of an individual's property.

Many times forfeiture is actually more costly to the taxpayers. Take for example this newspaper article dated March 29, 1998 from Raleigh, NC:

> "State education officials are putting the finishing touches on recommended changes to a new state law that takes cars away from drunken drivers and gives them to schools. Under the new law, school systems receive cars seized from people caught driving drunk on a revoked license. Once these people are convicted, schools can keep or sell the cars. But, since the law took effect Dec 1, 1998, school systems across the state have spent thousands of dollars towing, storing and insuring an estimated 420 cars per month. That adds up to 1,680 cars statewide. As of Thursday, only three had been sold, said Allison Schafer, legal counsel to the North Carolina School Boards Association. In Johnston County, educators spent $15,000 in March to comply with the law."

Once again proving the point that when the government gets involved, they usually end up wasting more money than they save. Now, not only are drunk drivers still on the roads, but the state has to take care of their predominately beat-up, old cars that really have no value.

Or consider Santa Clara County in California, where illegally changing lanes may result in the impounding of your car. In many cases the cost of getting the car out, may be more expense than the value of the car. Allegations have been made by the San Jose Mercury News that the city had mistakenly sold off cars without prior notice or made it very difficult and costly for individuals to get their cars out. Despite being ordered by a federal judge to tidy up their operation, the city continues towing away peoples cars that have just one outstanding parking violation.

Whenever you have increased governmental power, corruption will follow and the citizens will suffer. Take for example a case in 1993 in San Francisco. A gun shop owner, Norman Young, was arrested for having possession of assault weapons in violation of the new federal laws passed recently. He pled guilty and the weapons were supposed to be destroyed. However, it was later reported by the San Francisco Chronicle that an internal investigation had been started because the police were discovered to have been using the same weapons on personal firing ranges. It turns out the guns were collector's items, and since they were very expensive the police decided to defy the court order to destroy them. Upon learning that law enforcement personnel were using his supposedly illegal guns personally, Mr. Norman requested that the police give his guns back. His request was denied and the guns were later destroyed.

How about the War on Drugs? Forfeiture laws have been used for the last few decades to weaken the strength of major drug cartels. Regrettably though, the unelected representatives of those agencies have become corrupted by the power of the federal government; therefore, stories like the next one here will continue to plague our society.

The Palm Beach Post (Florida) ran a front-page story on Sunday, November 13, 1994 entitled "Family still fights for good name after Feds seized ranch 6 years ago." The story, written by Susannah A. Nesmith, features Donald Jones, 36, his sister Toni Wiersma, 40, and their 75-year-old mother Mildred Jones whose 4,000-acre family ranch was seized by then-acting U.S. Attorney Dexter Lehtinen in September 1988. The working ranch, valued at $6 million, is located on Brighton Seminole Indian Reservation in Glades County, near Lake Okeechobee.

The seizure--touted by Lehtinen as being the "largest federal property seizure in U.S. history"--was precipitated by the crash of a twin-engine Piper Navajo in February 1986. The badly burned crash victims were never positively identified and no drugs were found in the wreckage. Still, law enforcement authorities concluded that the plane was carrying drugs because metal grommets were found in the plane's remains. According to court documents, the grommets were similar to those used in the duffel bags drug dealers typically pack their drugs in. The Glades County Sheriffs Office later lost the grommets. Nobody in the Jones family was charged with drug dealing, nor were any of the employees on the ranch.

Amazingly enough, the plane did not even crash on the Jones ranch. It crashed about a mile from the ranch's western border. The ranch was seized because of the government's claim that the alleged drug plane was headed to the ranch before it crashed.

The government made the seizure after snitch Lazaro Fernandez, who was caught unloading drugs off a different plane, made a deal with the Florida Department of Law Enforcement to stay out of jail. Fernandez fingered 10 other men and gave the government the "probable cause" it needed to seize the family ranch.

Fernandez's story changed repeatedly from 1988 to 1993. At first he said that he had never been to the Jones' ranch. Later, he said that he did go to the ranch and saw a man named Richard L. Platt in a pickup truck near the alleged airstrip. By 1993, Fernandez stated that the man in the truck was not Platt, but Bill Wiersma, Toni Wiersma's husband. Fernandez also was caught lying under oath in a related criminal case in 1987.

In May 1994, U.S. District Judge William Hoeveler returned the ranch to the Jones family. Hoeveler wrote "It is of interest to note that, unlike the majority of the populace, Mr. Fernandez's memory seemed to improve rather than fade away with the passage of time, so that, remarkably, in 1993, he did what he couldn't do in 1988 or earlier: He identified Bill Wiersma."

Despite the return of their ranch, family members still don't think they received justice. Besides the $700,000 in legal fees they've expended, the family members say that the drug allegations have hurt the family's reputation. "I didn't step foot out of the house for three weeks," Mildred Jones said. "It was so embarrassing. I had never been in such a predicament."

The family has filed a slander suit against Lehtinen. They claim that Lehtinen, in a press conference held the day after the seizure, implied that they were drug dealers. At the press conference, Lehtinen is reported to have said: "These properties are assets of drug dealers. This is a major effort to take the war on drugs to the drug smuggler's pockets."

Judge James C. Paine dismissed the slander suit due to Lehtinen's prosecutorial immunity. The family is appealing the dismissal.

Donald Jones had this to say: "They say we're in a war, and in a war there's innocent victims. I guess we're the innocent victims."

It seems to me that the innocent victim here is our society's lost freedom. Individuals like the prosecutor here are part of the unelected representatives that can hide behind their prosecutorial immunity, slander innocent citizens and seize property all in an attempt to make themselves look more important. Thank God, the Senate refused Lehtinen's nomination for permanent U.S. Attorney in 1991. He later resigned.

Sometimes the price of over-zealous enforcement and the conflict of interest in governmental agencies is not just measured in money. Sometimes, it involves human life. Take for example the case of Don Scott in Los Angeles County back in 1992. This was a widely covered case with the information provided herein from the Los Angeles Times, The Las Vegas Review, and the Malibu Surfside News.

It seems on October 2, 1992 a task force comprised of L.A. County Sheriffs Deputies, DEA Agents and U.S. Park Service officers executed a search warrant on millionaire Don Scott's estate. The search was based on the information that 250 marijuana plants were growing on the grounds. In reality the 250 acre estate, which actually was in Ventura County, had been a coveted piece of land for some time. Federal parks officials had tried to convince Mr. Scott to allow them to incorporate his land into the scenic corridor natural park in the Santa Monica Mountains. Mr. Scott vehemently refused and thwarted multiple attempts by the government to seize his land through other means. DEA agents had planned to use the allegations of drugs to seize the property and turn it over the U.S. Park Services.

That fateful morning, armed agents busted into the estate at 9:00 a.m. frightening Scott's wife who begged law enforcement agents to not kill her. Hearing his wife in distress, Mr. Scott descended the stairs armed with a handgun. Realizing they were police, he agreed to surrender his weapon, but was gunned down as his arm was lowering. He died instantly.

During the raid, no drugs were found, but agents were sure to seize old maps and other historical documents Mr. Scott had collected that proved the land was a valuable historical site of the Chumash Indian tribe.

This is an example of the sad reality that exists when the government is given a free pass to seize peoples land for improper use. These are just a few stories of the negative effects forfeiture has on our society. There is no doubt that criminals should not be allowed to retain the wealth of their criminal behavior. However, if the courts find a person not guilty, why does the government insist on pursuing their property? For the money, of course. The government has a conflict of interest, and as it continues to grow, abuses of forfeiture are bound to increase, especially as the federal drug enforcement budget continues to rise each year.

# Governmental Waste: The Negligence of Our Leaders, The Price Tag of Big Government

The abuses of government do not lie solely in the hands of law enforcement officials. In fact, I was hesitant to include those stories because it may take away from the brave sacrifices our protectors make each day to insure our safety. My critique is not of the individuals in particular. My critique rests with the federal government, which inevitably encourages a system of conflicting interests. The men and women who have sacrificed their lives to enforce the laws did so under the orders of leadership who did not always have the interests of their employees, or the citizens of the United States at heart. That is the essence of my critique, the fact that, at all times, governmental actions should be taken only when it benefits the people.

Nonetheless, other abuses exist in this era of big government. They occur because unelected representatives feel as if they have a blank check that will always be cashed by the taxpayers. Forgetting their responsibility to frugally handle our resources, many individuals in government sign away large sums of money for wasteful items. Furthermore, many of them use this money for their own personal, political or organizational gains.

It is estimated that in Fiscal Year 1998, the federal government wasted over $30 billion dollars. This money was lost either to fraud or mismanagement. In response, the GOP House Appropriations Committee Chairman urged the House to not approve any further spending by the Clinton Administration until those problems were addressed.

Rep. Dan Burton stated, "Wouldn't we be better trying to fix the problems in existing programs before we start creating dozens of new ones?" A voice of reason in a time of expanding government. This voice apparently went ignored by the Clinton Administration when he announced his grandiose plans during the State of the Union address. If you need a refresher, look back in the last chapter and see just how much Clinton cares about 30 billion dollars that gets wasted every year.

Some of the major agencies cited for abuse included the Department of Housing and Urban Development. This is not a surprise if you remember my earlier section on how HUD makes pay-offs to special interest groups, and remains almost a decade behind on its contract auditing. It appears as if the unelected representatives sitting in the power seats of the Department of Housing and Urban Development do not believe they owe their bosses, the U.S. taxpayers, an explanation for their actions.

In the end, the defense they used was to blame Congress and politicians. Susan Gaffney, the Inspector general in charge of auditing HUD's yearly expenditure stated that,

> "HUD needs legislation to streamline its programs. Powerful interest groups surround HUD. They're not interested in consolidating HUD programs and they influence Congress."

I, for one, sleep less at ease knowing that everyone but the taxpayers and Congress have a say in how HUD is operated. Apparently our President does not care because he represents the powerful interests that allow HUD officials to get away with misappropriation and poor management.

HUD is not the only government agency that must assume the blame for this terrible waste of our society's resources. Some other examples of wasted monies include:

- One billion a year lost in improperly distributed Food Stamps.

- One billion a year in Supplemental Security income overpayments.

- 4.4 billion in fraudulent earned income tax credits.

- 365 million in losses from delays in selling of foreclosed HUD properties

Some groups allege that mismanagement and fraud actually cost even more than 30 billion dollars a year. The Council for Citizens Against Government Waste claimed in 1992 that up to 167 billion dollars is lost due to poor money management and appropriations. The reality of it all is that the National Deficit is a result of poor management, waste, and fraud.

The major problems this group identified with our country's spending is that:

- Spending and appropriations are based on political, not economical, priorities. This is very similar to my argument about the policy of protectionism. Log-rolling and political back scratching result in billions of dollars going to agencies and government contractors as personal favors.

- Large agencies, such as the Department of Defense, have little or no self-auditing procedures. Just in 1998 it was learned that the Defense Department required staff to produce a seven-volume specification layout for new raincoats. This form of wasteful spending is indicative of the Department of Defense. The reason for this waste is found in non-competitive bidding, unnecessary middlemen, shortened procurement cycles that prevent proper price research and an almost non-existent auditing procedure. This is the standard for almost every other major federal agency.

- Federal programs typically lack clear performance standards. As I talked about earlier, many agencies simply request money, but they are never forced to show that the money requested was utilized in a program that truly benefited the people. Fudging the numbers and developing statistics that look good can fool congressional appropriators who are forced to analyze thousands of appropriations bills each year. Many of these requests for money are based on deceptive accounting techniques that hide the true cost, and there is no way to know how much an agency is spending on a particular program. Therefore, with no way to prove if that program is successful, spending can continue to go on for years with little or no benefit to the people.

All of these sources of waste could be eliminated if the power was removed from large government bureaucracies and given back to local governments. These misappropriations are invisible because millions, even billions, of dollars are exchanging hands at any given time.

My personal favorite involves the recent assault against tobacco in this country. Trying to deflect political pressure from himself, Bill Clinton launched a campaign against smoking that was aimed at destroying the tobacco companies. In reality, no true benefits will ever come from this, and Bill is simply using high taxes and government lawsuits to try and put honest farmers out of business. However, despite his constant bantering about the dangers of smoking and the evils of the tobacco industry, Bill signs off on yearly subsidies for tobacco growers.

That's right; while federal negotiators attempt to extort 368 billion dollars from the tobacco industry for health related lawsuits the federal government is spending billions of dollars to subsidize American tobacco growers.

I find it hard to believe that our government could not use that money to help those farmers change over to another crop that would be in line with current policy. Or, more importantly, why doesn't everyone just tell Bill and the gang to get out of our personal lives and allow Americans to make decisions for themselves. That includes accepting the consequences of those decisions.

Each year, all of us gather together at the local post office to mail away our hard earned dollars to Uncle Sam. Most of us lick that stamp under the guise, or hope, that the money we send each year is going to better our lives.

There is no better program (except one administered at the State or Local level) I would rather spend money on than the compensation of victims of violent crimes. However, this is how the system, according to the U.S. Justice Department is supposed to work: (I am sure you will note the absurdity)

- Our money, in the form of tax revenue, is sent to Washington.

- The money is then distributed to the different states and the District of Columbia.

- Then the money is given to non-profit organizations in your local community

- Finally the money makes it into the hands of the victim.

That's a long road to take to get to your next-door neighbor. So, if that sounds inefficient to you, then you are correct. A Government Accounting Office (GAO) report found that in 1997 70% of the money allocated to this program was used to pay the salaries of federal employees.

In the end, after everyone, especially Uncle Sam, takes their share, nothing has been trickling down to the victims. Records show that in 1995, this multi-billion dollar program assisted not a single elderly individual who applied for federal aid. Everything was gone by the time it made it down to the community level.

All these federal agencies do is eat up the money before it ever reaches you and me. Sure, each of those people employed by the federal government are a citizen of the United States, and we do support them in their endeavor to succeed in life, but that was not the intention of this country. Our government was not formed to be the largest employer in the nation.

Once again, it has almost gotten to the point where no one is to blame. As government got so big, the inevitable conclusion was that bureaucracy was going to eat up all of the money collected each year. The only way to stop that is to end big government. For that we have to turn to our elected representatives, who sadly don't have much better of a track record.

# Our Representatives: Perpetuating the System of Misappropriation

Regrettably, those we choose to send to Washington, even if they try hard, have failed to change the system from within. I am afraid that it will not be as easy as some think; because the system of big government rears its ugly face everywhere. The end result is a bunch of elected representatives who are caught up in the system of federal mismanagement and growth. This combination is detrimental to the health of our political nation, and is a result of three major phenomena.

- Mentioned already, the fact that the system is overpowering, heavily established, and change usually only comes from those outside this system.

- Politicians engaged in pork-barreling projects that attempt to bring as much money home to the people in their districts regardless of whether or not the program is really beneficial.

- The primary decision makers in Washington being lobbyists and contributors who shape the decision making process of congressional leadership through dinner parties and blank checks.

The first of these aforementioned phenomena has already been well pointed out throughout this book. It is almost as if the federal government has become a living organism, feeding itself until it just keeps on growing into an uncontrollable monster. However, we haven't discussed much about the second item, pork filled appropriations bills. The infamous result of a zero-sum game where the loser is the American people.

# Pork- The Other White Meat
# of Government Waste

The federal government has become so large that everybody has got his or her hands in the cookie jar. Congressmen and Senators both exchange favors with each other in order to make sure the most money possible is appropriated to their particular district.

We, as residents of that district, tend to support their efforts to bring the money into our areas. The sad part is, we are assisting in the proliferation of big government when we encourage our representatives to take part in pork barrel spending projects.

Big government has made us all so dependent that we are no longer willing to give up the little scraps that we are handed off the table of the master. In reality, the federal bureaucracy eats up most of the money before it even reaches us, which makes us nothing more than beggars pleading "please sir, may I have some more?"

No matter what our representatives request in Congress, be it parks, roads, police, or other forms of federal subsidies and grants, they publicly call them a "worthy legislative initiative". However, behind closed doors they sip their brandies and talk about "bringing home the bacon".

In 1998 alone, lawmakers had requested over 114 million dollars in special projects for their districts, and many fiscal committee leaders say this estimate may be 25 million dollars short. Take for example Ellie Trueman who was asking for $300,000 to fund a therapeutic equestrian center for the disabled and at-risk youth at the Rickman Horse Park in her home state.

All of those programs that ate up 114 million dollars of our money were not funded for any other reason besides political back scratching.

Regrettably, we send our representatives to Washington in order to do this. In the voting booths, we support members of Congress who bring home "more bacon".

By encouraging this sort of behavior, we have overlooked the obvious fact: Why are we giving our money first to the federal government, only to have it returned to us after the federal bureaucracy has taken out a big chunk? The absurdity of it is frightening.

Instead of looking for ways to get the tax dollars back directly to the American people, we are paying for at-risk children to ride on horses. If this was such a good idea, why was it not funded at the state level? Furthermore, if the money never would have gone to Washington, the local community could have had the extra money to erect the same program at half the cost.

These types of practices go on at all levels of government, but come with the biggest price tag at the federal level.

Pork filled appropriations requests are the reason why there are billions of dollars being poured into federal subsidies for tobacco. On one side of Washington, the President and other "do-gooders" are leading the charge against the tobacco industry. They are systematically destroying the livelihood of thousands of people throughout the southern states. On the other side of Washington the U.S. Senate is voting to provide crop insurance, or subsidies, for tobacco growers. Senator Dick Durbin of Illinois was quoted as saying,

> "It is impossible to explain why the federal government is subsidizing the growth of a product the government tells people it is dangerous to consume."

Proponents of the subsidy say it is necessary to support farmers and make sure they do not go bankrupt. I say, they would not go bankrupt if the government would stop subsidizing production, setting price limits and persecuting those who choose to sell products on the free market. Government is the problem, not the land or the farmers.

# Big Government Means Big Abuse

Throughout this book, you will see that the federal government is like a child. If you give them an inch, they will take a foot. Every time we give the government more power, it opens us up for further abuse. All of the aforementioned abuses by governmental agencies are crimes against the people and the Constitution. If you agree with that statement, then you can only conclude that our current governmental system is unconstitutional and criminal.

The federal government is located far away from every American. Few people are plugged into the centralized system and most of us go on about our daily business forgetting that it actually exists. Meanwhile, the federal government has control of an absurd amount of our money and unelected representatives choose to spend it in wasteful and even oppressive ways.

As the federal government gets bigger, these abuses will continue. If the money, power and control is not returned to the states and local communities, more and more of our tax dollars will be lost in a sea of bureaucracy that operates contrary to the principles of freedom.

A big centralized government is a wasteful government. Furthermore, a wasteful government that controls too many aspects of the people's lives borders on an oppressive government and in a democracy that cannot be tolerated.

# <u>CHAPTER 3</u>

## The Loss of a Principled Society:

## The Myth of the Separation of Church and State

# A Nation Under God

Many individuals do not like to admit that the United States is a Godly country. There are those who seek to destroy all bastions of religion in our society and replace it with a form of neo-paganism, worshipping the self and loving nothing but material things.

These people have forgotten the long history of the United States, which was formed under God and flourished only because of God's will. People who believe this last statement have been told for some time now that their opinion does not matter. Those who choose to espouse the values of Christianity are rebuked and ordered to stay out of governmental affairs. The argument of the atheists and communists is that religion has no business in politics or government. They claim religion is dead and the people of America do not want it anymore. Well, they're very wrong.

Religion, and the belief in God, is as strong as it ever was in this country. It is simply in hiding from the oppressive forces that seek to defile anyone who attempts to include the principles of godly living in their daily routine. I have noticed that as we slowly stepped away from God in the public sector, we began to gain leadership that was not guided by a higher power. Thus, a nation has lost its principles and our leaders have become corrupted. Furthermore, Christians in the general public have become afraid to step forward and demonstrate their support of God because many people will call them fanatical, fascist, or simply ignorant. Let me be first to say that religion is indeed alive and the belief in God, and the principles he sets to guide our lives are still holding fast against the steady stream of criticism.

As Garry Willis writes in his book "Under God":

"Technology, urbanization, social mobility, universal education, high living standards-- all were supposed to eat away at religion, in a wash of overlapping acids. But each crested over America, proving itself a solvent or catalyst in other areas, but showing little power to corrode or diminish religion. The figures are staggering. Poll after poll confirms them: Nine Americans in ten say they have never doubted the existence of God. Eight Americans in ten say they believe they will be called before God on Judgment Day to answer for their sins. Eight Americans in ten believes God still works miracles. Seven Americans in ten believe in life after death"

Thus, those of us who continue to believe in God are not alone. An overwhelming majority of Americans believe in the principles set forth by the Ten Commandments. Regrettably, few of us are willing to reject the notion that the principles of God must be kept separate from politics and government. Many of us have been convinced by the socialists and atheists that the founding fathers intended for the Church to be separate from the State.

Godly men who saw it fit to include a Freedom of Religion clause in the original Bill of Rights founded this country. This is an extremely important rule that was made to keep the government from intruding upon and preventing individuals from practicing a religion of choice. Sadly, many have twisted the original words of the founders in order to restrict individuals from practicing their religion in the public sphere. The Freedom of Religion clause did not say that politicians and leaders in the public sector could not practice their religions; it simply said that the government could never force someone to adhere to, or deny a certain religion.

The media have downplayed religion, believing that bringing up morality with religious overtones would be unprofessional. Media personnel are trained and encouraged to avoid even talking about religious morality, instead we are forced to brush up each discussion with references to ethics and public decency rather than God's word. Many have claimed that there is a "liberal bias" in the media that results in this bias against religion. They attempt to prove this point by comparing the number of democratic to republican reporters. However, one may find a better understanding of the bias in the media against religion if you were to check and see how many people have liberal college training in areas such as Political Science and Sociology as compared to those who have been educated in Theology. Furthermore, you may find some of the bias is demonstrated if you compare the number of reporters who attend church as compared to the number that don't.

No matter how you analyze it, the fact remains that the media have been paramount in convincing the American people that religion should only remain in the private sector of the economy and the polity. I argue that this is a country of and by the people and therefore, if 80% of us believe in God, then we should include God in our government and in our daily lives.

The deleterious effects of a godless government are demonstrable in three major ways:

1) The acceptance of an adversarial legal system as the true foundation of justice. Thus, leading to a decrease in the nations sense of community, which results in increased disputes and disagreements.

2) A lack of morals and principles in the leaders who have ascended through the ranks and have never been checked by the media for they're lack of moral principles.

3) A lack of morals and guiding principles for young children in our schools, when an overwhelming majority of parents want this but cannot afford to send their children to anything but a state-controlled school.

All of these effects have resulted in a society lost in the desert, searching for direction. Our children, the future leaders of society, are not provided with a moral education and our current leaders, who serve as the models of future leaders, are becoming more corrupt. Sadly enough, if anyone ever tries to confront our leaders about their dishonest and immoral habits, they are criticized for being a religious zealot, rather then the true god-fearing, freedom-loving American they are.

# Setting the Record Straight: The Truth About the Constitution and the Church

When I first decided to write this book, I was very hesitant about including a discussion on morality in a book about governmental intrusion and constitutional freedom. Although I saw the need in this society for more principled leaders and religious education, I had been convinced by many that the Constitution forbade any form of religion inside of government. I wanted to stand up for bringing God back into the schools, but I feared violating the 1$^{st}$ amendment. I wanted to encourage our political leaders to make morally based decision, but I did not want to violate the separation of church and state. This led to quite a dilemma.

However, as I began to research this subject more, I soon learned the truth about the protection of religion clause in the Constitution. I also learned that the "separation of church and state" is nothing more than a philosophical interpretation of the Constitution and not written in stone.

Simply stated, the Constitution guarantees the right of individuals to practice any religion they choose without government persecution. This means that the government cannot have an official religion that everyone must adhere to. Furthermore, this also means that as long as you can prove that your religious beliefs are well founded, the government cannot impede your ability to practice your religion. (Unless of course your religion involves harming others, then the state must take an interest in the protection of another)

The Constitution never stated, anywhere, that a politician cannot use their personal religious beliefs to guide their leadership decisions. In addition, it was never stated anywhere that religious philosophy cannot be utilized in legislation. The fact remains that we live in a democratic republic, and, as long as the laws we create do not harm other members of our society, then the majority rules.

The Atheists and Communists have convinced those of us who believe in God, and accept the morals that his word has set up for us, that religion has no place in the public sector. How many times have we heard about a controversy over a nativity scene in front of a city building? There is nothing in the Constitution that says that if the current mayor of a particular city is a Christian, and they wish to put up a nativity scene, that this action is depriving anyone of the freedom to practice or not to practice a religion. This is especially true if a majority of the local citizenry support the nativity scene. If the community doesn't like it, they can vote the mayor out of office. At no time, however, is anyone forcing them to practice a particular religion. There is absolutely no harm done to individuals who do not have the same beliefs. Despite this, courts continue to rule in favor of the godless and order people to give up their religious beliefs and practices.

It has gotten to the point that no one is allowed to talk about religion in public. Workplaces have rules against employees talking about religion among themselves. Businesses forbid their employees to even mention God to a customer. A teacher in a school is not allowed to mention God in the classroom.

The United States has forced religion into only the private sector. This is not the way it was supposed to be. Look at our pledge of allegiance:

"I pledge allegiance to the flag, of the United States of America, and the to Republic for which stands. One nation, under god, indivisible, with liberty and justice for all."

I have heard children in public schools who are forced to omit the "under god" part of the pledge. This is just one example of how the removal of religion from the public sector is very recent. Those who try to argue that this is what our original founding fathers had intended are dead wrong, and they know it too.

The atheists in this country refuse to accept the fact that

God has always been an integral part of American society. Since the beginning of the first major settlement, to the signing of the Constitution, America has been a country grounded in Christian principles. These principles made us into the great super-power we are today, and if we turn our back on God, we will see the decline continue as it has in the past decades.

Thomas Jefferson, one of our most important founding fathers, was a strong supporter of a Unitarian country. He believed that the teachings of Jesus were universal and that it was man who twisted the words into something impure. This strong view led some to criticize him for being anti-religious and even an atheist, but analysis of his writings proves differently as Garry Willis points out in his book "Under God". Some of the writings Jefferson sent to others included the following quotes:

> "If nothing had ever been added to what flowed purely from his (Jesus) lips, the whole world would at this day have been Christian... Had there never been a Commentator, there never would have been an infidel"

This quote clearly shows that although Jefferson was critical of some organized religions, his belief in God and the principles Jesus bestowed upon man held true. In fact, he hoped for an America where everyone would accept these principles in both the public and private sector. He wrote further:

> "Had his (Jesus) doctrines, pure as they came from himself, been never sophisticated for unworthy purposes, the whole-civilized world would at this day have formed but a single sect."

On the subject of America and religion he wrote:

> "I rejoice that in this blessed country of free inquiry and belief, which has surrendered its creed and conscience to neither kings nor priests, the genuine doctrine of only one God is reviving, and I trust there is not a young man living in the U.S. who will

not die a Unitarian."

It is undeniable from statements like this, that Jefferson fully intended the public sector to remain full of discourse about the principles of Jesus. How else could everyone in this country end up converting to Christianity? Jefferson believed that the freedom won by Americans in the Revolutionary War would give everyone the chance to see the greatness of Jesus' principles. His vision was for a united country, truly under God. He encouraged the expansion of his Unitarian Christian ideals and wrote in 1822:

> "The pure and simple unity of the creator of the universe is now all but ascendant in the Eastern states; it is dawning in the West and advancing towards the South; and I confidently expect that the present generation will see Unitarianism become the general religion of the United States."

Jefferson intended the government to stay out of religious affairs. However, he did not foresee his own words being utilized by some government officials to actually usher in a philosophy of the "separation of church and state" that made government discourage religious involvement in the public sector. Jefferson also did not foresee the creation of a federal government as large as the one that exists today, and therefore did not realize that the end to his Unitarian dream would rest in the government he helped create.

Many today use the words of Jefferson to support the belief that the freedom of religion clause was created to protect Americans from religion. This misguided belief fails to realize Jefferson's distinction between religious principles and organized religion. This fundamental error is one of the major justifications for the current separation.

In addition to Jefferson's works many opponents to religion in America today use the philosophical beliefs of James Madison as support of the separation of the church and state. Once again, taken out of context, Madison's words could also be interpreted as being anti-religion and, thus, calling for the removal of religion from the public sector: He wrote the following on the subject:

"1)   Since faith depends on evidence, not on coercion, man cannot alienate the right to follow conscience, nor can God abrogate his demands on the individual conscience, nor can God abrogate his demands on the individual conscience; so that civil society has no cognizance (jurisdiction) over religious faith.

2)   If civil society in general has no such cognizance, no organ of it can have any.

3)   Partial establishment can lead to absolute establishment.

4)   Free exercise of conscience is an equal right for all.

5)   Civil magistrates are incompetent to judge of religious matters, even if they had a right to.

6)   Religion is not helped by establishment,

7)   But is hurt by it,

8)   As is civil society.

9)   Establishment would hinder immigration,

10)   Foster emigration,

11)   Disturb good social relations,

12)   And retard Christian evangelization.

13)   Attempts at enforcement would weaken government,

14) Since there is no clear public consensus on the matter.

15) To deny religious freedom would weaken other rights."

In reality, Madison was attempting to protect religion from government, not vice versa. Therefore, he too supported Jefferson's notion (in some respects) that the government should never infringe upon an individuals right to practice a religion. Nor, should there be any official government religion. But, once again, Madison acknowledged the fact that America was a Christian country and that religion should not be prevented from entering the public sector.

Regrettably, today there are Supreme Court Justices like Sandra Day O'Connor[1], and other powerful people, who have taken it upon themselves to no longer recognize America as a Christian nation. These people have used their positions of power to cause government to impede the progress of religion in the public sector. Individuals like Justice O'Connor, who give merit to frivolous lawsuits concerning the protection from hearing religious views in public, have been important players in the destruction of a once principled nation.

The Constitution never gave anyone the right to not be offended by someone else's religious views. Furthermore, it was not intended for someone to use the uttering of "under god" in a pledge of allegiance to sue a public school district for thousands of dollars. The separation of church and state and the eradication of morality in the public sector have begun a decline in American quality of life.

In the next sections of this chapter, I will discuss two major problems, mentioned earlier, that have resulted from this loss of principles. I urge you to keep in mind the fact that the

---

[1] Sandra O'Connor said in 1989 that the belief that America is a Christian Nation is questionable in modern society, as reported by the New York Times.

current practice of keeping God out of the public sector is only based on a philosophical interpretation of the Constitution and is also a recent occurrence. If we succeed in forcing our government back to the principles of freedom it was founded upon, and prevent it from impeding the word of God in the future, the negative effects can be turned around.

# Adversaries rather than Neighbors: America Into the 21st Century

The first major problem that has resulted from a loss of societal principles is a reduction in the sense of community. Regrettably, in the United States, citizens have stopped caring for each other on a day-to-day basis. The same self-love and selfishness that has decreased Christian values has also made each person an island in this nation.

In early societies, the community was the most important factor in the success of any village. Hunting and gathering societies had rules and traditions that encouraged individual members to place the good of the community, over the desires of the self.

Jesus, when he came down to us in the form of man, reiterated these values that had long served godly men. Jesus encouraged us to "love one another" and give "our earthly possessions" to those who needed them more then we do. Christ taught us to have charity and faith in God. These are the principles of any good community.

These principles continued to be utilized throughout the centuries, and even into the colonial era. When individuals first came to America and set up the original colonies, each member of a specific colony relied on the others for support. The realization was that if one member did not have enough to eat, then their services would be lost due to illness or death. The end result being an overall loss to the community that was detrimental to survival.

Modern society has allowed us to forget how important our neighbors are. Supermarkets provide nourishment, large residential areas provide shelter, and close family friends provide support. As our country became larger, and more bureaucratic, individuals began to put their trust in the federal government rather than their community. Worse yet, they had begun to put their trust in hedonistic material wealth and not in God. As principles vanished, so did the community, and the chaos we see today ensued.

Today, our country has become overrun by the adversarial legal system. Instead of resorting to Christian principles, we have embraced secular society's way of dealing with disputes and daily functions. Whenever, there is a problem, we utilize the courts to obtain a resolution, and because this system is adversarial, it rubs off onto our daily actions. We have become a society wrought with disagreement and violence.

The violence is best demonstrated by our high crime rates. True, they have fallen in recent years, but violence among our youth is still ever present. Instead of working out differences, children resort to beating, shooting, raping and killing their peers in order to get what they want. Our prisons have over 1.5 million people in them and our jails have even more each year that spend time behind metal bars. One out of every four black men in this society will spend some time in jail before they are 25, and 1 out of every 5 young girls will become pregnant, and either kill their baby through legalized infanticide or raise them without a father present. These are only a few statistics that show the decline of our people in general.

The lack of community and widespread disagreement is best represented by the lawsuits we see brought to the courts each year. I thought I would share a few of my favorites that at first brought a chuckle, then a tear. I was not crying for the people involved in the lawsuits, however. I was crying for our loss of community. You'll see what I mean as your read on:

1) A minister and his wife sued a guide-dog school for $160,000 after a blind man learning to use a seeing-eye dog trod on the woman's toes in a shopping mall. Southeastern Guide Dogs Inc., is a 13-year-old guide-dog school. It's the only one of its kind in the Southeast, and the organization raises and trains Seeing Eye dogs at no cost to the visually impaired. Carolyn Christian and her husband, Rev. William Christian, brought the lawsuit. Each sought $80,000. The couple filed suit 13 months after Ms. Christian's toe was stepped

on and reportedly broken by a blind man who was learning to use his new guide dog, Freddy, under the supervision of an instructor. They were practicing at a shopping mall. According to witnesses, Ms. Christian made no effort to get out of the blind man's way because she "wanted to see if the dog could walk around me". (Houston Chronicle 95-10-27)

So much for Christian principles in this case. Even someone claiming to be a man of God encouraged this blatantly non-Christian behavior. An organization devoted to the betterment of the needy in society may be put out of business because someone lost his or her sense of community.

2)  A woman was treated by a psychiatrist from March to November 1988, became romantically involved with him, and subsequently married him in October of 1989. After more then five years of marriage they divorced in 1995, at which time the woman sued her ex-husband for psychiatric malpractice and negligence, claiming that the romantic or sexual relationship between them started before the formal psychiatric treatment ended. She contended that her ex-husband had breached the standard of care as a psychiatrist by becoming romantically involved with her, and sought general, special and punitive damages.

3)  A woman was playing golf and hit a shot that ricocheted off railroad tracks that run through the course. The ball hit her in the nose and she won $40,000 because the golf course had a "free lift" rule (this allows golfers to toss ball which land near the rails to the other side). The woman alleged that because the course

allowed a free lift, they were, in effect, acknowledging the rails to be a hazard.

4)  A woman went into a Northridge discount department store to buy a blender. She decided to take the bottom box from a stack of four blenders from an upper shelf used to store extra stock. When she pulled out the bottom box, the rest of the boxes fell. She sued the store for not warning customers from taking stock from the upper shelf and for stacking boxes so high. She claimed to sustain carpal tunnel syndrome and neck, shoulder and back pain.

5)  A college student in Idaho decided to moon someone from his 4th story dorm room window. He lost his balance, fell out of his window, and injured himself in the fall. Now the student expects the University to take the fall; he is suing them for "not warning him of the dangers of living on the 4th floor."

6)  A jury awarded $178,000 in damages to a woman who sued her former fiancé for breaking their seven-week engagement. The breakdown: $93,000 for pain and suffering; $60,000 for loss of income from her legal practice, and $25,000 for psychiatric counseling expenses.

This next one, in my opinion is the worst. It is, by far, the best example of a loss of Christian principles in our society that tops even the guide dog story.

7)  A woman driving a car collided with a man who was riding a snowmobile. The man died at the scene. Since his snowmobile had suddenly cut in front of her, police said she

was free of blame. She then sued the man's widow for the psychological injuries she suffered from watching the man die.

8)  While climbing a mountain, a young man slipped and fell 90 feet and sustained injuries. The mountain rescue unit, which has saved hundreds of lives over the past 30 years, worked with a physician and a paramedic to mount a difficult nighttime helicopter rescue. The rescuers probably saved the man's life... but he turned around and slapped them with a $12 million lawsuit.

9)  A woman dropped some burglar bars on her feet. She claimed that her neighbor, who was helping her carry the bars, had caused the accident. The neighbor's insurance company offered to settle dispute by paying her medical bills, but she refused. She wanted more and sued for damages, including "pain and suffering". The jury took only 17 minutes to unanimously decide that the woman was fully responsible for her own injuries. The innocent neighbor had to pay $4,700 in defense costs. The two are no longer friends.

10) A man was invited to his parents' house to celebrate the Fourth of July. He became intoxicated. And when one of the fireworks he brought with him to the party did not ignite, he went over to inspect it, and it exploded in his face. He sued his parents, the coworkers who sold him the fireworks and his employer.--- So much for Honor thy Father and Mother.

11) A drunk driver was speeding, careened past a detour sign and crashed. He sued the engineering firm that designed the road, the

contractor, four subcontractors and the state highway department that owned the property on both sides of the road. Five years later, all defendants settled for $35,000. The engineer was swamped with over $200,000 in legal costs.

12) A New York appeals court rejected a woman's lawsuit against the company that makes the device called 'The Clapper", which activates selected appliances on the sound of a clap. She claimed she hurt her hands because she "had to clap too hard in order to turn her appliances on;" I couldn't peel potatoes (when my hands hurt). I never ate so many baked potatoes in my life. I was in pain." However, the judge said she merely failed to adjust the sensitivity controls.

13) John Carter, a New Jersey man sued McDonald's for injuries he sustained in an auto accident with one of their customers. He claimed the customer who hit him did so after spilling the contents of his chocolate shake (which he purchased from McDonalds) onto his lap while reaching over for his fries. He alleged that McDonald's sold their customer food knowing he would consume it while driving and without announcing or affixing a warning to the effect "don't eat and drive". The court concluded that McDonald's had no duty to warn customers of obvious things which they should expect to know, but refused McDonald's request for attorney's fees stating that "the plaintiff's attorney was creative, imaginative and he shouldn't be penalized for that." This case was in the court system for three years, underwent appellate court review and cost McDonald's over $10,000.

Why are our tax dollars and courts being tied up with these petty disputes? More importantly, why have others not seen that this lack of community and increased unchristian and argumentative behavior is a result of a loss of principles?

We have thrown God out of the public sector and look what were left with. Petty arguments, wasted tax dollars, high crime rates and criminals attempting to make villains out of our protectors. Without God, there is no principled behavior, and without principles, there is no community. I dare add, without community, there is no America.

# The Corruption of Our Leadership

The second major result of a loss of religion and God in the public sector is the corruption of our leaders, and the failure of the American people to become enraged and take action against those who live the life of the ungodly.

Not all politicians have become corrupt, and some have only been corrupted to a small degree, but it is undeniable that the American people reaped what they sowed when it came to government.  By allowing those in power to interpret the Constitution, and the words of the founding fathers, incorrectly, God has been all but eliminated from anything in the public sector.  This is especially true when it comes to government, because the liberal press vilifies any god-fearing public figure for being a "religious fanatic" or an "overzealous moral crusader" who will take away your freedom. Their actions quickly destroy any chance that an openly religious contestant for public office will get elected.

It is the honest politicians, who know that freedom lies in God, that we truly need in power.  Ones who respect the individual citizens and realize that they not only answer to us, the constituency, but to God for their actions.  This is quite a deterrent when many politicians today act above the laws of man.  It is no wonder many of them do not want to act in a Christian manner, or let religion into the government, because they fear judgment by a power they cannot usurp.

The United States used to be a model for other countries to admire.  It used to be the third-world nations that had corrupted rulers and unprincipled leadership.  However, it is now Americans who must lower their heads in international discussions about political corruption and immoral behavior by major office holders.  As Tim Snyder writes in his essay "What Americanization Has to Do With America":

"Today as disillusion accompanies deeper acquaintance, the embassy's flag is no more than a curiosity. In 1989, America was a model of democracy and rebellion against imperial power. As an American I was asked about Paul Revere, Thomas Jefferson, and the Constitution. In 1998, I'm asked about Paula Jones, William Jefferson Clinton, and the Fifth Amendment. Precisely because the Czechs and Eastern Europeans expected so much from American Politics, their disappointment is painful to observe."

For those of you who do not realize or believe that our political system has become corrupt, just look at these examples. The *Seattle Times* reported in 1998, that Thomas Stewart had made millions of dollars in illegal financial contributions to various public election campaigns. The judge for the case stated that ". . . he had knowingly violated federal election laws." After being caught, of course, Stewart admitted to his wrongdoing but the men who received his illegal donations to their campaigns were not removed, nor were they forced to pay back the money. After all, it was the federal government investigating the federal government. How is this failure to punish the crooked politicians supposed to dispel the general consensus that politicians are in the pockets of the rich?

In another example, the *Kansas City Star* reported in 1996 that a federal investigation into local and state political corruption was advancing quickly. One councilwoman, Jeanne Robinson, resigned and pled guilty to a felony mail fraud charge. Cleaver, the mayor of Kansas City, stated, "The stench of corruption hangs over this building . . . everybody knows we have a problem . . . but (corruption) is neither unprecedented in Kansas City, nor uncommon in public life." Four council members are expected to be prosecuted as a result of this probe. Which, by the way, was conducted by federal authorities, raising the question again, who is watching them? Certainly not state and local oversight committees.

In 1995 it was reported in the *Los Angeles Times* that state Senator Paul Carpenter had been sentenced to 7 years in prison for political corruption. While in office, Carpenter committed mail fraud, money laundering and obstructed justice.

When asked to explain himself to the court, and the people, he simply replied "No, your honor." Keep in mind that he is only an example of someone we were lucky enough to catch. How much corruption goes unseen each year, or has become accepted as normal by the American people.

The stench of corruption befouls the ranks of our esteemed federal congressional leaders. Imagine if you will an actual American company that is currently operating in the United States. It has approximately 500 employees. The following are basic statistics about those employees:

- 29 have been accused of spousal abuse
- 7 have been arrested for fraud
- 1 has been suspected of murder
- 19 have been accused of writing excessive bad checks
- 117 have bankrupted at least two businesses
- 3 have been arrested for assault
- 71 cannot get a credit card due to bad credit
- 14 have been arrested on drug related charges
- 8 have been arrested for shoplifting
- 21 are current defendants in lawsuits in 1998 alone
- 84 were stopped for drunk driving

This company is the United States Congress, or the 535 members of the House of Representatives and the Senate. This is the same group of people who continuously propose multiple legislative initiatives that seek to regulate our lives and ensure that we "stay in line". These are our representatives, supposedly the best and the brightest in the nation. These are our leadership whom we entrust with our futures. When the media slammed the door on godly, outspoken Christians in public office it flung open the alley door for the corrupted and immoral to waltz in.

It has been noted in the past stories how the Federal Elections and Investigation Committees have overseen and caught the state and local corruption. But, I wonder about how well they do with their own people. The New York Times wrote in 1997, that the Federal Election Commission has been pretty generous in their approval of questionable actions by federal politicians. Let's see what you think about it.

The Federal Election Committee approved using campaign money for the following:

- Baby-sitting services for Rep. Jim McCray, while he and his wife were out speaking.
- Rep. James Walsh hauling his wife and children ages 12 and 16, to the 1996 GOP convention in San Diego. Walsh said the kids went for his political benefit.
- Moving costs for congressional retiree Charles Wilson, to bring furnishings, artwork and memorabilia from his closed Lufkin, TX office to Washington, where he joined a lobbying firm; and for in-office Kiki de la Garza to move office and household belongings back to Texas.
- The purchase by Alfonse D'Amato's campaign committee of thousands of copies of the New York Republicans book for supporters.

This was all money supposedly earmarked for election campaigning and not for personal benefit. These are all examples of small loopholes in a system that reeks of corruption but has been doctored up to become socially acceptable.

In a speech in 1994 in front of the Congressional Institute for the Future, Louis Harris, a public opinion analyst, stated:

" As a people, we are more skeptical, even cynical about our leadership in all sectors-private as well as public-and our sense of powerlessness and alienation, if you will, has never been higher. I've been measuring both for the past 28 years. First, alienation, measured by such terms as belief that "the rich get richer and the poor get poorer, most people with power try to take advantage of people like myself," "what I think doesn't count much any more," "the people running the country don't really care what happens to me," and "I feel left out of the things going on around me." Back in 1966, 29 percent in the aggregate reported such feelings. It went up to 36 percent in the 70's, to 44 percent in the 80's, and now has reached 61 percent."

Where do you imagine all of these negative feelings came from? This corruption in the political and public sector has led Americans to lose hope and trust in their leadership. This leadership has lost the faith of the people, because they lost their faith in God. The encouragement of no religion in the public sector, has led to little more than corrupt politicians and disgruntled citizens. Only God can bring it back.

# Bill Clinton: Taking the Cake of Corruption

Most of us have watched the trials and tribulations of William Jefferson Clinton throughout the last 6 years. There are very few people that have not heard about Whitewater, Monica Lewinsky, and Paula Jones. However, these are only the tip of the iceberg when it comes to the corruption that Bill Clinton takes part in.

I too have heard the allegations that Clinton had people murdered and such, but there is little proof to these allegations (although I would not consider them out of the question considering his track record). When writing this book, I was motivated by the fact that Bill Clinton was one of the primary reasons why this country was losing its principles, its freedom and its direction. I really believe that if the people learn about the truth, before the next election, something can be done to stop the decline of America and the freedom it brings to us all. This starts with principled leadership, which Bill Clinton is definitely not. This is the reason why I picked and chose stories that you may not have already heard. These stories are just as serious as the others and they are 100% true. My only thought while I was reading about these facts was: "Why were these not plastered all over the media?"

Bill Clinton has lied to the American people, extended the control of government, ushered in an era of government reliance, and taught our youth that a criminal, liar, and adulterer can make it all the way to the top. Would you want your child imitating Bill?

In the search for more money, Bill and his buddies concocted a heck of a good scheme in 1997. They were able to turn ten thousand dollars into 27 million. Quite a feat if you ask me. But, looking deeper, I learned they accomplished this task by using your tax dollar investments. Bill and his Democratic Party fund-raisers performed some amazing investment tricks that shamed the finest accountants on Wall Street.

I ask you this, how could you throw a multi-million

dollar fund-raiser for only $150? In my humble opinion, it would be utterly impossible to impress the rich folk with only a $150. That is, of course, unless you utilized the white house, the secret service, and thousands of governmental employees to help pay the bill. You see, the Democratic National Committee only paid around $10,000 in order to use the White House, supplies and labor as well, to host 70 fund-raising coffees.

Some of these fund-raisers really do lend credence to the idea that Clinton and Gore have re-invented government. The total cost of one coffee, or the amount the Democratic National Committee reimbursed the White House (the U.S. taxpayers) for was equal to 55 cents a cup. Yet, that cup of coffee would sometimes raise up to $400,000. I'd like to see my local coffee shop pull off that stunt. In the end, the White House was able to raise over 27 million dollars to help support their big government party campaigns, all at the cost of the American taxpayers. Maybe Bill thinks that taking down big government means just making everyone work for him rather than the American people.

By the way, unless you want the same thing to continue for the next 8 years, you all better think twice about electing Bill's little protégé Gore into office. It seems that Gore has learned from the master, and he and Tipper have taken the opportunity Bill has bestowed upon them to hold 28 little coffee meetings of their own. Of course they did not just remain in the White House. They felt no need to reimburse the owners (the American people) for the use of the Old Executive Office Building and the Naval Observatory for their fund raising campaigns. Bill Clinton is truly making government work for himself, but what about us?

Bill continues to claim that he supports the dismantling of the over-extended federal government, despite actions that prove his comments to be blatantly false. He can sit there and lie to the American people, just like he lied to the courts in his Paula Jones lawsuit, and just like how he lied to the American people when he said he did not have an affair. I had no idea that a president was allowed to cross his fingers when he was speaking to us.

Nonetheless, he still continues to support large spending programs and expansive regulatory agencies while he claims that the era of big government is over. The Detroit news on January 17, 1997 reported that

> " The president says he wants an activist government to soften this transformation (the transformation from an industrial based economy to an information/technological/service based one, such as extending free public education to include two years of college)."

This is totally absurd; an activist government is exactly what we do not want. An activist government attempts to get involved in every aspect of our lives. It is a socialist government that throws out the principles of freedom, self-reliance and religion and replaces it with big government programs, high taxes and stifled economies.

Clinton has also said that there should be a: minimum wage increase, health care coverage for uninsured children (mandated of course through a corporate and small business tax), increased environmental regulations (that will stump economic growth), and government intervention in state propositions that end racial discrimination (such as proposition 209 in California which simply stated that race and sex can no longer be utilized in selecting a person for a position). Bill wants more regulation, more control in federal hands, more of your money and less freedom for all of us. This prompted Slate, an Internet magazine, to write in 1997:

> " when Clinton keeps announcing the 'end of big government' one wonders whether this is not one more of his placatory phrases. For he plainly remains a believer in activist government-- even if the scope of his activism is, for the moment, limited."

I see it differently than that. Bill Clinton is nothing more than a snake oil peddler who robs people of their money. In all of his speeches, he only says what he thinks the American people want to hear. Bill Clinton is the finest actor of our time, for he plays the role of a dutiful politician so well that the American people line up to believe him. No one is concerned about whether or not he backs up those statements. When the Republicans began to turn the pressure up on the Democrats to end big government, Bill said, "The era of big government is over." But, whenever there is a problem in the United States, Bill comes on the TV like a late night infomercial and sells us a 27 billion dollar spending fix-it solution to that problem. No matter what the concern is, Bill has the cure. Government spending can fix the family, it can replace god, it can cure a broken heart and it will save our children.

The American people want to believe him, because if he were telling the truth, then we would all sleep better at night. Now, there are too many Americans who do sleep better (falling prey to his lies and deceit) because his approval rating is still incredibly high, but that is only because he mixed a little laudanum in with his snake oil. His words are still lies, and they will only end up hurting us all in the end. He is the biggest liar of them all, and the American people do not call him on it. If god was guiding our government, I doubt that lies like that would be forgiven so quickly.

Clinton's unprincipled behavior goes on however, with no one to stop it. Proof of this unfettered advancement of Bill's illegitimate goals can be found in a story published in the Washington Post back in December 1997. It seems that a federal judge had ordered the government (once again using our tax dollars) to pay $300,000 in fines because of a cover-up that involved both the White House and the Justice Department! It is no longer hard for me to believe, but some of you may find it hard to swallow that the same federal agency supposedly devoted to the cause of justice was guilty of withholding essential evidence to a federal court that was probing the health care reform task force. Which, by the way, was lead by none other than Bill's wife Hillary.

It appears that the task force had become overrun with special interest lobby groups. Ira Maganizer, Clinton's health care advisor, had made false statements to a federal judge during an earlier inquiry that allowed the task force to keep some of their documents and meetings closed to the public. Ms.

Maganizer had assured the judge that the task force was comprised of governmental employees who had only the interests of the nation at heart. As it turns out, Bill and his wife had sold out this task force to health care special interest groups who wanted to get their grubby hands on a plan developed to use American tax dollars for the welfare of the American people.

What had happened was that the Association of American Physicians and Surgeons sued the government and claimed that because there were so many special interests involved in the task force, the meetings should be held in an open forum. Bill and his supporters held them off for years until they were finally ordered by the courts to produce documents. When they did, they produced them with the slow resolve typically seen out of Bill and his other corrupted buddies on Capitol Hill. It was the lawyers from the Justice Department that knowingly refused to allow incriminating documents to come to light in this lawsuit. These documents were only lawfully released after the task force was disbanded, the tracks leading to the White House were covered up enough not to implicate Bill or Hillary, and the American taxpayers were out over 15 million dollars. In the end, the health care task force was only another way Bill let special interest groups into the halls of power and used his position to lie to the American people and the courts.

I regret to bring up some of the already common knowledge stories, like Paula Jones, but it has become necessary in order to demonstrate Bill's level of corruption. You see, the reason why Bill loves big government, is because if he is in control, he can use that power to invade our lives and make sure no one is ever able to hurt him. He has tried to hide behind the presidency to withhold vital information during his impeachment hearings, and he uses government money, resources and facilities to raise the money necessary to keep himself and his friends in power. In addition to this, it appears that Bill likes to wield other governmental agencies like swords against his enemies.

Several days after refusing to settle her sexual harassment case against President Clinton, Paula Jones was informed she was being audited. 21 Republican members of Congress immediately wrote letters of protest, calling the audit "retaliatory and politically motivated." There have been so many audits of those whom the Clinton Administration perceives as enemies that Congress has launched an investigation into the politicization of the IRS. The administration maintains that these allegations are groundless and that there is no correlation between the audits and the enemies of the Clinton Administration. I beg to differ with the assertion that these are all just coincidences.

Among the conservative organizations that have been recent targets include: the National Rifle Association, Americans for Tax Reform, the Heritage Foundation and many others. Many of these groups have complained, citing the fact that no liberal organizations have been selected for audits. But, once again, the White House claims only a coincidence.

The plot thickened though when Billy Dale was fired from the White House travel office in 1993, supposedly because of disagreements with Hillary. He was audited shortly thereafter. Furthermore, it just so happens that the head of the IRS was none other than Margaret Milner Richardson, a close personal friend of Hillary's.

If you still think it's a coincidence, try this on for size. In 1996, the IRS began auditing the Western Journalism Center. It just so happens that the Western Journalism Center was the only media outlet targeted for "action" in a 1994 White House memo concerning the coverage of administration scandals by the press.

Still think this is all just a coincidence? Well, there is more. In July of 1996 Patricia Mendoza yelled "You Suck" at President Clinton while he was campaigning in Chicago. Within a month she was notified that she would be audited. The IRS also upped the ante by threatening to seize all of her property. Ms. Mendoza did not lie down, and began to publicly criticize the Clinton Administration for causing this all to happen. The end result was that the IRS blamed the mistake in auditing her on the computer and dropped the whole matter. I ask this question: If she really was a tax evader, I mean after all, the IRS was about to seize her property, then why wasn't she so guilty after she pointed out the unlawful connection between her statement and the audit? Probably just a coincidence.

Finally, remember the last story about Hillary and her

little corrupted health care reform task force. Well, Kent Masterson Brown, one of the individuals who filed suit in that case which eventually opened up the secret files, was audited shortly after filing his lawsuit.

No wonder Bill wants a big government, because I have already shown that he has the IRS and the Justice department under his belt. In reality, men like Bill Clinton do not want to have to answer to a higher power like God. Sure, they go to church so the camera can see it, but men like him are afraid of what religion would do in the public sector. Unprincipled men like him would be exposed for the evil they represent and would be thrown out of power. Then, the juggernaut of big government that was created as their personal play toy could be used to lock them away forever.

Sadly, without God, without morality and without principles, when our leadership had a chance to throw him out, they allowed themselves to be corrupted by the system, and they left him in power. So now, he can continue to raise money for his buddy Gore by using your tax dollars, he can use the Justice Department, the EPA and the IRS as his lap dogs to attack anyone who opposes him, and he can continue to set up a large federal government for his right hand man to take control of in the year 2001.

There is no doubt that you will see William Jefferson Clinton's name used throughout this book. He has become the symbol of big government and the corruption that now hangs like an evil stench all over Washington. He is the purest example of a corrupted politician. He is also a good example of what the American people get if they tell God to get out, and let evil men walk through the doors.

Although Bill is almost gone, we still have to deal with his lead minion, Al. If we elect Al Gore in the next election, we can expect to have another liar in the oval office. The Investor's Business Daily reported in 1999 that Al Gore was attempting to "Reinvent Bad Government". It seems that Al Gore was misusing statistics to try and prove that he and Bill had made education more effective in this country. The Investor's Business Daily reported that Al Gore said:

"I am proud to report to you new evidence that our efforts are beginning to pay off. For the very first time, reading scores have improved for each of the three grades measured by the National Assessment of Educational Progress, fourth grade, eighth grade and 12th grade. This is great progress, and we're proud to report it."

What Al Gore failed to mention was that this was only since 1994. The reality of the situation was that some scores actually dropped below the levels in 1992 (when Al and Bill took over). Despite this small increase from 1994, the Investor's Business Daily reported that still "38% of fourth graders, 26% of eight-graders and 23% of 12th-graders scored below the most basic measure for reading at grade level in 1998."

Al Gore utilized the findings of this assessment to spearhead his initiatives to give more money to the U.S. Department of Education. He funded more of his worthless programs and used lies and deceit to gain the public's support. I believe that this is reprehensible and so does the Investor's Business Daily's editorial staff, because they stated in the conclusion of their article:

"The founders dedicated themselves to the principle of limited government to restrain politically self-serving officials. The founders did not want America to place politics before truth or personal liberty."

We all know that Bill and Al do not care about the Constitution or the people; they just care about their own political ambitions. On judgment day, God will hold them accountable for their lies, but we must hold them accountable on earth as well.

# Morality and Youth: A Necessary Combination for the Future

With all the problems facing our society, we collectively must turn towards our youth, in the hope of a brighter future. Sadly, however, the light of our youth is fading quickly, overtaken by the grim reality of secular society. Children are failing to follow the ten commandments of life, which in the end has led to a degradation of our country.

This loss of values among children is a direct result of the removal of God from the public sector. Furthermore, increased violence at schools, higher juvenile delinquency rates, higher dropout rates, teen pregnancy, drug use and anarchist ideologies have resulted.

As a society, we have forced God out of the schools and replaced it with other more pagan religions. We have removed Christ and invited the Satanists, the Communists, and the Anarchists to help shape the minds of our youth. This is all a result of removing God from our schools.

Once again, when writing this book, I was perplexed by the notion of the separation of church and state. I could not advocate the governmental regulation of a particular religious dogma. This in turn, caused me to contemplate a solution to our lack of values in the schools. When the smoke cleared and the dust settled in my mind, I realized that I had personally been looking at the issue all wrong.

The key here is not to put God back into public schools, but to take the government out of our schools. With no government, there would be no need to restrict religious freedom in the schools and parents who wanted their children to learn principled and moral behavior could do so. In addition, those parents would not be forced to see their tax dollars used to promote atheistic principles, while having to pay for their own child's Christian education out of their own pocket.

There is no doubt that the whole country has seen a problem with our children. Time magazine reported in its May 24, 1999 issue that schools are beginning to start classes in

character. The curriculum of these classes is based on the six pillars of character: Trustworthiness, Respect, Responsibility, Fairness, Caring and Citizenship. They have begun to teach these in almost every state. As Andrew Ferguson writes:
"Some form of it (character education) is being taught in all 50 states."

On the surface, this seems like a great idea (although the six pillars of character are nothing more than Christ's words changed over to secular terminology). However, when one looks deeper into the issue, the eventual demise of these types of programs is foreseeable.

Once again, the government is instituting these programs. Just think of it, the entity that has created all of the abuses, problems and degradations of freedom in the United States is going to teach our children ethics and character. Maybe Bill Clinton will give a traveling seminar on how a person of low moral character can easily ascend to the highest office in the federal government.

Despite this obvious flaw in the program, our tax dollars are being shoveled into these programs. Time magazine writes:

> "Last year the federal Department of Education handed out $5.2 million to schools for character education; the figure is expected to double in 2000... Last week Senator Pete Domenici, New Mexico Republican, proposed legislation to provide an additional $125 million over five years for character education programs."

As much as I respect the Senator for trying to get morals back into the schools, he, along with most others, are simply missing the point. Big government is the problem, not the children. It's the federal Department of Education, sticking their noses in local affairs that prevent our children from getting a good education. What we need is government out of the business of teaching our children. With no government intrusion, there would be no more compulsory atheistic teachings.

I think Dan Quayle said it best when he expressed his

own ideas on how to proceed: "I suggest students start with the Ten Commandments." I am sure there are people out there who would like to crucify him, but he is dead right. Regrettably, as long as he represents the government, he could never accomplish the goal of getting the Ten Commandments back into the classroom. Therefore, what we must do is get the government out of the schools, get our hard earned tax dollars back, and allow each parent to have the choice to get an education for their child.

Despite the ardent criticism of liberals, communists and Clintonions, the issue of school vouchers is gaining popularity in this country-- and it's about time! For those of you who are unaware, a school voucher program consists of dividing up the amount of money, per capita, a school district has to spend on each student. Then, that money is given to each person with a child. This gives that family the choice to send their child to whatever school they want. If they choose to support the public schools, then so be it, they can continue on with their "character education". However, if a family wants their children to learn about real morality and true character, they can use their own tax dollars to send their child to a school that promotes Christian principles.

Some would have you believe that this program would hurt children. These people are only those that have lost the confidence in themselves. They are the ones who freely hand over the control of their lives to the government, hoping someone else will take care of all their problems. They are the ones who believe they can make it without God. All a school voucher program asks for, is the right to choose how your own child will be educated, with the money that was set aside for them. That's it.

In a Phi Delta Kappa research study in 1997, it was found that 44% of Americans support returning government monies to individual parents in order to give them the freedom to choose. Furthermore, 82% believed that the government should help financially support a child who is being educated, by the choice of the parent, in a parochial school. This is what the American people want, so why doesn't it happen?

I'll tell you why, it's the unelected representatives

sticking their noses in our business again. Think about it, if each state and local school district turned over the choices to the parents (and the tax dollars) that would put the U.S. Department of Education right out of business. There would no longer be the need for that giant bureaucracy in Washington. There would be no more need for lobbying over federal expenditure issues in regards to education. The federal government would be cut out of the issue all the way. Just think how much extra money that would free up to be given to the direct education of our youth.

The unelected representation love keeping God out of the schools, and your tax dollars in their pockets. Instead of making a decent living, they live like leeches on the backs of Americans sucking the money and morality out of our families and our children. A bureaucrat in Washington cares nothing about your child's education. They care only about their paycheck and the prominence of their status in the over burgeoning federal government. Therefore, although 82% of us believe that the government should get the heck out, our tax dollars are continually wasted on these nonsensical federal programs. It's so absurd, it's mind-boggling.

Over 70% of Americans say that the federal government should play little or no role in the education of our children. Despite this, we continue to see spending patterns like the aforementioned. More and more money is being pumped into our local schools and all the people want is choice, nothing more.

Vouchers are the crown jewel of the school choice movement, which encompasses not only privately funded scholarship programs but also school choice and charter schools. As a whole, this movement is a worthy heir to the legacy of the Civil Rights Movement because it shares many of that movement's fundamental qualities: it is a moral crusade reflecting a struggle between the individual and the state; it is politically explosive; and its fate will largely be determined by the courts.

Vouchers will allow low-income families the opportunity to send their children to the school of their choice, public/private or secular/religious. The pinnacle argument is that parents, not the federal government or even the state governments, or even the local school boards, know what is best for their children. Vouchers offer children of crime ridden and impoverished areas the opportunity to seize the necessary building block of success- a good education. How can we call it "public education" when the people are not given the freedom to choose just how that education will be administered. This is a prime example of how the arrogance of the state collides with parental rights. The assignment of children into secular, godless education camps is something we should expect out of the communists, not a free society like America. Just as America is a land of freedom, diversity and choice, so should our educational system. I think Grover Norquist says it best when he states:

> "In the old days, George Wallace stood in the schoolhouse doorway and told children they could not come in. Today, the foes of school choice stand in the doorway and say to the grandchildren of George Wallace's victims, "You cannot get out".[2]

Even many liberals have seen the selfishness of the system rearing its ugly head in this situation. The teachers unions and the Department of Education are afraid of losing their stranglehold on the American youth. Many find it perplexing their unreasonable attitude towards school voucher programs. As liberal journalist E.J. Dionne has said,

> "Within the poorest of neighborhoods with the poorest public schools, there ought... to be a willingness on the part of both teachers unions and liberals to experiment with public vouchers... Surely progressives, with their long history of favoring public innovation, ought at least be open to some experiments along these lines."

Despite this outcry, the passing of voucher legislation

---

[2] "The Choice Crusade" by Gregg Vanourek

faces incredible opposition. Scare tactics by those who leach off our tax dollars fool Americans into striking down these legislative measures when they come up. I am sure you and I are not surprised to learn that the U.S. Department of Education spends almost 10% of their yearly budget on lobbying efforts. One of their biggest expenditures is in opposing vouchers. So, I ask you, whose interests are they looking out for? Furthermore, whose money is going to not only pay their salaries, but also help them insure their right to deny Americans freedom of choice?

The Supreme Court, the interpreters of our Constitution, has struck down some voucher laws, but they have let some stand. It appears as if there are three major rules that must be followed if a voucher program is to be considered Constitutional.

1. Financial support for religious schools must be provided to the parent or child, not the institution.

2. Any benefit accruing to a religious institution must be the result of individual choices made by parents or children, not the government.

3. Funds must be religiously neutral and made available to all regardless of whether they attend public private, or parochial schools.

This is all I am asking for. I do not want the government forcing children into religious concentration camps; however, I do not want them to force America's children into secular concentration camps. Return choice back to individual parents; preserve the Constitution, and a strike a blow against those bureaucrats in Washington who think only of themselves and not the welfare of our children.

In the end, removing God from the public sector, removed God from our classrooms. It has turned our city streets into crack houses and war zones. Those in the government are trying to fix it, without realizing they are the problem. The American people want choice not "character education".

Remember what Thomas Jefferson and James Madison were trying to do; they were trying to save religion from government, not the opposite. The expansion of the federal government and, to some extent, the state governments, into our schools has thrown out God, thrown out morality and stalled the future growth of a free nation.

# Never Too Late

The true Christians throughout America in the past and today have served the needs of the people. They have protected our country in times of war and in times of peace. They have educated our children in both knowledge and morals. Today, organizations like the A.C.L.U. (American Civil Liberties Union) help foster the destruction of the $1^{st}$ amendment by suing god-fearing people. They have been misguided and remain in ignorance about the true meaning of the $1^{st}$ amendment.

I remember a story from World War II about a pilot who lost a wing and both engines during combat. He flew his plane in and landed while praying and asking those around him to pray as well. He landed that plane, "on a wing and a prayer". I bet you, the A.C.L.U. would have sued him for this. Why doesn't the A.C.L.U. come to the aid of those who trust and love God? Christians should be just as protected from governmental intrusions as atheists are. The A.C.L.U. and all other Americans need to get their priorities straight.

The time to strike back is now, not later. God was never intended to be stricken from the public view. Without God, we have turned into an adversarial society, pitting neighbor against neighbor in a battle for limited resources. This, instead of Christ's way of sharing. Without God we have elected leadership who are without decency or morality. Individuals who have corrupted our public institutions and seek only to serve their own unethical interests. Without God, we have unleashed modern society upon our children and have stood back idly as they have become lambs to the slaughter.

All of this has happened because we let snake-oil peddlers convince us that the 1st amendment was intended to protect the government from religion. When, in reality, the 1st amendment was designed to protect religion from government. We are a godly nation, founded by men of faith, it is time to demand those values be brought back into the public sector. Only then will we truly be "One Nation, Under God, with Liberty and Justice for all."

# The Bill of Rights or The Ten Commandments?

"We the people of the United States, in Order to form a more perfect Union, establish Justice, insure domestic Tranquility, provide for the common defense, promote the general Welfare, and secure the Blessings of Liberty to ourselves and our Posterity, do ordain and establish the Constitution for the United States of America..."

The task of creating a framework by which a great nation may flourish was not completed overnight. The ratification of the U.S. Constitution was delayed until 15 years after the Declaration of Independence. Long after the British troops had surrendered their arms at Yorktown and returned to England defeated and removed from the American coast.

Many times, people ask why it took so long to produce the framework of this society. Throughout the past 200 years, a multitude of historical scholars and political theorists have investigated and debated why the Constitution took so long to complete. They have found that at the time, there was a great debate about how large and/or powerful the new government of the United States should be. Many were very frightened of a powerful centralized government, and at many times, the United States looked like it may flounder and fail because an agreement could not be reached. However, despite this enormous difficulty, the framers of the original Constitution worked diligently to produce a firm foundation upon which a society, founded in liberty, could be preserved for centuries to come.

Thus it is logical to conclude that one of the major factors that elongated this process was because many great minds had come together to design a document that would stand the test of time. The final result was the Constitution, and more importantly, the Bill of Rights.

The Bill of Rights set down in stone ten rules that the

government must abide by. Although named the Bill of Rights, it was more like a list of rules that restricted the actions of the federal government. There is no doubt that the Constitution never would have been ratified if the original Bill of Rights had not been included. The American people needed to know that the federal government would never grow out of control and become like a tyrannical king.

This, in my opinion is one of the greatest ideas ever conceived. So often we hear about laws that govern the people. Most people believe that the government, by law, should control the people. In many ways, we have lost the notion that the people control the government through the Constitution and the Bill of Rights.

For those of you who do not know, those who cannot remember and those who do not care, I have included in this book the ten rights bestowed upon us by our founding fathers to "secure the blessings of liberty...".

For those of you who have forgotten or have made the active decision to not care, I suggest you read through this next section carefully. As you are reading, I am sure you will begin to realize, or remember, just how important these rules for government are. You may also begin to question whether or not the federal government of today is abiding by these rules.

I have also included, for a little assistance, a brief layman's description of the amendment. Some times the jargon utilized at the time may seem a bit cumbersome, and I have never claimed to be a scholar, therefore, it took me time to fully understand what some of these amendments truly meant. I thought I would share my interpretations with you.

## Amendment I

Congress shall make no law respecting an establishment of religion, or prohibiting the free exercise thereof; or abridging the freedom of speech, or of the press; or the right of the people peaceably to assemble, and to petition the government for a redress of grievances.

*In other words:*

The government should never be able to tell you what religion you must practice, nor should they be able to stop you from freely worshipping God. In addition, we have the right to speak freely, join groups and speak out against any governmental action.

## **Amendment II**

A well-regulated Militia, being necessary to the security of a free state, the right of the people to keep and bear Arms, shall not be infringed.

*In other words:*

Don't let anyone lie to you. This amendment states very clearly that a U.S. citizen should have the right to possess firearms, with no restrictions. There is no other way to interpret the statement "shall not be infringed". Some argue that the statement "well regulated militia" refers to the state regulated militias that currently exist. These people are wrong. These state regulated militias are still under the power and control of the state governments. When this amendment refers to the militia, it is referring to individuals like the minutemen who faced the overwhelmingly powerful forces of the British at Lexington and Concord. This amendment insures that those who keep and bear firearms to preserve freedom can never be considered criminals. Take note of the statement, "right of the people", not of the government, or an extension of the government. A well regulated, people's militia can only be maintained by allowing unfettered access to firearms. This is necessary to maintain "the security of a free state".

## Amendment III

No soldier shall, in time of peace be quartered in any house, without the Consent of the Owner, nor in time of war, but in a manner prescribed by law.

*In other words:*

This amendment, brought about in a time when King George had forced colonists to house and care for his troops, may seem unimportant today. However, one must see the other meaning behind this amendment. It sets up boundaries that ensure the privacy and sanctity of the home. This amendment clearly states that the government cannot use a person's home or property for its own gain without the consent of the owner. It is directly related to the next amendment.

## Amendment IV

The rights of the people to be secure in their persons, houses, papers, and effects, against unreasonable searches and seizures, shall not be violated, and no warrants shall issue, but upon probable cause, supported by oath or affirmation, and particularly describing the place to be searched, and the persons or things to be seized.

*In other words:*

This amendment expands on the protections afforded to U.S. citizens in the 3rd amendment. It solidifies the individual's right to be protected from governmental intrusion on their private property. According to the 4th amendment, an agent of the government may not invade your personal property without the express written consent of a judge, or other legal public servant. Furthermore, a judge may not issue a warrant unless there is reliable proof that some specific illegal items are contained in your property, or that you are involved, or have been involved, in some illegal act.

## Amendment V

No person shall be held to answer for a capital, or otherwise infamous crime, unless on a presentment or indictment of a Grand Jury, except in cases arising in the land or naval forces, or in the Militia, when in actual service in time of War or public danger; nor shall any person be subject for the same offense to be twice put in jeopardy of life or limb; nor shall be compelled in any criminal case to be a witness against himself, nor be deprived of life, liberty, or property, without due process of law; nor shall private property be taken for public use, without just compensation.

*In other words:*

This amendment covers a vast array of issues. First of all, it sets up the rights of the accused in our society. Before a person can be tried for a serious offense, their case must be presented to a Grand Jury, comprised of other citizens, who will determine whether or not the government has enough evidence to accuse this person. Secondly, this amendment sets up the framework for a protection from "double jeopardy". "Double jeopardy" in this case, is the act of bringing formal criminal charges against a person two times for the same crime. The 5th amendment forbids this practice, and holds that if a person is found not guilty of a crime, they should no longer be subjected to any criminal sanctions for the offense. Third, this amendment gives us the right to not answer any questions police, prosecutors or judges ask us, if they are attempting to prove us guilty of committing a crime. Finally, this amendment clearly states that we should never lose our life, liberty (freedom), or property without our day in court, which is what due process is. In addition, the 5th amendment strengthens the rights of property owners and privacy when it restricts any governmental agency from seizing personal assets without just compensation. Just compensation being the fair market value, in addition to the personal costs, of any piece of property that a citizen possesses.

## Amendment VI

In all criminal prosecutions, the accused shall enjoy the right to a speedy and public trial, by an impartial jury of the State and district wherein the crime shall have been committed, which district shall have been previously ascertained by law, and to be informed of the nature and causes of the accusation; to be confronted with the witnesses against him; to have compulsory process for obtaining witnesses in his favor, and to have the Assistance of Counsel for his defense.

*In other words:*

The 6th amendment sets up the groundwork for a citizen's day in court as guaranteed by the 5th amendment. This amendment provides for the right to be judged by a jury of one's peers. In addition, every citizen is guaranteed the right to confront anyone who accuses them of wrongdoing as well as to present evidence and individuals who are willing to assist the accused in proving their innocence. Finally, this amendment guarantees our right to have a lawyer advise us of our rights and how we should travel through the nightmare of the American court system. That way, governmental agents cannot use their knowledge of the system to oppress those of us who are not as learned in the law.

## Amendment VII

In Suits at common law, where the value in controversy shall exceed twenty dollars, the right of trial by jury shall be preserved, and no fact tried by a jury shall be otherwise re-examined in any Court of the United States, than according to the rules of common law.

*In other words:*

The 7th amendment explains that in civil matters (involving money or property) an individual has the right to his day in court, in front of a jury, if the disputed amount is in excess of $20. Of course, today, that has changed a little bit, because $20 in 1789 is about the same as $500 today. Furthermore, this amendment states that if you are successful in winning your case in court, the individual can only appeal your decision to higher court, according to the rules of common law. They may not simply go to another city and try again.

## Amendment VIII

Excessive bail shall not be required, nor excessive fines imposed, nor cruel and unusual punishments inflicted.

*In other words:*

Let the penalty match the crime. A citizen of this country is protected from spending life in prison for stealing a pen from work. Furthermore, a citizen of this country is protected from being tortured and maliciously harmed no matter what their actions are. Liberals have twisted this amendment in many ways today, but in its purest essence, this amendment was designed to stop government agents from excessively punishing decent, honest citizens for minor infractions of the law. You will see an example of the governmental violation of this amendment in chapter four when I talk about the overzealous agents of the Environmental Protection Agency.

## Amendment IX

The enumeration in the Constitution, of certain rights, shall not be construed to deny or disparage others retained by the people.

*In other words:*

This was a magnificent amendment included by the writers that exemplified their belief that the Bill of Rights was a living document. They knew very well that they could not include every conceivable protection from governmental intrusion in ten amendments. Thus, the 9th amendment asserts that if a protection from government already exists, government agents may not ignore that law because it was not included in the Constitution. These ten amendments were not totally inclusive, and the framers wanted to make sure the government would not utilize loopholes in the rules they created in order to defeat the "spirit", or implied intention, of the Constitution. I am positive they would be saddened today if they could witness how government agents use loopholes in the Constitution everyday to destroy the rights of the citizenry.

## Amendment X

The powers not delegated to the United States by the Constitution, nor prohibited by it to the States, are reserved to the States respectively, or to the people.

*In other words:*

The Constitution was made a relatively short document on purpose. The framers did not want an overwhelmingly strong central government. Therefore, the federal government was only created to "establish Justice, insure domestic Tranquility, provide for the common defense, promote the general Welfare, and secure the Blessings of Liberty to ourselves and our Posterity...". Anything else was supposed to be delegated to the States. The 10th amendment is like a small government clause in the Constitution. It was designed to restrict the federal government from becoming too large and imposing its control over the individual state governments.

Many of you have probably never heard of the rules set forth in the 9th and 10th amendments. The reason for this is obvious. The federal government, as large and powerful as it is today, exists contrary to the rules set up by the framers of the United States Constitution. It is in direct violation of the 9th and 10th amendments and it has soiled the noble intentions of the original founding fathers. The federal government has, in many ways, ceased to be a government controlled "by the people".

I am sure that many people, as they read this section, had thought about ways in which the federal government bypasses these rules set up to govern their actions. Some of you may have used these examples of governmental intrusions as ways to discount the validity of the Bill of Rights. I strongly caution you against this oppressionist logic. Instead, I believe that any example you thought of while reading this section, that proves the government violates these rules, should encourage you to read on further into this book and begin the slow realization that we, as American citizens, are slowly losing, or have already lost, some very valuable protections.

In the beginning of this chapter, I brought up the question of why it took so long to develop these rules by which governmental oppression could be controlled. One of the obvious answers to this question was the fact that this document was designed to stand the test of time. I am sure many of you will agree that few documents, or sets of rules, have stood the test of time. People always change, societies always change, and the world continues to grow and expand. However, there is one document, or set of rules, that has stood the test of time: The Ten Commandments.

These rules, set forth by God- the greatest framer of freedom and justice, are still considered universal, although some people choose to reject them. I don't believe that it is by mere coincidence that there were an original ten amendments, just like there were an original ten commandments.

"1.  I am the Lord thy God, which have brought thee out of the land of Egypt, out of the house of bondage.  Thou shalt not have no other Gods before me.  Thou shalt not make unto grave image, or any likeness of any thing that is in heaven above, or that is in the earth beneath, or that is in the water under earth;  Thou shalt not bow down thyself to them, nor serve them.

2   Thou shalt not take the name of the Lord thy God in vain.

3.  Remember the Sabbath day, to keep it holy.

4.  Honor thy father and thy mother.

5.  Thou shalt not kill.

6.  Thou shalt not commit adultery.

7.  Thou shalt not steal.

8.  Thou shalt not bear false witness against thy neighbor.

9.  Thou shalt not covet they neighbor's possessions.

10. Thou shall not covet they neighbor's wife."

Over the years, the prophets and Jesus added to these laws that Godly men have utilized to pay homage to the creator. Just as the Constitution has increased its amendments to match the changing beliefs and attitudes of a changing society. However, the original Ten Commandments are still solidly intact, and they still have tremendous applicability to today's modern world, much like the original ten amendments should not be discarded as the world changes and new challenges befall the people.

In a time when morality is at an all time low, we must all collectively turn to the original rules set forth by God to govern us as people in his world. Furthermore, at a time when the size and control of government has reached an all-time high, we should turn to the original ten amendments, or rules, set up by our founding fathers, to regain our freedom.

There is no mystery then about why there were 10 original amendments. The godly men who created these rights believed strongly that the symbolic number of ten would continue to flourish well into the future. They would be saddened by how apathetic the American people have become today, just as how saddened God must be with our deviation from the morality of his law.

The two lists of ten should be hoisted up all around our nation. In every school, every governmental building and on all the streets. The Ten Commandments and the Ten Amendments of the United States Constitution. Only then will they serve together as an important reminder that under God, there will be liberty and justice for all.

# <u>CHAPTER 4</u>

## The Deterioration of The Constitution:

## Case Studies in the Erosion of American Freedom

# Case Study #1:
# Firearms- The Insurance
# Policy of Freedom

One is hard-pressed to watch TV, open a newspaper or read a magazine without seeing some reference to firearms. This is especially true in today's world where violence and crime have grabbed the attentions and captured the fear of many Americans.

While writing this book, the people of the United States were dealing with a terrible tragedy. In April '99, Columbine High School in Colorado was the sight of a brutal massacre. Two heavily armed, well-organized students entered the school grounds and began a killing spree that resulted in 15 deaths, including the two gunmen. A nation bemoaned the loss of the innocent, sung the praises of heroes and wallowed in self-pity over the loss of a facade called the "American Innocence".

Immediately following this tragedy, I heard a lot of debate about what should be done to thwart future tragedies of this sort. Some of the more positive things I heard were increased moral teachings in schools and the re-integration of God back into our daily lives. There is no doubt that a loss of faith and devotion to God's word was a causal factor in this terrible tragedy. However, amidst some of this intelligent and progressive debate I saw the signs of a disturbing trend in this country: the call for increased gun control. Measures were introduced into Congress that were actually termed the "Columbine Initiatives".

Utilizing burgeoning public support spawned from the mediazation of this terrible tragedy, gun control advocates were able to begin a systematic attack on the 2nd amendment. The first bill, a law to require background checks at gun shows, an extension of the already existing Brady Law, was first defeated in the Senate. However, rallying public support and challenging the will of 80 million gun owners, Bill Clinton kicked the initiative back to the Senate. Bill Clinton manipulated the

American people, through the media, to get another one of his anti-2nd amendment measures passed. Let me also point out that at least one of the guns used in the killings was purchased by a *friend* of the gunmen who had a spotlessly clean record. How could this law have possibly prevented Dylan Kleibold and Eric Harris from getting the guns?

After all the smoke cleared, the gun was blamed for this terrible tragedy. Let's all just forget about the fact that these two kids built bombs in the garage and bedrooms of their parents' homes. Ignore the fact that local law enforcement officials failed to take decisive action when these children were threatening other children in that school. Be oblivious to the notion that the principal of Columbine High School ignored possible gang activity in his school. Forgive the teacher of the class for which they comprised a video acting out their future violence. Finally, and most importantly, forget the fact that two young adults with murder in their hearts pulled the triggers of those weapons. If you can do all that, then you may be able to blame the gun.

As always, the liberals in this society are looking for someone, or something, to blame, besides of course, the people guilty of the crime. I ask, why can't we blame the kids that committed this heinous act? Let's blame the deranged, godless children who fired those weapons. Have we become so backwards in this society that self-determination is no longer true. There are too many people out there who are constantly looking for someone else to blame for their mistakes and shortcomings.

Out of fear, and a lack of personal responsibility, too many Americans have turned to the government for answers. We have sacrificed our land, our God, our rights and now they want our guns. There is no way that the weapon I keep in my house had any responsibility at all for the deaths in Colorado.

Believe me, I weep for the innocent lives slain in this massacre. However, I also weep for freedom. If we, as citizens in this free nation, lose the right to "Keep and Bear Arms", then there is no way we can ever stand up to an oppressive government. Of course the government is afraid of guns, it's the one insurance policy we have as citizens that those in power can never step over into fascism. This is why or founding fathers, in their wisdom, placed it high atop the list of necessary rights for insured freedom from government oppression.

The Columbine massacre was just one piece of a larger issue that has been plaguing Americans for some time. There have been quite a few school shootings in the recent years, as well as other incidents of violence that have gripped the nation's attention. However, despite the efforts of many activists and quite a few irresponsible politicians, gun control has not been able to make much headway in the past 10 years. Nonetheless, slowly but surely, the anti-freedom fighters calling for gun control have eroded away, piece by piece, the rights of the 80 million gun owners (legitimate) in this society.

This is indeed dangerous times for freedom. The governmental regulation of the 2nd amendment is truly a "slippery slope" that leads to the pathway of fascism. Now, gun control activists have changed their tactics to those successfully utilized by the Clinton Administration to strangle the tobacco industry. Individuals and governments claiming that the excessive use of cigarettes harmed them sued the tobacco industry. Now, I don't know about you, but I remember the warning labels on the sides of cigarettes. I remember that even though I have been around for some time, I was told that smoking was addictive. The fact is, individuals chose, despite the risks, to smoke cigarettes. Now, the tobacco industry is being held liable for that.

The same tactics are being utilized to sue gun manufacturers. Governments and individuals are suing gun manufacturers claiming that they are responsible for any deaths resulting from the use of a gun. These actions have received tremendous support from the Clinton Administration. Continuing on his path of criminal and oppressive actions, Clinton has spearheaded this assault on tobacco and guns. Gaining a majority of public support, Clinton is like a prostitute. If enough people are willing to pay him, and he is doing something that appears to make certain liberals satisfied, he will take a course of action that is irresponsible and oversteps the boundaries of federal intrusion.

His view of the "New World Order" turns out to be nothing more than the "One World Order". He has convinced the American people that this is the answer. Part of that "One World Order" is the handing over of our liberties to multi-national organizations, such as the United Nations. One of the first steps in the oppression of the American people is making us so scared that we peacefully hand over our weapons. I assert that all of you who believe that the "One World Order" will solve the problems of war and violence better think twice. The "One World Order" will be the end of liberty; the end of self-determination and it will usher in an era of governmental dictatorship and bury freedom in a deep grave.

So, Clinton has worked for almost 7 years to erode our rights so that he can shape America into the form of this One World Order. Therefore, following his example, other liberals are doing his dirty work for him and are using civil lawsuits to attack gun manufacturers for marketing weapons that ended up being used in the commission of crimes. Once again, our courts are actually hearing cases were the most important fact is being ignored. A person, a human, had to pull that trigger and point it at another.

Therefore, in the midst of this most dangerous time, we all must become more educated about, and more wary of, government actions to pull apart the framework of freedom. Therefore, in order to start off this discussion on gun control, I felt that a brief history of the gun in America might just shed a little light on this increasingly dark subject.

## Americans, Guns and Liberty

There is no doubt that guns were created, designed and intended to kill. There is no denying the fact that we live in a violent world. However, freedom is not something you are given. Freedom is something you take, it is self-determining. True, not all of us have to fight for freedom everyday by using violent means, but the fact remains that there are people out there, in this modern world, who would take away your freedom in a heartbeat. Sometimes it becomes necessary to either stand up for the freedom one already has, or strike out and seize liberty from the claws of the oppressor.

When the cry of "The British are coming!" rang out across a fledgling nation, early pioneers of freedom did not lock the doors and dial 911. They did not walk up to their new government and ask for the military, or the police. When that cry rang out, the freedom fighters of a new nation grabbed the muskets they had stashed away in hiding.

You see, the British Monarch knew very well that he could keep the American colonists under his thumb if he did not allow them to have weapons. After all, why do you think we called the "Boston Massacre" what we did instead of the "Battle of Boston"? Because we did not have guns and the British did; we were massacred and the British lived.

In order to achieve his oppressive goals of de-arming the American colonists, the King ordered warrantless searches and issued decrees outlawing guns. Therefore, when the time of battle came, the only ones who stood out on the roads at Lexington and Concord were so-called "criminals". These early pioneers of freedom were common citizens, like you and me, who kept arms in their homes, prepared for the day when they would have to strike a blow for liberty. There is no doubt that the reason why we are free today is because we had guns.

Julian S. Hatcher, Lt. Colonel U.S. Army, wrote in 1938 as contained in the book "The Rifle in America" by Phillip Sharp:

> "To every red-blooded American the rifle is a weapon with a deep and romantic appeal. The rifle was developed from a mechanical monstrosity into a marvel of precision by our pioneering forefathers of colonial days, and had no small share in gaining them their freedom. In fact, it was the War of the American Revolution that first brought the rifle prominently before the eyes of the world as the one firearm that made marksmanship possible."

The importance of the rifle was quickly recognized by this new nation. Through an Act of Congress on April 2, 1794 three new arsenals were built to manufacture and store weapons for the people. The Army was very small and our country relied on the volunteer militia. In other words, Congress wanted to pay for, and build facilities that would make weapons *more* accessible to the common citizen. That way, in 1812 when the British came back for round two, the young government could once again call on its citizens to form militias and stand up to the aggressor. This time, our minutemen were called upon to defend the freedom that had been won by their fathers approximately 25 years prior.

Maybe it's the fact that no one has invaded the U.S. since then which has made us complacent and forgetful of history. This is why we do not remember the fact that when the government needed our help, they tried to make guns as easily obtainable as possible. Now, however, when we pay almost half of our paychecks each year in taxes, tariffs and government charges, we are discouraged from owning guns, forming militias and standing ready to beat off oppression. It's peculiar how, as government increased in size and stature, the more the leaders in government wanted to discourage the private ownership of weapons. Could this reason be the same as King George's?

Nonetheless, the gun continued to be a necessary element in the progression of American interests. Despite what people like Bill Clinton want to tell you, it has always been necessary to defend American interests, and not the interests of the "One World Order". True, some of our guns today are pointed at countries like Iraq, which threaten control of our oil supply. But, we are also involved in the United Nations' "police actions" such as the war in Yugoslavia, where America has absolutely no interest, except for those of the "One World Order".

American dedication to the production of the finest weapons was demonstrated throughout time, and there is no doubt that American manufacturers are the best in the world at producing fine, precision style weapons. This has been a valuable asset in our time of need. For example, in WWI, just as trench warfare entered its most stagnate stage, it became necessary to develop a portable machine gun. This way, advanced firepower could be brought to bear on entrenched enemies who lied in wait across those bloody fields of battle. The French were the first to develop the worst piece of junk in history, which would jam after firing only half of its clip. American innovators were once again called upon to produce another weapon that would serve our men in the field, which Remington did successfully.

This innovation is in addition to the already expert production of rifles that existed for many years before WWI, and culminated in the production of the Springfield Model 1903 rifle. This rifle was, arguably, the finest in production at the time. As proof of this, it was found that although the U.S. was only involved directly in WWI for the last year, 877,000,000 .30 caliber service cartridges were produced for use in the war during that time period. This is over 200,000,000 more cartridges produced for the Springfield rifle as compared to the comparable British model. This differential in cartridge expenditures existed, despite the fact that the British were involved in WWI from the onset of hostilities. The point being, the American made Springfield rifle was the most popular and therefore the best.

These stories of expert production continue on into the future, when even today, the United States is the leader in the production of firearms and munitions. This is one of the major reasons why U.S. Military actions have been overwhelmingly successful in the past and will continue to be in the future.

This long history, and much more detailed than contained herein, of dedication to the production and design of firearms is proof positive that one of the necessary requirements for the maintenance of freedom in this world is the production and possession of firearms. Some liberals say this next statement with a cynical, sneering tone to their voice, but I take great pride in the following fact: The long history of gun design, production and use in America has led to extensive ownership and expertise among individual citizens. Therefore, the citizens of the United States of America are the most heavily armed and readily trained group of citizen militia throughout the world.

Like I said before, some liberals will think that the aforementioned statement should scare us all, but I disagree. In fact, I am scared only by one fact, that there are citizens of this country who are willing to place their freedoms in the hands of those in government. This is not a personal attack against all government officials, police, military etc.... However, our country was not founded with the intention of handing over all control to an over-extended federal government. In fact, the Civil War in the 1800's was fought mostly because of an over-extended, northern, industrial based federal government that had utilized its power to enforce federal law over state law. Although I am personally happy that this great nation did not split, I find it undesirable that the northern victory also encouraged the continued expansion of the federal government. One of the unintended consequences of the preservation of the Union was the silent endorsement of increased federal intrusion into state rights.

So, with that said, our little history lesson has ended. However, the issue is just beginning. We must turn our attention now to the current battle over gun control. Keep in mind the lessons learned from history: freedom is not something given, it must be taken, with force if necessary and protected like the delicate brainchild it is.

## A Struggle for the Right to Defend Freedom

The assault against the 2nd amendment is a full scale one, with millions of uninformed individuals attempting to demonize 80 million legitimate gun owners. Each year, individuals who are just plain ignorant attempt to blame guns for increases in crime, violence, and a loss of principles.

I have already discussed in this book the true cause of these problems, a loss of God and the principles his word espouses, but some people want to find another reason. Therefore, they utilize high profile cases, and over-eager government agencies to try and erode the right to keep and bear arms.

Laws are being passed and expanded to control every aspect of gun ownership. Soon, there will be no way to own a gun without the government having a profile on you. Gun ownership was not intended to subject a citizen to government observation and tracking. In fact, the authors of the Constitution wrote the 2nd amendment to encourage citizens to maintain firearms. They knew that the only reason why we were free was because we had guns, and during the fight for freedom, certain people had to risk criminal prosecution by maintaining secret armories.

Those who support gun control try to convince the American people that guns are the reason for violence and high crime rates. In reality, crime rates have actually gone down without the assistance of gun regulation. This includes a marked decline in violent crime. Examine the tables below that describe crime in the state of Ohio over the past 16 years. Ohio has typical crime rates for the rest of the country.

**Graph 4-1:** **Index Offenses in the State of Ohio between 1980 and 1996**
(Source: Uniform Crime Reports)

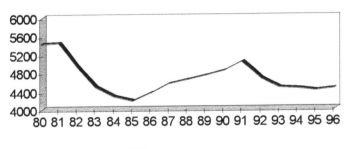

Rate Per 100,000

**Graph 4-2:** **Rates of Homicide in the State of Ohio between 1980 and 1996**
(Source: Uniform Crime Reports)

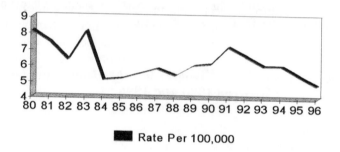

Rate Per 100,000

**Graph 4-3:** **Violent Crime in the State of Ohio between 1980 and 1986** *Raw Numbers*
(Source: Uniform Crime Reports)

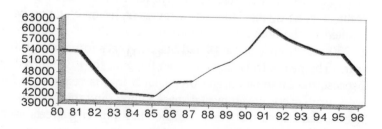

Violent Offenses

You can see that crime typically goes up and down, on a roller coaster ride. Criminologists have identified hundreds of different causes for these patterns, and none of them involve firearms. Crimes, even violent ones, will be committed whether or not firearms are available. Individuals who choose to break the law will continue to do so despite any efforts to limit their access to firearms.

Gun control advocates fail to realize that the gun can do no harm in and of itself. It takes a person with evil intentions to misuse a firearm. It is nothing more than a tool, just like the hammer and the pen. Both of the aforementioned can be used for evil purposes, but we do not hold those instruments responsible for the wrongdoing of evil men.

Take for example the pen. The number one reason why Adolf Hitler was able to subjugate the people was because he orchestrated one of the most successful propaganda campaigns in the history of the world. Here, he used the media, in all forms, to spread his words of hatred, bigotry and world domination. The end result was millions killed and murdered throughout WWII. Did anyone ban pens, magazines, newspapers, radio or TV because of this? Absolutely not, because they were just the instruments utilized by an evil man to accomplish evil goals. We realized the positive benefits of these instruments and understood that they cannot harm anyone unless misused.

We must learn to view guns in exactly the same light. In fact, guns are responsible for far fewer deaths, resulting from criminal actions, than the pen throughout history. Guns have resulted in the homicide of approximately 300,000 people over its 220-year history in the United States. That's less than 1,100 a year. The pen is truly mightier than the gun, for it is utilized to dispense the information and propaganda that is responsible for every war, every governmental mass killing, and the mounds of bigotry and hatred that force violence into our city streets each day. No one talks about banning the pen, but they may start to limit what you say if you no longer have the ability to defend your freedom.

I personally like this little saying:

First, they destroyed the 4th amendment in order to wage the war on drugs; I did not say anything because I was not a drug dealer, nor had government agents broken into my house unlawfully.

Second, they weakened the 5th amendment in order to make it easier to prosecute criminals and punish them by seizing their property; I once again had little to say because I was not a criminal and could not believe my land would ever be seized.

Then, they passed laws to eradicate the 2nd amendment and I said little because I did not own a gun and I was afraid of crime.

Now, they have taken away the 1st amendment and I can't say anything about it.

It is indeed a slippery slope we scale when we began to dismantle the protections the Constitution has given us. There are absolutely no valid reasons for gun control. The support for anti-gun laws originates either out of highly charged, emotional events that shock the senses, or out of the fear many of us have towards crime.

Gun control advocates lie to the American people and try to tell them that tougher gun control will result in lower crime rates. This is not true. Law enforcement agencies have time and time again tried to tell politicians and gun control lobbyists that tougher gun laws will not reduce crime. Take for example an article in the Calgary Herald back in 1995 that was written about the recent increase in gun control throughout the province of Ottawa, Canada.

Police in this situation were backing softer gun laws and Scott Newark, the executive officer of the Canadian Police Association stated,

"It would be wrong to criminalize a fairly large

segment of society that has been completely law abiding for what is regulatory noncompliance."

True criminals will not be stopped by government regulations. All of these laws are dancing around the real issue, which is addressing crime and passing laws that are designed to catch criminals. Whether you pursue legitimate gun owners or not, it will have no effect on the crime rates in our society. Criminals will continue to work outside the system.

As I write this book, tougher gun laws are being passed because America is outraged by the Columbine High School massacre. Gun control advocates have utilized this tragedy to con the American people into believing that tougher gun laws would have stopped this tragedy. This is blatantly false.

These anti-freedom fighters demonize those of us in this country that try to stand up for the 2nd amendment. Gun control activists are constantly trying to enact more regulatory laws concerning guns that will inevitably criminalize those of us who choose to exercise our Constitutional right to keep and bear arms.

Just like with the EPA and the wetlands, which I will get into later in this chapter, the government will enact a web of outlandish regulatory requirements that will end up tripping up legitimate gun owners.

Take for example a current proposal in Congress (June 99). This bill, called the Lautenberg Referendum, will require the registration of guns if they are given or sold to family members. How many of us have handed down the family shotgun to our son, or given our daughter a handgun to protect them from the trash of society? Few people will know about this law, and will not comply with it. Then, the ATF and other law enforcement officials will have the freedom to come busting down our doors and continually harass those who want to keep and bear arms.

## The Credibility of Our Government

The credibility of our government has been seriously

questioned by major events in the past decades. Most notable is the assault on WACO back in 1993. In 1993 it was reported by the Fort Worth Star that U.S. Representative Steve Stockman, a freshman republican in 1993, had said that the assault on WACO was a ploy by president Clinton to gain support for his assault weapons ban.

Mr. Stockman was brave enough to report the truth to the American people. Under a barrage of propaganda from Bill Clinton and Janet Reno, the American people had collectively vilified the individuals inside of WACO. But, according to men like Mr. Stockman, this was simply not true. Mr. Stockman stated in 1993:

> "What had these people done to provoke the government to do this? The answer to that question is a frightening one indeed. WACO was supposed to be a way for the Bureau of Alcohol, Tobacco and Firearms (BATF) and the Clinton Administration to prove the need for a ban on so-called 'assault weapons'. Clinton and other gun control advocates felt that an incident had to be encouraged to happen to build congressional support for banning assault weapons."

Whether or not these allegations are true, it is an incontrovertible fact that Clinton utilized this tragedy to further his assault weapons ban and appear tough on crime. In reality, the assault weapons ban has done nothing to reduce crime and it has had very little success.

In 1997 the Los Angeles Times contained an article titled "Crackdown on Assault Weapons has Missed Mark". They reported that:

> "Assault weapon laws are so filled with vagaries and political undercurrents that police say they are often stymied in trying to crackdown on the illegal gun trade. Among other things, it is often impossible to distinguish between weapons that are lawful and those that are not."

The BATF and Clinton wanted the laws written loosely so they could have free range to persecute as many legitimate gun owners as they wanted. Andrew Molchan, the president of the national gun dealers association has stated:

"The whole assault thing is 99% hysterical. Clearly, most assault weapon owners are law-abiding gun collectors or target-shooting enthusiasts who handle their firearms with caution and believe that the 2nd amendment guarantees them the right to bear assault weapons."

Before we start passing even more laws that restrict gun ownership, we should look at the success of the laws we already have in place. No gun laws have had any effect on reducing crime, preventing violence, or arresting those who sell weapons with the intent of hurting the people.

Gun law advocates will not be happy until they have eradicated gun ownership all together, and they are not afraid to say this. They are willing to give up their right to defend themselves because of hysterics and emotionally charged arguments from people who have been victims of heinous, violent crimes.

Please don't think that I dismiss the feelings of those who are victims of violent crime. I am just appalled by the way gun control advocates utilize the emotions of decent Americans to advance their own fascist agenda of destroying the Constitution.

Members of the National Rifle Association, over 3.5 million strong, are individuals who have spent their hard earned money to protect everyone's rights and freedom. For these sacrifices they have been vilified in the media, and rightist militia groups are highlighted as examples of why we should not have 2nd amendment rights.

In 1995, appearing on CBS's Face The Nation, Wayne LaPieffe, then NRA executive, stated:

" We have never had anything to do with these

paramilitary-type groups you see on television. The NRA has never provided any type of support for those organizations."

Bill and the boys in Washington are simply afraid of having honest Americans own guns. They are afraid that they do not have the total control and power they once thought they had. Guns are the only things that insure the fact that the American people are running the show. It is a caution flag to any government agent and official that they cannot tread on us. I personally hope the day never comes where it will be necessary to fight our own government for freedom. However, I happy to know that if and when the time comes, I'll have a good weapon at my side. If not, we will end up like massacred Chinese freedom fighters in Tianenman Square.

The ban on weapons has even gone so far as to try and prevent young men and women from competing in rifle team as a sport. In January 1999, it was reported in New Jersey that gun control fanatics had tried to shut down High School Competitive Shooting Teams. They claim that allowing children to fire weapons in competition is "sending the wrong message about guns."

These gun control advocates will stop at nothing until your 2nd amendment rights are stripped from you. They do not deny this and use this piecemeal legislation, such as the assault weapons ban and the Brady Bill, to slowly chip away at the foundation of gun ownership. They want to slowly harass gun owners and vilify 2nd amendment protectors so that Americans who are afraid of crime and do not own guns will sit back idly while their rights are taken away.

But could those law enforcement officers calling for gun control be hypocritical? Just recently, it was a subject of national news that police stations around the country had been selling their used weapons to local gun dealers to raise extra money. When the guns for sale were illegal in their state, they would sell it to a dealer in another state. So much for law enforcement's cries of "keep guns off the street!" Not only were used handguns sold, but machine guns, and in one case a *grenade launcher!*

A good example of the ignorance typical of many gun

control advocates involves the debate over a .50 caliber gun. As I watched *CBS This Morning*, an advocate for banning the gun said that it was a threat to safety and should be abolished. The opponent replied that the gun was *six feet long*, and weighed more than 30 pounds. The gun control advocate then claimed the gun could be used by drug dealers to blow up a school bus (as if a drug dealer would ever want to do this). The owner of the weapon, apparently with clearer head, pointed out that the gun had *never* been used in a crime of any kind. So why all the fuss? The gun is awkward and heavy, and has never been used for an evil purpose. So where's the danger?

The actions of gun advocates in the past have achieved no discernible positive effects on our society. Take for example, the Brady Bill, heralded as the gun control law that would protect the people. This measure has failed miserably. The law has absolutely no impact on crime. Consider the following:

- 93% of criminal predators do not obtain their guns from a gun dealer.

- As stated by the General Accounting Office in January, "criminals can easily circumvent the Brady law by purchasing handguns on the secondary market or by having friends or spouses without a criminal record make the purchase from dealers"

- Over 50% of denials under the Brady Law are due to administrative mistakes, parking tickets, traffic violations, or reasons other than felony convictions.

- The law has resulted in only three incarcerations during the first year and a half.

- According to GAO, "proponents of gun control acknowledge that criminal records checks alone will not prevent felons from obtaining firearms."

So I ask, why did this law get passed in the first place? It was passed for only one reason, to begin the slippery slope towards total regulation of gun ownership. Bill Clinton rallied public support and began his campaign to whittle away at the 2nd amendment.

It also appears that the Clinton regime is not above taking credit for legislation they had nothing to do with:

(AP-WASHINGTON, DC) -- The White House has embarked on a deliberate campaign of deception and misinformation, in a "win at all cost" effort to impose more federal restrictions on lawful, peaceful gun owners, charged Wayne LaPierre, Executive Vice President of the National Rifle Association.

Referring to comments made this morning by White House spokesman Bruce Reed, LaPierre said, "When Bruce Reed was in short pants and Bill Clinton was running for Governor of Arkansas, the NRA was on Capitol Hill lobbying for passage of the national instant background check on firearm purchases. For the Clinton-Gore Administration to attempt to take credit for that instant check is deceitful. When the law was passed in 1993, it was the NRA who supported the mandatory instant check system, while Bill Clinton and Al Gore opposed it."

LaPierre also blasted the Administration's claims today, after the White House stated the background check had stopped more than 400,000 felons and prohibited persons from purchasing a firearm.

Making such an attempt has been a federal felony, subject to ten years in prison, since 1968. "If that's true, where are the prosecutions?" LaPierre asked. "The truth is they had zero prosecutions in 1996, zero in 1997, and one in 1998."

"They've only prosecuted 11 people nationwide in two years for illegally giving a gun to a juvenile.

With that kind of dismal record of enforcing federal law, it's no wonder Bill Clinton and Al Gore are trying to mask their record with lies and misinformation," LaPierre said.

Yesterday, reading from a written speech in New Orleans, Al Gore said that juveniles under the age of 18 can currently walk into a gun store or pawn shop and purchase a handgun -- when, in fact, current federal law prohibits anyone under the age of 21 from the retail purchase of a handgun.

Gore's staff later admitted the "mistake," after reporters questioned the statement.

"If you're the Vice President of this country, trying to run for President, you'd better at least be aware of current federal law before you try to push for new laws," LaPierre said. "Members of Congress don't like being misled any more than the American people. And this is a matter of important public policy and a constitutional right. This is not a time to play fast and loose with the truth. It is a time for accuracy and honest debate."

Bill Clinton and Janet Reno have been major players in the harassment of legitimate gun owners. Using the BATF as a club to bludgeon the people, they have systematically attempted to harass and criminalize decent law-abiding Americans who want nothing more than to be left alone. The Nazist tactics of the BATF, and the fact that they are under the direct control of Bill Clinton, are the best proof to show that a man like Clinton is dangerous to a free society. His goal is to strip away the last protection of freedom that the American people have. I am sure Al Gore hangs around on the same platform.

You be the judge of whether or not government has overstepped its boundaries. Most of you know about Waco and Ruby Ridge, but I have included a few more stories for you to peruse and determine whether or not your government is acting in your best interest.

## The Abuses of the BATF

Almost two decades ago Congress investigated the criminal Bureau of Alcohol Tobacco and Firearms (BATF) in hearings before the Subcommittee on Treasury, Post Office, and General Appropriations of the Senate Appropriations Committee. The final report called the BATF's enforcement tactics "constitutionally, legally, and practically reprehensible" and said there is "little doubt that the Bureau has disregarded rights guaranteed by the Constitution and laws of the United States."

In particular, the report found of the Bureau of Alcohol Tobacco and Firearms:

- "It has trampled upon the 2nd Amendment by chilling exercise of the right to keep and bear arms by law abiding citizens."

- "It has offended the 4th Amendment by unreasonably searching and seizing private property."

- "It has ignored the 5th Amendment by taking private property without just compensation and by entrapping honest citizens without regard for their right to due process of law."

- "Approximately 75 percent of BATF gun prosecutions were aimed at ordinary citizens who had neither criminal intent nor knowledge."

Sadly, little has changed over the past 20 years. Armed with new gun laws, and a green light from the White House, the BATF has remained out of control, operating outside the boundaries of the Constitution. Despite the obvious criticisms of the late 70's and early 80's, the budget for the BATF has steadily increased over the years. Although kept in line by Presidents

Reagan and Bush, the BATF has been unleashed upon the public by the Clinton Administration.

The BATF has become Clinton's lapdog to help further his public agenda of gun control. Ruby Ridge and Waco, where ATF actions were called "irresponsible" and "improper" by congressional review, are just the icing on the cake. The BATF stands as a symbol of a government bent on the destruction of the Constitution and the eradication of American Liberty.

Dan Clifford and William Gazecki, both respected reporters, pointed out in a 1998 documentary that the actions of federal authorities during the Waco standoff were reprehensible, and even criminal. The reporters most damning evidence was a piece of infrared footage of the siege that suggests government personnel fired automatic weapons into a burning building were women and children were trapped. This was not a product of some Hollywood wizardry, or the product of a conspiracy nut. It comes from videotapes shot by FBI nighttime surveillance teams. The tapes show bright flashes of light bursting near military tanks at the perimeter of the raging Waco inferno.

Regrettably, a liberal media that tends to support gun control chooses to stigmatize individuals who ask unpopular questions about the illegal tactics of federal enforcement agencies, especially the BATF. However, they cannot succeed in this situation, because two independent analysts, one a ranking physicist who supervised the U.S. Army's Night Vision Lab, concluded that those flashes could only be interpreted as blasts from automatic weapons shot into the building and possibly at people trying to escape the fire.

The documentary also discloses 911 calls and home videos of Branch Davidian members that portray articulate, intelligent and sympathetic people under siege. The warped body of an 8-year-old shows the toxic havoc wrought by six hours of continuous BATF gassing into the Branch Davidian's homes. The BATF used a chemical warfare agent that contracts muscles so violently it snapped the child's limbs like broken popsicle sticks.

The shredded, charred body of an adult appears to have been crushed beneath the treads of a tank, which U.S. Attorney General Janet Reno defends in congressional testimony as a "non-assault" vehicle akin to "a good rental car."

The documentary is full of horrendous pictures that sum up the attitude of some of the most powerful unelected representatives in this country. The documentary depicted Federal Agents flexing their muscles and bragging before the cameras that they are "honed to kill". It also has the footage from a phone conversation where a Davidian was pleading with negotiators to keep vulgar soldiers from mooning children in the windows.

Then, a final image that made me realize how the media has become part of this horrifying assault on American liberty. Reporters clowning around in a kick line on the outskirts of the Branch Davidian's estate while 21 children under the age of 14 were huddled inside awaiting their death sentence.

This assault, designed to protect children from abusive parents, was a farce. The widely claimed evidence of child abuse was never documented. The entire crime scene was destroyed. The BATF successfully "misplaced" crucial forensic evidence such as local coroner's records and the bullet-ridden front door of the Davidian's home.

As I write this chapter (September, 1999) new evidence in the Waco tragedy has come to light, following a lawsuit by the victim's families. Newly "found" tapes of orders given to launch the incendiary canisters into the compound were just released. On the tape, someone expresses concern that the devices might land in standing water and go out. This is significant, because it supports the "conspiracy buffs" contention that those canisters could easily have combusted, and started the fire that destroyed the compound, something that Reno's camp has always denied.

Janet Reno's actions are also in question. It could be that after all of the lies and cover-up, the truth may finally emerge from the ashes.

But Waco, after all, is an example that we're all familiar with. It's the stories that go less noticed by the media that continue to show the BATF's true colors.

As reported in the *Milwaukee Sentinel* on March 9, 1995:

"An Agent of the federal Bureau of Alcohol Tobacco and Firearms was assigned administrative duty Wednesday pending the outcome of an internal investigation into allegations he held a gun to the head of a man in a downtown tavern, an ATF spokesman said.

The 43-year-old agent appeared in the district attorney's office Tuesday, but no charges had been issued Wednesday.

The agent allegedly threatened a man at the Gas-Lite tavern, 775 N. Jackson St., Monday evening. The agent was not arrested.

The agency's Office of Inspection is investigating the incident, said Jim Kuboushek, an ATF spokesman in St. Paul, Minn."

*******

As reported by the *Washington Times* on April 13, 1995:

"The hilltop home of gun-show promoter Harry Lamplugh in the wooded central Pennsylvania town of Wellsboro was raided by several agents of the Bureau of Alcohol, Tobacco and Firearms last May.

The encounter was a nightmare out of a Gestapo handbook, say Mr. Lamplugh and his wife, Theresa: Agents waved automatic weapons in their faces, damaged their property, took medical and family records, seized guns and $ 2,000 in cash, and even caused the death of pets.

In court papers, the federal government has called

the charges of harassment and brutality "outrageous and utterly false."

But no one in the Lamplugh family has been charged with a crime. And ATF doesn't dispute that at least $ 18,000 of the Lamplugh's property was seized and listed for forfeiture and that personal documents have not been returned.

The couple and their attorney, Robert Sanders, have been unsuccessful in trying to open a court affidavit justifying the search and describing why the Lamplughs were being investigated. With federal income taxes due Monday, the Lamplughs have not regained any business records.

In an interview, Mr. Lamplugh said the federal agents were on a "fishing expedition".

He thinks the ATF was searching for records of people who sell guns through the 40 shows he promotes in the Eastern United States each year and for the names of the 70,000 members of the Borderline Gun Collectors Association, which his family runs.

Another motive hinted at in court papers filed by the family in an effort to get property back is political retaliation against Mr. Lamplugh for setting up gun shows at which "cruel and personal" criticism of the Clinton administration and the ATF is exchanged."

\*\*\*\*\*\*\*\*\*

These stories are all too typical. Remember back in the earlier chapters when I offered proof that the Clinton Administration arranges "random" harassment of critics by utilizing government agencies. It is not a surprise that Bill had a part in the harassment of a legitimate businessman. I never once heard of a law that made it illegal to criticize the government, or one that justified the Nazi tactics of "jack-booted thugs" who hoot and holler as people get burned alive in a building.

The list of abuses goes on. Take for example this report contained in an April 28, 1995 issue of the *Washington Times:*

> "The 1992 arrest of Louis Katona III, 34, of Bucryus, Ohio, a real estate agent, part -time police officer and gun collector.
>
> In 1990, he lent a military style grenade launcher to the ATF for use in an unrelated prosecution, but it was never returned.
>
> In May 1992, ATF executed a search warrant at his home. During the search, Mr. Katona said his car tires were flattened, his firearms were intentionally damaged and his pregnant wife was manhandled so roughly she had a miscarriage.
>
> That September he was charged with 19 felonies relating to having falsified documents used to record the purchase of firearms. When the case went to trial in April 1994, U.S. District Judge George W. White directed a verdict of not guilty- asking on the record, "Where's the beef?"

Clinton's Administration has been standing in the shadows, encouraging the BATF in its assault against the Constitution. Al Gore himself suggested in 1993 that the BATF should be merged with the FBI in order to give it more police powers.

Do you remember earlier when I discussed how the DEA first started? Its roots were also in the Department of the Treasury. The Treasury Department has always tried to get its hands on the lucrative aspects of law enforcement appropriations. This example, as well as the other abuses of the BATF, perfectly sum up how a governmental agency can take on a life of its own. Working outside the boundaries of the Constitution and the will of the people, the BATF can exercise a terrible conflict of interest to perpetuate its own prestige.

The sad part is, the American people are the victim in this struggle to obtain departmental prestige and job security. Take for example a 1996 raid in St. Louis, Missouri.

In this particular case, more than a dozen heavily armed law enforcement officers in black SWAT uniforms busted into a St. Louis area home and held a couple at gunpoint, turning the house upside down in a weapons search.

Once inside, instead of turning a handle to open the door to the kitchen, they kicked it in, breaking the frame. The agents were yelling "ATF" but no one in the family was sure what that meant.

"There were no guns in the home and never had been," reported the *Washington Times* in May of 1996. "The family who lives there was innocent. ATF officials admit raiding the wrong house."

The Mueller family may never have known there was such an agency as the BATF. But, after that fateful day, the Muellers came face to face with the horror that many gun owners have experienced over the years. After tearing apart the house and terrorizing the family, the Mueller's received no apology and were left with a totally ransacked house.

There is an awful lot of criticism flying around about the BATF. Many representatives in Congress have tried in vain to limit the appropriations of this controversial agency. This reputation as a Nazi-like agency, is well earned by the efforts of those in the BATF. The officials and agents of the BATF have worked very hard over the years to earn their reputation and they must be proud of it because they make no effort to change.

Take for example these couple of stories:

- Remember the racist "Roundup" in Tennessee that found several BATF agents in attendance. Apparently, agency officials had known for years about the racist overtones at the Roundup and just ignored the fact. The men were allowed to attend in their official capacity with the full knowledge of BATF officials.

- How about in 1995 when the BATF shocked many Americans when they announced they had successfully computerized 60 million gun dealer records? They had accomplished the task of creating a centralized database that had the names and addresses of millions of gun owners throughout the country. Individuals who exercised their Constitutional right to bear arms were profiled by a government agency so they could be monitored.

Some members of the BATF even admit that they have been wrong in the past. In January of 1993, CBS ran a *60 Minutes* special story on the BATF. During that interview, Mike Wallace was stunned when Bob Huffman, a BATF agent, stated, "the people I put in jail have more honor than the top administration in this organization."

Despite all this criticism, Bill Clinton requested in 1996 that the BATF receive a 28 million dollar increase in yearly appropriations. He personally likes the job they're doing, because they are doing exactly what he wants them to: Harass and discourage legitimate gun owners so he can advance his agenda of total gun control. Bill Clinton apparently has no problem with allowing government agencies to break laws and violate the most important rules of our society. He ignores any wrongdoings by his minions and increases the spending of an agency devoted to the destruction of freedom and justice.

The BATF has little problem with breaking every law we hold sacred in order to achieve their goal. They even encourage their agents to lie in court, under oath.

On October 18, 1995, Thomas A. Busey, the Chief of the National Firearms Act Branch of the BATF, made a training video for all agents of the BATF. In this video, he openly admitted that BATF agents routinely lie during forfeiture cases. Furthermore he was instructing other agents to do the same.

In every forfeiture case, a BATF agent must testify that

the firearm seized was not listed in the NFRTR or the official registry of any Title II firearms in the United States. Only after the agent testifies that he or she has completed a full search of this registry and found no record of registration, can the weapon be legally seized. Mr. Busey explained in his video the procedure for testifying in court:

> "Our first and main responsibility is to make accurate entries and maintain accuracy of the NFRTR. When we testify in court, we testify that the database is 100 percent accurate. That's what we testify to, and we will always testify to that. As you probably well know, that may not be 100 percent true... So the information on the 728,000 weapons that are in the database has to be 100 percent accurate according to the courts. Like I told you before, we testify in court (that the NFRTR is 100% correct) and, of course, our certifications testify to that too, when we are not physically there to testify."

Mr. Busey, after he informs all BATF agents to commit perjury goes on to actually cite the true reliability of their NFRTR:

> "...when I first came in a year ago, our error rate was between 49 and 50 percent, so you can imagine what the accuracy of the NFRTR could be, if your error rate's 49 to 50 percent."

In other words, Mr. Busey is well aware that the information his agents use to seize our personal property is only right half of the time. Fully aware of this, he instructs everyone in the department to perjure themselves so that they can bypass our 5th amendment rights and seize property illegally. He is suborning perjury, and no one in the federal government was attempting to stop him.

Only after the tape was ordered to be released to the courts were the injustices committed against thousands of gun owners overturned. Still, however, there are many gun owners who had their weapons destroyed, paid stiff fines, or even spent time in jail because BATF agents perjured themselves.

The most frightening aspect of this story is the fact that it was later learned the BATF had reports of an inaccurate NFRTR as early as 1979. Simply put, the BATF had been suborning perjury for almost two decades.

Another case that is very disturbing involves Laura Kuriatnyk, a mother of four, who was harassed by a neighbor who then falsely accused her of brandishing a firearm at him in 1996. Later, Mrs. Kuriatnyk was terrorized when local, state and federal law enforcement personnel (including the BATF) raided her home and held the family at gunpoint for several hours while they searched the house. The BATF even pointed a machine gun at the head of Mrs. Kuriatnyk's six-year-old daughter.

The abuses continue on, and Bill Clinton only asks for more money to support his shock troops. The BATF has become uncontrollable and is a government agency that no longer answers to the people.

Just look at a story contained in the September 30, 1998 issue of the *Detroit News*:

> "Two ATF special agents face criminal charges stemming from a raid where one agent allegedly kicked a suspect in the head and both tried to cover it up.
>
> Alcohol, Tobacco and Firearms Special Agents Regan J. Scott and Joel J. Kirkpatrick were indicted earlier this month by a federal grand jury on charges they abused their positions and disobeyed orders by participating in a raid with Detroit Police on Oct 7, 1996.
>
> Scott faces the additional charge of kicking Arthur Bruce Norris, the target of the raid, in the head hard enough to injure the Detroit man, the indictment said."

Members of the BATF are encouraged to disrespect the

rights of American citizens. They are told to break the rules, such as committing perjury, in order to rob decent law-abiding Americans of their right to bear arms. This is an undeniable fact. I cannot believe that we as Americans continue to sit back and allow an organization like this to run free throughout our country. Furthermore, I cannot believe we allow our current leadership to remain in office when the rights guaranteed to us by the Constitution are being openly trounced.

How about when the BATF decided to raid the North Carolina Military Museum on June 28, 1994. The curator of the North Carolina Museum was the target of the raid that was justified by the information received from a "confidential informant". With search warrants in hand, BATF agents seized about twenty disabled fully automatic firearms, all legally registered to the curator, inert artillery shells on display and about 100,000 rounds of small arms ammunition.

Agents claimed the shells contained powder residue, yet were clearly labeled "EOD MRT". Agents also claimed that the ammunition could have been stolen from the military. It appears as if the BATF's printout of the Class III firearms he had registered was inaccurate (not a surprise) so they simply seized any weapons they could not personally identify.

The agents came across an RPG launcher (inert of course, with the operating devices welded over) and allowed a member of the news crew to shoulder it while videotaping. "'This is the kind of communist bloc weaponry that prompted the raid", an ATF agent told reporters later.

The BATF has become the perfect example of big government gone wrong. The people in this organization have forgotten that they serve the Constitution and the American people. Their organization has been allowed to forcefully destroy the rights of too many American for too long, and it must end immediately. Only then can we hope to protect the 2nd amendment.

I just can't understand why we continue to support a department that has never accomplished any constitutional or worthwhile function. It only stands to reason that local Sheriff's departments can effectively achieve the same tasks the ATF is supposed to accomplish. These are the elected officials of the people and if their actions go beyond the scope of the Constitution and the will of the people, they can be removed from office. Just think about how effective your local Sheriff's department would be at fighting crime and illegal gun ownership if all that money we gave to the ATF each year was funneled into your local communities. Remember, over 25% of the money we send to Washington is lost to mismanagement, waste and needless bureaucracy. If we just kept that money in our local counties and townships, local law enforcement would accomplish twice as much as the BATF could ever imagine doing. In addition, the citizens would maintain control of those in power because we could remove from office any sheriff who got out of line.

Given these facts, there is absolutely no reason for the BATF to exist.


## The 2nd Amendment: A National Treasure

We must continue to fight day in and day out, for the right to keep and bear arms. No matter what, gun control is a slippery slope towards the eradication of public gun ownership. The owning of guns is the most important way a people can guarantee they will never fall victim to government oppression.

How can we trust a government that already utilizes oppressive tactics to harass and arrest legitimate gun owners and dealers. If they are utilizing these tactics to take away our guns, what will they be doing once we can no longer defend ourselves?

Americans must stop listening to those that call gun advocates "fanatics". Those who wish to preserve the right to own guns are not ignoring the crime rates, or the violence in our schools. They are closely watching the federal government in order to make sure that a democracy will exist to deal with the problems of crime and juvenile violence.

I think it is best to end this section of chapter four with an essay by Peter March, a columnist with the *Daily News Worldwide*. He states, in words richer than mine, how important opposition to gun control is for Canadians and Americans. He reminds us that freedom is tenuous at best, and that governments should never be trusted. We must always maintain a way to dispose of a government if the democratic process breaks down and evil powers attempt to take away our liberty.

# By Force, If Necessary

By: Peter March

Remember that, as far as guns go, the government, not criminals is the potential enemy. Hence, we should not let the government know who has guns, who has the ammunition. The government should not be allowed to know what kind of guns are out there - nor how, nor when, nor where they might be brought together to form a citizen army. Political freedom is only secured by genuine power, and such power is ultimately secured only by force.

For where a citizenry loses the ability to counter government force with an adequate force of its own, it loses the ultimate guarantee of its freedoms and rights. Human freedom is always and only, threatened by other humans who are prepared to use force. Against this threat, a wise citizenry will retain sufficient power to fight back, to fight any government that threatens its freedoms.

The prime minister asks why we allow the registration of pets but are unwilling to register our guns. The answer is that we do not rely on cats and dogs for our freedom. Guns, however, are the essential tools of power, they are the fundamental tools of self-defense. The government knows that and keeps a good supply for itself (And don't say such guns are only for "outside forces"). Think of your local police force, and by golly, remember OKA, by God remember the FLQ "crisis" when an unrepentant "Liberal" was quite ready to declare the War Measures Act in peacetime.

No doubt Canadians will accept gun control. They will not notice that this will mean the government can quickly and effectively collect all the guns in the country. They will not see that by this measure they lose the fundamental guarantee of citizen freedom against the abuses of power by government. They will accept the argument that there is no use for a gun other than hunting, collecting and target practice. Like innocents who want to believe in the goodness of their elected representatives, they will deny themselves the protection they need from these very representatives.

Guns are needed in citizens' hands not for hunting or protection from criminals. Such uses are scarcely worth the cost of the weapon. Guns are needed against that evil day when the government becomes the enemy of the citizens. Won't happen here? Won't happen in the USA? Why not? Why are we immune from the abuse of power by government? We must be different! What is it? Genes that make us better? Our special history? Do we have a new and wonderful culture safe from the political disasters that have afflicted all other cultures in the past?

What many in the United States understand in their bones is that the right to have a gun, a well functioning gun, is a crucial right    Because the American "balance of power" that political scientists talk such rubbish about is not between the legislatures, the judiciary, and the executive branch: the vital balance is between established authority, wherever it resides, and the power of the citizenry. In America, the great balance must therefore be between the citizenry on one hand and that mass of powers that combine to restrict citizen freedoms. The presidency, the judiciary, the legislatures, and powerful civil servants.

The balance that matters is not between those in power but between those in power and those who have relinquished their power, temporarily, on the understanding that their freedom is respected. And the citizenry must retain the ability to regain that relinquished power, by force, if necessary.

The same is true in Canada.    Yet we have no understanding of the issues. The National Rifle Association is not a bunch of cranks, it is a bunch of people who in one way or another understand enough about history, enough about human nature, to know that, ultimately, we must be prepared to defend citizen freedom with a gun.

We act as if we are naive about humans and about the troubles they get themselves into, and about their willingness to violate one another's rights. We act as if we are naive about ourselves.

There is no question that most governments will feel mystified and even hurt when citizens insist on the right to keep guns. Those who are in government are bound to feel offended when we do not give governments that ultimate trust involved in disarming ourselves completely. But we should be firm. History speaks clearly of the need of all citizens to be prepared to defend themselves against the abuse of power by governments.

Not today, of course, and not tomorrow will you need a gun. Perhaps not in your lifetime. The need will arise only when Canada evolves into a country where a government abuses its power. Against that sad day, and despite the human cost, we should hang on to the right to own an un-registered gun.

# Case Study #2: The EPA and the Destruction of the Right to Own Property

So far in this book, I have told you about numerous stories that shed a negative light on a large federal government. Members of the unelected representation have become hell bent on: 1) protecting their jobs and 2) taking away your liberty. Every time we hand another one of our liberties over to the government, those unelected representatives get another job, more tax dollars, and more security. It has become a self-perpetuating cycle of dominance that is only getting worse.

America has been a land of opportunity for me, just as it should be. I have been relatively successful in life, because of the freedoms that the Constitution provided. One of the most important freedoms is that of property ownership. In America, a citizen is entitled to own property and thus, use that property to benefit himself. Ownership of property has long been a source of freedom. Looking back through history, one can see that fascist societies usually consisted of government owned, controlled or operated property. The only way a lord, dictator or fascist can control the people is to control the land.

When the United States was first born, a large portion, over 50% of the people were farmers. Nearly everyone was tied to the land in some way. Slowly, over the years, farmers have dwindled in number and proportion to the rest of society. Nowadays, many of us live in large urban areas and have no idea where the meat, milk and grain products we find in our supermarkets come from. Land, and the farmer, have become less center-staged. Nonetheless, the role of the farmer is still the most important (after all, without food we would all die) and the need for privately owned, controlled and operated land is vital for the health of our freedom.

In the last four decades, farming employment dropped from just under 8 million to a little over 3 million. The number of farms has gone from 5.8 million to 2.1 million. In the last 20 years, the percentage of the rural workforce employed in farming has gone from 14.4 percent to 7.6 percent. Even by including agricultural services, forestry, and fishing, the numbers have gone from 15.3 percent to only 8.5 percent.

Today, only about 5 million people, less than 10 percent of the rural population, live on farms. In addition, in 1990, 58 percent of U.S. farm operator households received wages and salary (averaging nearly $30,000 per reporting household) from off-farm employment.

*Farming's "double-edged sword": increases in productivity mean fewer workers are needed.*

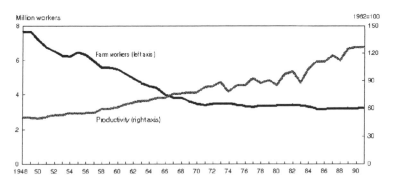

An American way of life is slowly disappearing. Iowa reported this year that 6,700 of its farmers were driven out of business due to economic pressures.

Too many Americans, the same who have accepted the large federal government, have forgotten the importance of individual land ownership. Slowly, but surely in this society, land is being taken from the individual citizen and turned over to government control. True, the deeds may not change hands, but each day more and more land is placed under the control of the federal government and individual citizens are being robbed of their rights.

You read earlier about federal abuses as it pertained to suspected drug dealers. Those stories were absolutely horrible, but many of us, including myself, could at least take some comfort in the fact that drug enforcement actions also attempt to stop a scourge upon our society. Although this does not condone the illegal seizing of an innocent individual's land; it at least justifies, to some extent, the existence of the Drug Enforcement Agency. What would you say, however, if I told you that there was a government agency that had no other purpose than to control privately owned land, without any discernible benefit to our society?

A group of unelected representatives, loved by Bill and Al in the White House, have begun to usurp the rights of millions of Americans by telling individuals how they can use their land. In addition, unfair, persecutory actions by this group have led to hundreds of complaints of abuse and millions of lost dollars. This agency is the Environmental Protection Agency.

Believe me, I have heard all of the talk about destroying the planet, and saving mother earth. I personally love land and do not believe that anything should be done to harm it. But, I was saddened to learn that the EPA has little to do with the protection of the land. In reality, this agency is comprised of individuals who wish to rob you of your right to the free ownership of property. This agency has become an affront to freedom.

I know most of you right now do not believe me. In fact, many of you may call me myopic for talking bad about an organization supposedly designed to protect the environment. Let me first say that protecting the environment is vital, but a federal government that has a track record of ripping off the American people and taking self-serving actions to perpetuate the prestige and size of its own bureaucratic organizations should not do it. Secondly, the only way you will truly understand what I am trying to say is if you bear with me, and learn a little bit more about what the EPA has done.

I am going to begin a story about the EPA that many of you will find hard to believe. I understand this, because our current leaders in the White House lie to you each night and say that the actions of the EPA are in the best interests of the American people. I tell you they are wrong, and they are lying. The money we spend annually in the EPA could be better put into the local community's efforts to reduce pollution and protect the environment. Regrettably, however, the American people have become convinced that the United States is on a highway to environmental destruction, and therefore, we should trust the EPA to make all the right decisions. Well, here is the truth, and it may be a little hard to swallow.

Shakespeare once wrote in Hamlet, "Something is rotten in the state of Denmark." Well, I say, something is indeed rotten in America, and it is the green movement supported by the EPA. The facts show that the environmental movement has been taken over by those who seek to gain political power through it. Those people, like Al Gore and the members of the EPA, seek only to destroy key elements in American society such as: individualism, free enterprise, private property rights, the right to bear arms and the moral foundations our society has been built on. The green movement is an excellent barrier to hide behind because the American people have become increasingly concerned about the environment.

The president of the National Wildlife Federation, Mark Puttent, said in December of 1998 that:

" The 1998 Endangered Species Act has been the catalyst for a profound change in how we view the land and it has helped bring about an unheralded revolution in land use."

What he should have said was that it brought about a silent revolution in regards to public control over privately owned land. This "unheralded revolution" was little more than a covert revolution against American ideals. The goals and beliefs of the Green Party and the green movement are nearly identical to the goals of the Clinton/Gore Administration. Furthermore, it seems that their values and morals are about the same.

They both seek to use the government to control the land, and force individual citizens into a cooperative lifestyle involving government funded and supported life necessities. Look at our society already in the past 25 years. There is now a federal organization for every facet of our lives, and with the help of the green movement and the EPA, those who seek to socialize our society will be able to achieve this by the eradication of personal property rights. As Lenin once wrote:

"The only task that remains is to organize the
population into co-operative societies, with most of
the population organized in cooperatives, socialism
will achieve its aim automatically... the system of
civilized cooperatives is the system of socialism."

In other words, get people to hand over their autonomy
and their control of the property, and they will fall into the hands
of anyone with a socialist agenda. No wonder the EPA and the
green movement are so well loved by the socialist Clinton
Administration, it has become a perfect disguise for their
philosophy of governmental socialism.

So many of you ask, how can the EPA, the green
movement and the Clinton Administration take away an
individual's right to own and control private property? My
answer is: slowly, under the color of law, and without regard for
the Constitution. The best way to show you is through
examples.

The following story about the erosion of personal
property rights was taken from the *Bakersfield Californian* on
April 29, 1994:

"Bakersfield Businessman E.G. Berchtold couldn't
have been more shocked when he received the
official document from the U.S. Attorney's office.
'The United States of America vs. One Ford
Tractor."

A $50,000 tractor and disc Berchtold Equipment
Co., had sold recently to a customer had been
confiscated by the U.S. Fish and Wildlife Service.
Berchtold still has a sizable financial interest in the
equipment.

What the document didn't say, but what Berchtold
later learned, was that it was the tractor driven by
Taung Min Lin when he allegedly ran over and
killed several endangered Tipton kangaroo rats about
20 miles southwest of Bakersfield.

Lin, an El Monte-based businessman and an owner
of Wang-Lin Farms hic., is the first farmer in Kern
County to face prosecution under the Federal
Endangered Species Act, said Karen Kalmanir,
assistant U.S. attorney in Fresno.

'Our concern is not only the tractor we might lose,'
Berchtold said. 'All of us are losing our rights. The
government is doing whatever it wants to do with us.
What people don't realize is that this could be their
house if they happened to kill some endangered
species in their backyard."

The story continues on to say that Berchtold still has
financial interest in the tractor, because the farmer accused of
this action will not be able to pay of his loan if he is thrown in
jail. It seems that this farmer, who had no idea there were
kangaroo rats lying around, is facing two years imprisonment
and a $200,000. fine. All Berchtold did was sell a tractor to a
person who accidentally killed a few rats. As a result, he is
facing serious financial loss, and this is not even mentioning the
criminalization of a decent law-abiding farmer.

This is a concern of any businessman, and Berchtold put
it right when he said all Americans should be concerned. Fred
Starrh, an active member of the Coalition to Promote and
Preserve Private Property Rights has said:

"Farmers are finding that land they've owned for
years but haven't used has become Federal Reserve
(under the endangered species act) and there is
nothing they can do about it."

This is one story, but there are many more, and I believe
the only way to drive the point home is to keep on telling the
truth. Something Clinton has a hard time doing.

A very sad story is the one of Billie Vatalaro, a woman
sick and dying who wished to move to a dream house to spend
her final days.

Back in 1994, the Orlando Sentinel reported that Ms. Vatalaro had purchased 10 acres on the shores of Lake Rouse in Central Florida. She had planned to build two homes on the land, one for herself and one for her daughter. She spent a large portion of her life savings, $130,577 on the land. Sadly, however, she never saw her house built, and had the pleasure of spending the last painful moments of her life fighting a state bureaucracy who refused to let her build on her own land.

It appears as if the land she had purchased with her life savings was considered a wetland under federal law, and she was therefore prevented from building anything there. Of course, the federal government never offered to give her back her life savings, even though it was their regulatory actions that made her land worthless and unusable. Her son, Ron Vatalaro was quoted as saying,

> "I saw my mom go from when she bought the lot-she was out there happy, planting plants and starting the landscape- to when right before she dies she was in a wheelchair, on oxygen. The people with the government are cold, callous. Like, if you're a raccoon we care, but if you're a human being, we don't."

The government keeps on playing their little games, even as someone dies. She had used up her life savings , and there was no way to get it back. The state government, forced into action by the EPA, was responsible for robbing this woman of her property and destroying her "pursuit of happiness" during her last days. This crime could not be compensated by any amount of money, but the family hardly even got an apology or any form of monetary compensation. A hardy "tough luck" was all the environmentalists and government bureaucrats had to say.

I have already stated that the ownership and use of land is vital to the pursuit of the American Dream and is strongly supported by the Constitution. However, the case of logger Ken Davis is a different story. He owns 2,800 acres of forested land in the Northeast. He intended to cut that timber down to generate revenue, but the EPA stepped in and said no. It appears that cutting down any more than 40 acres of land has become nearly impossible. There have been regulations placed on his land that "hold the land hostage". Therefore, he cannot use that land for a multitude of purposes unless he jumps through thousands of bureaucratic "hoops" in order to gain permission from the EPA. Even if he was to file all the correct paperwork, there is absolutely no guarantee he will be allowed to use his own land.

After being harassed by the EPA, Mr. Davis came to the terrifying realization that the private ownership of property in the United States is slowly becoming abolished. In response to this environmental menace, he has formed a group called POST, to fight governmental control of privately owned land. To him, this issue is not about timber; it's about property rights. He has been robbed of the value of his land, and the government should either pay for it, or allow him to use it for whatever purpose he wants, as long as it does not harm another person.

The EPA is undaunted by these kinds of complaints and actions because they have the might of the federal government behind them. It is very strange, how our own tax dollars can be used to erode our constitutional rights. To me, this is incredibly absurd. The individuals already mentioned in this chapter were forced to fight the injustices of the federal government with their own money, whereas the EPA used our money to defend their unconstitutional actions.

The frightening list of governmental abuses goes on. In 1996 the Telluride Ski Resort was ordered to pay 1.1 million dollars for illegally bulldozing acres of land for development. The fine was for nothing more than failing to obtain the proper permit from the EPA before they began their project. That is 1.1 million dollars for not following bureaucratic nonsense and red tape and just doing what you want with your own land. In addition, the EPA ordered the Telluride Resort to replace the land they had bulldozed to its old condition, a process that will cost them another 1.3 million dollars.

The Telluride executives had no idea that they needed to obtain any form of a permit. They simply decided to develop land they already owned. The real scary part of this story is that they were discovered to be in violation of the obscure rule by the

U.S. Army. That's right, the U.S. Military is involved in inspecting and investigating violations of EPA regulations, especially when it comes to wetlands.

If I recall, my tax dollars were supposed to be paying for an army to protect me from outside governmental intrusions. I shudder to think that the U.S. Army is operating in the United States to deprive individuals of their freedom to control their own property. This is not what our original founding fathers had in mind.

## Wetlands- The Big Issue

At a first glance, most of the land seizures by the EPA involve violations of wetland laws. I examined these laws as close as possible (there are actually over 200,000 pages of legalize). It is undeniable that our sources of fresh water rely on healthy wetlands. The destruction of all wetlands will definitely result in major damage to our environment. However, the EPA, the Clinton Administration and the green movement have taken this issue too far.

The EPA claims that over 100,000 acres of wetlands are being lost each year. However, they do not cite any reliable sources for their information. Wetlands may act as reservoirs and water purification systems, but so do man-made structures. Furthermore, rivers and streams act as natural purifiers of our water. Our water is cleaner today than it was 30 years ago, so if there is that much degradation of wetlands, as the EPA claims, how can our water quality be increasing? The EPA is only saying this because they are caught up in a conflict of interest. Their jobs rely on their ability to frighten the American people.

In reality, wetlands many times cause floods that result in damage to property and the loss of vital topsoil in farming regions. This is because wetlands are already saturated to the point where no more water can be absorbed into the ground. Man made reservoirs not only perform the same functions of wetlands, but they also prevent floods and other forms of water damage. The EPA is desperately clinging to wetlands because this issue has opened a door for them to destroy our constitutional rights and increase the power and prestige of their organization. There are many other tactics that can be utilized to protect our water supply, but the EPA only investigates ones that keep their organization center-staged.

Wetland regulations have been expanded so far to include almost every piece of undeveloped land in the United States. Even some developed land falls under its regulation. If water is standing on a piece of your land for more than one week out of a calendar year, it is considered a wetland. Therefore, before you can do anything to change the face of that land, you must obtain a permit from the federal government. Failure to do so will result in imprisonment, outlandish fines, and public humiliation. Furthermore, the EPA and the federal government have reserved the right to tell each individual citizen what they can and cannot do with the land that they legally own. Each year, thousands of applications to develop land are denied by the EPA because they will potentially destroy wetlands.

This fact, coupled with the fact that a large percentage of undeveloped land is considered a wetland, gives the government dejure control over most of our land.

Bill and the boys in Washington are encouraging the EPA to more strictly enforce the wetlands, and other anti-constitutional environmental regulations.

In 1997 the Boston Globe reported that Clinton sent his lap dogs to Boston in order to find out why there had not been many civil prosecutions occurring for environmental violations. It was reported that the EPA in the area had been working along side local industry and property owners to achieve a reduction in pollution through education and incentives. Bill and the boys took issue with this, and ordered the local administrator to "reinvent environmental protection in New England". The end result was more prosecutions, increased land seizures and an adversarial approach to environmental regulation. Keep in mind that the *Boston Globe* also reported that pollution levels had been at an all-time low since 1975, before these oppressive measures were taken.

The fact is, the EPA is nothing more than a group of unelected representatives utilizing their power to promote their own department. There is an incredible conflict of interest involved in this scenario. Years ago, they made it illegal to put sand in sugar, this was obviously necessary to regulate those who sought to rob individuals of properly measured purchases. These were necessary laws and they solved the problem expediently. However, the EPA, so to speak, is now attempting to put sand in the sugar just to justify their existence. In other words, they are crying wolf to scare the American people into giving up their 5th amendment rights to own property.

The EPA and the federal government have a long history of "Cry Wolf" scenarios. Take for example the following:

- Two weeks before Thanksgiving in 1959, minuscule amounts of a potentially cancer causing weed killer were discovered in some cranberries grown in Washington and Oregon. Government officials issued flash alerts to local papers in New York and Washington, and before one could stop and think about it, the people were panicking. In reality, there was absolutely no contamination, as later tests reported, but that year, cranberry sales plummeted, including cranberry juice from other regions in the country.

- Daniel Puzo, who covers food safety issues for the Los Angeles Times reports that the recent trend is for the EPA to center their efforts on watching out for pesticide contamination in produce. The EPA has jurisdiction over the matters pertaining to pesticide contamination and therefore, they spend billions a year watch dogging the industry. However, the real danger in foodstuffs is from food-borne microbes like salmonella and E-Coli. The end result is billions wasted each year in checking for pesticides while millions get sick and thousand dies from food-borne microbes. The EPA led the charge and spends your tax dollars on efforts that produce few instances of contamination. Mind you, the farmers or marketers themselves, not the EPA, discover most of those contaminations.

- In the 1980's, the EPA led the charge to enact the SuperFund laws to help clean up polluted sites. However, 20 years of efforts, and billions of dollars spent have resulted in little clean up. Only 15% of the 1300 sites identified by the EPA have been completely cleaned up. The EPA used scare tactics to compel politicians to give them over 13.5 billions dollars, but they did little to actually clean up the sites they claimed were "vitally dangerous" to the environment.

The EPA also helped foster the asbestos scare of the 70's and 80's. In reality, asbestos was a danger to those who worked in industries that utilized asbestos based raw materials. However, the danger to most Americans was nominal. Despite many studies that concluded asbestos was "not a risk in the non-occupational environment" the EPA still falsified reports and made inflammatory comments to local media. This, is in turn, caused the 1993 panic in New York City that involved the city schools. Even though there was absolutely no risk to the students, the EPA used scare tactics on parents to enrage them to the point where they compelled school officials to spend 130 million dollars on asbestos removal. Classrooms opened two weeks late for the 1 million school aged children that year who were "in no more danger from asbestos in school than on the streets."

In 1987 the EPA even admitted in a report to the General Accounting Office that, "Overall, EPA's priorities appear more closely aligned with public opinion than with our estimated risks." In other words, the EPA is in the business of creating a panic and then heroically coming to the rescue of the American people. The price being a few more billions in funding and increased regulations giving them control over many more facets of our lives.

The issue of the wetlands is not that different from this. In reality, the wetlands issue has become another "Cry Wolf" scenario utilized by the EPA in order to gain more power. Only now are critics beginning to examine the issue more closely. It was reported in the January 12, 1998 issue of the *Baltimore Sun* that the 4th U.S. Circuit Court of Appeals had struck down the federal regulation of wetlands, ruling that the federal regulations were overstepping the bounds of the federal government's control. The federal government is only allowed to regulate inter-state waterways, not the backyards of all Americans. Despite this, the U.S. Army, the EPA, the White House, and the green movement continue to impose more stringent federal regulations onto the American people. The result is a destruction of our 5th amendment rights. Just look at some of these next stories.

Lois Jentegaard lives in a crumbling house on 335 acres of land that is near the Columbia River. Beginning in 1938, she and her husband began accumulating this land slowly throughout their marriage. Her land is part of a panoramic view that can often be photographed by individuals in Crown Point State Park. Congress loved the view so much that they decided in 1986 to designate 264,000 acres, including her property, as a national scenic area and protected wetland.

In 1988, Lois' husband died and the property quickly began to get dilapidated. In an attempt to raise money, Lois decided in 1992 to sell off some of her land to help renovate her home. She just wanted to sell of 20 acres of pastureland to raise necessary funds. However, because of the 1986 congressional action, she was forced to seek approval from the EPA and the federal government in order to sell the land. Her request was denied. In one swoop of a pen, the United States Congress devalued Lois's land and offered her nothing in exchange for compensation.

Hiding behind wetland regulations and laws, the government and the EPA defend their actions claiming that the preservation of nice scenery takes precedent over Lois's right to own and control her property. Her property is now absolutely worthless to her and her family, and a bank will not even loan her money on the property because the government has determined it can never be developed.

When Lois sued only to receive compensation for her

loss of property, her claim was thrown out of court. Gary Kahn, an attorney for the government was quoted as saying, "It may not be fair to all people, but any piece of legislation will affect some people more than others... It's the price you pay for living in a democracy."

If you find this statement as bewildering as I do, then you can understand the frustration thousands of Americans are facing each year. The government stepped right in and took Lois's property for their own use without ever consulting her. She was told that she may be able to develop the land, but only after mounds of paperwork was completed, specifications were analyzed and approved, and thousands of dollars in fees were paid.

Mr. Kahn, just like the rest of the EPA boys, simply believe that the government has the right to take whatever they want, and the increasing number of environmental regulations each year make that easier and easier. The end result is the destruction of an individual's property value without any compensation.

Daffel Harting of Washington has become a convert to the property rights movement. He was told in 1993, that the property he had owned since 1948 could not be turned into an apartment complex. Laws enacted in the 80's turned his land into a federally protected reserve. He was offered no money in compensation for the devaluation of his land, but the government "effectively confiscated my land" and robbed him of his retirement he had planned on for 30 years.

How about Carl Ruestig, also of Washington, who owns a 200-acre tree farm? Twenty-five years ago he could have sold off his land as one-acre plots to develop homes. Then, it was re-zoned into only 5-acre lots. Then all of the sudden the Federal Growth Management Act said that his property was now a "designated forest". The end result was that he could only sell of his land in 80-acre plots. Even though Carl has no interest in developing his land, his property value has diminished substantially and he feels that the government is illegally telling him what he can do with his land.

In another story, John Welch of King County Washington, lost his entire life savings because of one regulation. He had planned to divide 10 acres into 42 homes, but wetland regulations stopped him from doing so. He lost over 4 million dollars in the deal and is now stuck with paying taxes on land that is totally unusable and is worth a quarter of what he originally paid for it.

The horror stories continue. Take for example the quiet port town of Port Bolivar, Texas. Here federal bureaucrats are threatening to put an old man in jail because he wants to spend the last years of his life by the sea. The billboard this man was ordered to place in front of his house best summarizes the heinous nature of this story. This billboard, measuring ten feet high and twenty feet across is a sadistic form of punishment that announces to the world that this old man has supposedly sinned against the U.S. Army and the EPA by depositing "illegal fill material" on his property. The billboard instructs all that his terrible sin has resulted in a big fine and the order to repair the supposed "damages" to the environment.

This particular incident started when Marinuis Van Luezen, a 73-year-old immigrant, decided to build his dream home on 20 acres of land he had legally purchased. In fact, he had owned it for more than 20 years. When he filled in the land to build the home, the U.S. Army and the EPA hauled him into court for the violation of Section 404 of the Clean Water Act (i.e. the wetlands regulation that supposedly allows the government to seize our land).

The reality of the situation is that section 404 of the Clean Water Act says nothing about wetlands. It simply says that a person must obtain a permit before filling in any navigable waterway. This however, has not stopped the EPA and the U.S. Army from harassing thousands of Americans whose land is in no way considered a navigable waterway. The federal regulatory program has taken on a life of its own and the goal is to rob Americans of their land.

All Mr. Luezen did was fill in a one half-acre section of land 50 feet from highway 87. Because of this terrible crime he has to put this large billboard in his front lawn, and place $350 dollars in a special account each month for eight years. At the end of those eight years he will have to use that money to move his house.

The EPA treated Mr. Luezen like he was a rapist or murderer for filling in a 1/2-acre plot of his own land. This land, by the way, was already located next to a bait camp and campground that had long destroyed the beauty of the land. In preparing to prosecute him, federal officials hid in bushes, video taping his every move. As Jonathan Tolman wrote in the *Wall Street Journal*:

"Unaware that the microphone on the camera was recording their conversation, the cameraman said at one point: "O.K., I think I've got him." This was greeted with a chorus of "All right!" "That's great!", and "Good! Good!" from other three Corps employees on the stakeout. One would have thought they were staking out a drug kingpin or Mafia don."

The EPA takes good, honest Americans who are attempting to live out the American Dream, and turns them into criminals. Many of us believe that the Constitution protects us, but these EPA thugs, with the U.S. Army and Clinton Administration backing them up, have successfully destroyed the 5th amendment and taken away the right to own property.

Furthermore, the EPA rarely has scientific proof backing them up. Even the U.S. Court of Appeals in Washington believes that the EPA "...was arbitrary and capricious and amounted to an unconstitutional delegation of legislative power."[3]

If you still need more proof, take for example the 1995 case of John and Josephine Bronczyk in Minnesota. They had owned 160 acres of farmland since the Great Depression. After the dust bowl era, John and Josephine's family was happy to allow a natural wildlife preserve to develop on their land, where pheasant and waterfowl visit each year. After many years, out of nowhere the Department of Natural Resources wishes to stick its head in the mix.

At the urging of the EPA, the Department of Natural Resources has designated more than half of the 160-acre farm as protected wetlands. This forces the Bronczyk's to spend their

---

[3] As contained in "Protecting Us From The EPA" by Eric Peters.

own money to comply with thousands of regulations that now dictate how their land can be utilized. The government has told them that this land must be opened to the public. In essence the government has robbed them of the right to restrict access to their land. In return for this regulatory designation, the government offered no compensation. Effectively, they stole their land, put it under government regulation and control, and gave the Bronczyk's nothing in return.

One of my favorite (and most disturbing) cases involves a Baptist preacher who is facing up to a year in jail in Michigan. This god-fearing man did not violate one of the commandments, nor did he harm another person. His crime was filling in a horse pasture that had, unknowingly to him, been designated a protected wetland. In his own words, "We have not been prosecuted-we've been persecuted."

The government has persecuted this man, and now, this man of God faces a year in prison, a one thousand dollar fine, and a bill for the clean-up effort that may run into the hundreds of thousands of dollars. The amazing part of the story was that the Preacher had purchased the 4.6-acre plot from the Department of Natural Resources. When he paid them the money, they never once mentioned any sort of wetland protection or restrictions on how the land may be utilized.

Amazingly enough, it was only after he began to cut down trees and build his house that water began to settle on the ground. The land was not a wetland until he altered it himself. Then, as soon as he altered it back into usable land, the government stuck their head in and took his land and freedom away from him.

The price of an over-zealous federal government and an illegal environmental policy continues to rise. Take for example the case of Frank LaDue, a 73-year-old man who decided to plant a small garden and some evergreen trees in his own yard. He has been involved in a dispute since 1991 with government officials regarding his creation of a rich topsoil base utilized to grow the trees and garden. The government alleges that he destroyed a protected wetland in order to create the tree and flower garden. The total size of the garden was less than 1/2 acre. Because of this, he was slapped with a $5,000 fine for planting his trees and garden, and he refuses to pay it. Here is one man standing against the strength of the government, defiantly opposing the destruction of the 5th amendment.

Mr. LaDue is lucky, compared to others in a similar situation. Take for example James J. Wilson in Baltimore, Maryland. Back in 1996, he was sentenced to 21 months in a prison for violations of wetland laws. I ask you to keep in mind that recently, a man convicted of gross sexual imposition in the city of Columbus, Ohio received an 18-month sentence. His victim was the sexual molestation of a 6-year-old boy. Mr. Wilson's crime was punished more severely. He was put in prison longer than a child molester because he was caught filling in 70 acres of privately owned land that had been determined, without his knowledge, to be federally protected wetlands.

Mr. Wilson is just one of over 250 individuals and corporations who have been given stiff fines and prison sentences between the years of 1990 and 1994. Their crime, developing their own land. Paul Kamenar, an advocate for those charged with wetlands violations claims:

> "As far as we can tell, not a single fish, bird or sea lion was either killed, injured or even threatened. It's like being sentenced to prison for jaywalking. To have a first time offender sentenced to jail for almost two years is a complete waste of tax dollars and is excessive punishment."

Despite the inability of any government agency to concisely define exactly what a wetland is, or prove federal jurisdiction, the witch-hunt continues. In 1995, Nicholas Codd set out to build his dream home in Maryland on a piece of property he purchased 30 years ago. He tried, in many different ways, to work with the regulations that were enacted after he had made this purchase. He agreed to put the home on stilts. He agreed to make the home smaller, but the government staunchly refused all of his modifications. In the end, the government ardently stated that he was not allowed to develop his land in any way. In order to compensate him for his loss, the government gave him nothing but years of legal battles.

Over the years, the numbers of cases like the ones listed above have increased steadily as the size of the EPA has also increased. Thousands of lawsuits are filed each year in which individuals attempt to get the government to compensate them for the devaluation of their property and the legal expenses they incurred in fighting the illegal seizure of their property by government agents. However, even the Federal Courts, who in some cases sided with those who accused wetland regulations of being too vague, have made it almost impossible for Americans to receive compensation from the government when their land becomes devalued or controlled by the government due to changing environmental regulations.

Take for example a case in Lansing Michigan in 1998. This case involved a developer who sued the government for the devaluation of his land. Bob Jones, president of the JFK Investment Co. had filed suit against the state government to receive compensation for the 5.1 million dollar devaluation of his property that occurred after his land was placed under a 1993 wetland regulation. He first won his lawsuit at the local level, but a Federal Circuit Court of Appeals overturned that ruling and said that the government is not liable for compensating individuals whose land value had been depreciated through governmental regulation.

In essence, this court ruling, and others like it throughout the 80's and 90's have given the government a free pass to steal away an individual's land value and make no effort to compensate them for the loss. Many property rights activists have noted this trend, and say that these are early signs that the federal government is over-stepping their bounds and violating the 5th amendment. I happen to agree with this belief.

Only in a dictatorship can the government change the rules on a private citizen and steal away their wealth and land. It frightens me when we have cases like the one involving Kathleen Kenny. She failed to obtain the proper building permit that was necessary to construct her retirement home. Some obscure environmental regulation necessitated filing additional paperwork when Ms. Kenny decided to build her home on top of an old chicken coop. Ms. Kenny now has a criminal record and a fine of 1.5 million dollars hanging over her head.

Throughout the incident, Ms. Kenny filed every document she was told to and spent thousands of dollars that she was assured would smooth over the situation. However, public officials routinely dismissed her filings or claimed that documents had been "accidentally lost" in a sea of bureaucracy.

In the end, Ms. Kenny fought back and learned that the reason for her problems was actually two corrupt bureaucrats who were utilizing these unsubstantiated regulatory violations to inflate their own pocket books. It seems that no one was assigned to watch those who were employed to watch us. When it was proven that there was a conspiracy to commit governmental fraud by agents involved in her case, she was awarded a $33,000 settlement.

The most startling fact however, was that the previous violations and fines were not removed from her record. Even though it was proven that she was a victim of fraudulent regulatory actions, she is still supposed to pay the 1.5 million-dollar fine. Furthermore, she still has a criminal record. A victim of the unelected representatives in our nation, Ms. Kenny has kept a good heart and relishes in the victory she won by exposing the fraudulent practices of those entrusted by our government to oversee environmental regulations.

## The Increase in Government

Many different environmental regulations and policies (The Clean Water Act, The Clean Air Act) have spawned an incredible growth in governmental agencies. The EPA and the Department of Ecology have grown 400% in the past 12 years, both in personnel and yearly expenditures. It appears as if a circular logic is at work here. Many are not sure what came first, the incredible number of regulations or the enormous bureaucracy charged with the task of enforcement.

As Richard Davis, head of the Washington Research Council said in 1993:

"Has the growing maze of regulation spawned the growth of the DOE and EPA, or has the agencies' growth spawned the maze of regulation? What they need to ask is, do these regulations work? And how much is enough?"

The fact is, no one has ever taken the time to independently analyze whether or not the enormous numbers of regulations currently in effect actually help the environment. The duty of analyzing the efficacy of enforcement is left in the hands of the EPA and other environmental watchdogs. The end result is a perfect recipe for conflict of interest.

Here, we have an entire branch of the government, stealing citizens' land away at an alarming rate, and no one in power is questioning their tactics or their ability to actually protect the environment.

In the 1980's, during the tenure of Ecology Department Director Christine Gregoire, some shocking revelations were made. The Director of one of the most powerful environmental regulatory agencies said that,

> "It's almost a religion to make people comply no matter what (with environmental regulations). A lot of environmental officials do not know how to deal with people. Many Ecology employees viewed the environment, not people, as the client. You run into a real problem when you think like that, because then the questions becomes, who are you accountable to?"

Ms. Gregoire admitted that most environmental regulatory agencies view success in their department by how many fines are issued and how much property is seized or forced into compliance. The issue of whether or not the air is cleaner, or the water is clearer has become lost in the overzealous persecution of decent, law-abiding Americans.

One can understand why this is the case when the leadership in the White House also judges the efficacy of environmental regulations by how many rights are stolen away from citizens. Remember earlier when I talked about the fact that Bill and Al had criticized the New England Region EPA

Administrator when he tried to actually clean the air by obtaining compliance through partnership and education?

Too often our politicians are willing to give the EPA total control of setting policies when dealing with environmental issues. This means that no one is watching the EPA. As Eric Peters points out:

> "When Congress amended the federal Clean Air Act in 1990, it authorized the EPA to create regulations that would meet the requirements set forth in the act. However, the act never specifies in any meaningful way what, exactly, constitutes "clean air" or "healthful" environmental conditions: instead there are vague platitudes about "protecting the public health" with "an adequate margin of safety." Thus the EPA was effectively given carte blanche to make up its own definitions and standards."

The EPA immediately changed the rules and suddenly hundreds of communities were considered in violation of the Clean Air Act, although just a day before they were considered in perfect compliance. The EPA went way over the line and their actions were not under control. When congress trusts criminal organizations like the EPA, Eric Peters says it only "passes the buck to unaccountable, often overzealous regulatory bodies".

Bill, and other politicians who strongly support the green movement, want nothing more than to expand the governmental control of the land. This, as I have pointed out multiple times throughout this book, is the first step towards communism and the destruction of freedom.

Despite multiple cases of constitutional violations, Clinton still pushes onward in his fight to destroy the American Democracy. He has issued a "no net loss" policy in regards to wetlands, and has ordered his governmental lap dogs to seize control of as much land as possible. In the wink of an eye, Clinton destroyed all of the Bush Administration's efforts to reduce the over-zealous, and illegal, regulation of privately owned land.

Ignoring the fact that the federal government can only

regulate navigable waterways and interstate rivers and lakes, the Clinton Administration has increased the power of the EPA and the U.S. Army to increase sanctions against individual landowners who choose to alter their own property to suit their needs.

All of these actions are being taken when no one is concerned about whether or not the seizure of private property is even helping to protect the environment. I may be even more willing to accept some governmental intrusion if there was a clear and present danger to the stability of the world. However, the filling in of a few mud puddles on my own land is not a danger to the stability of the ecological system.

This whole environmental regulatory scam is nothing more than another part of Bill Clinton's scheme to increase the size, power and control of government. He, and other politicians like him, believes that big government is good government. The more tax dollars they have and the more control they have over our individual lives, the happier they are. It just amazes me how people like him can get on TV and tell the American people the era of big government is over. It's just beginning and Big Brother is adopting a Big Sister, the EPA, to help erode our civil liberties.

## The Greenhouse Effect

We hear a lot about the effects of global warming, and you'll probably hear a
lot more about it in the 2000 election from "Mr. Environment" Al Gore.

But what if all this fuss and bother is all over some extremely shoddy science? A growing number of scientists are now saying that we may have been misled.

First of all, the US government spends $2.1 billion a year on global warming research. According to an article in the *Washington Post* by Ross Gelbspan, there are 2000 climate scientists (there are only about 60 people in the United States with a Ph.D. in climatology). That's a million dollars per scientist, per year. Is that enough money for each of them to exaggerate the problem just a bit?

Secondly, the global warming thesis evolved from a 1990 study by the first Scientific Assessment of the United Nations Intergovernmental Panel on Climate Change (IPCC). They used a computer simulation of planetary climate, ran using data on the present concentrations in the atmosphere of greenhouse gasses. They added that their simulation is "generally realistic on large scales."

Critics pointed out, however, that the "largest scale" of simulation of planetary climate would be the average surface temperature, and it was pretty obvious, even back in 1990 that the computer was predicting much more warming than had actually been observed. The "generally realistic" models were predicting that the globe should have already warmed between 1.3 degrees and 2.3 degrees Celsius, with the higher figure for the Northern Hemisphere. Since the late 19th century, it has only warmed about a degree and a half.

Then the scientists backtracked and claimed that if it wasn't warming as much as it was supposed to, it was due to sulfate aerosols, which are tiny bits of dust emitted during the burning of fossil fuels. Apparently, these tiny particles of dust are reflecting away the sun's radiation.

Patrick J Michaels, writing for the University of Virginia at the Cato Institute, reported all this in June of 1997. Michaels says that the scientists are desperately trying to avoid writing this letter:

"Dear Mr. Vice President:

We are sorry, but we goofed. Thanks for the $$. Hope you get your carbon tax.

Yours truly,
The Consensus of Scientists"

Instead of admitting that their calculations had been wrong, the scientists have backpedaled quickly, and claimed an effect that apparently they hadn't considered in their "generally accurate" model had interfered with getting the "true" results they were seeking.

Even if the changes had occurred as predicted, Michaels, who is a professor of environmental sciences, doubts that they would have been as catastrophic as claimed.

Both critics and proponents of global warming agree that human activities such as burning coal and driving cars have changed the amount of warming radiation about 2.5 watts, which is 1/4 the power of a good flashlight. The question is how much this affects the environment. Very little, says Michaels. He went on to say:

> "Warming up the planet's coldest air masses clearly creates little harm, because no plant or animal can feel the difference between -40 degrees and -35 degrees . . . It's no threat. It's pretty hard to melt ice caps at temperatures that are way below freezing."

Most recently, scientists at the prestigious Weizmann Institute in Israel have found evidence of a 'natural' global warming in equatorial Africa that took place between 350 BC and 450 AD.

Not to mention the fact of the satellite measured temperatures. These measurements are accurate to .01 degrees Celsius, and have found a *cooling* trend since they started taking measurements in 1979. The old models used by the UN predicted a warming of .35 degrees. And it's just not happening.

Who's to say that this isn't a natural cycle of our weather patterns? Humans haven't been monitoring the earth's climate for very long. We could very possibly be deluding ourselves into thinking that we have created a "problem" that is naturally occurring.

It makes one think of the islanders that believed that their lack of sacrifice had angered the volcano gods into punishing them with lava. . . . Putting human cause behind natural events.

Global warming certainly deserves more study before we accept that we have a problem. Billions shouldn't be spent on a problem that "might" exist.

## Eco-Scam and the New World Socialist Order

Each year that Clinton-Gore remains in power, the support for environmental preservation continues. This increase in popularity and support continues despite the fact that scientific evidence does not support the drastic conclusions that Clinton-Gore environmentalists espouse.

This next section is quite long, but I implore you to read through the horrors contained herein. If the stories I have already mentioned have not convinced you of the illegal government actions in the name of saving the environment, then maybe these stories will.

I have compiled for your information various stories that demonstrate how government agencies hide behind poorly worded environmental regulations to steal away citizen's rights. I ask you only one question: How can all these people be wrong?

This list is not all-encompassing, but it does paint a good picture of how the government over-regulates and oppresses good, decent Americans and forces them to become criminals because of poorly worded and unconstitutional regulations. I have broken down this part into three sections that each represents a major facet of environmental regulation: wetlands, endangered species, and clean air/water.

As you read through them, never forget that this may be you someday.

### Wetlands & Water Regulations

I have already written a great deal about the unconstitutional and illegal behavior of the EPA. However, one must consider the fact that the recent trend in federal regulations has extended itself to the state agencies. All of the stories contained in the next segment are a direct result of the over-zealous tendencies that the Clinton-Gore administration, along with the EPA, fosters in the United States. It is not the environment that is in danger, rather the rights of the American people are under attack.

Howard Dean had owned 4.8 acres of property in New Baltimore, Michigan that was zoned for commercial use. The Michigan Department of Natural Resources turned down his application to fill in a portion of the land in 1988. The denial was based on the fact that a portion of Dean's property was deemed to be a federally protected wetland.

However, according to the books, Michigan's wetlands laws hold that any piece of land less than 5 acres is exempt from wetlands regulation. Despite this, the Michigan Department of Natural Resources decided that the small portion on Dean's land was a part of a larger network of wetlands that needed federal protection. Michigan was, in effect, closing the barn door after the cow had escaped because every other landowner in his area has already developed their land any way they wanted to, despite the fact that each of their properties contained some federally protected wetlands. In the end, government regulators arbitrarily robbed Mr. Dean of 80% of his property.[4]

James J. Wilson, a Maryland developer, was sentenced to twenty-one months in prison, fined $1 million, and his company fined $3 million after he created lakes and open spaces on a 50-acre wetlands site he was developing in St. Charles.

The government pursued this action against Wilson even though it acknowledged that his actions "had no adverse environmental impact." In fact, in 1979 the Army Corps of Engineers had *approved* Wilson's original plan and the required environmental impact statement he filed. He did everything according to the book. But in 1990, the Corps changed its mind and ordered him to stop development in one particular area of the land. Wilson had the construction stopped as ordered and promptly filed a lawsuit against the Corps for expropriating his land without compensation.

Then, in 1995, the Corps charged Wilson with violating the Clean Water Act. After a seven-week trial, he was found guilty of four felony counts of violating the Act.

---

[4]-*Defenders of Property Rights*

Wilson is currently preparing a legal challenge to the constitutionality of the government's wetlands regulation. The Corps maintains that it can regulate as a wetland *any land that is ever wet*, which pretty much covers everything from an ocean to your driveway after a rainstorm. The "wetland" that Wilson was developing in St. Charles was actually dry as a bone for most of the year.[5]

Robert Brace was a farmer in Erie County, Pennsylvania. He found that he was being fined $ 10,000 and faced the loss of the use of 30 acres of his farm because he tore down a beaver dam.

It all began in 1987 when the beavers constructed a dam across a drainage ditch. Because the dam made the surrounding area soggy and unusable, Brace did what anyone would do: removed the blockage.

Then, one morning, he noticed several men wandering around on his property. It turns out they represented the United States Fish and Wildlife Service, the Army Corps of Engineers and the Environmental Protection Agency.

Even though Brace was simply trying to protect the farm, which had been in his family for four generations, they accused him of damaging a wetland and threatened him with fines of up to $68 million.

Brace told the court that the government had violated his 5th Amendment property rights. Although he won the first round of his federal suit, Brace lost on appeal. Besides paying the fine, he spent thousands in legal fees.[6]

Back in the 1960's an unnamed citizen in Iowa dug a 1-acre pond on a piece of land he owned in the center of the city of Urbandale. He had built this pond so that his family and friends could swim and fish.

He decided to sell the property to a developer in 1990, and at this time, he attempted to fill in the pond that he himself

---

[5] *Max Boot in "The Wetlands Gestapo", published in the Wall Street Journal on March 3, 1997:*

[6] *David Brown in the "10th at Heart of Suit over Land Use" published in the Pittsburgh Tribune-Review on July 4, 1997:*

had created. Then, the Iowa Department of Natural Resources stepped in and informed him that he could not fill it in, and claimed that the artificial pond was a federally protected wetland and thus they had full control over it. A year of negotiation passed by, and finally, the state settled the issue by allowing the owner to fill in the pond, as long as he made a large "contribution" to a group that was building new wetlands outside the city, to replace the "wetland" that he wanted to destroy.[7]

Gaston Roberge of Old Orchard Beach, Maine purchased a 2.8 -acre lot in 1964, he says, "as an investment for our retirement years, when we wouldn't be earning anything." Over a decade later, Roberge allowed local officials to dump excess fill dirt on his lot.

In 1986, Roberge tried to sell his land, but was informed by the Army Corps of Engineers that the property was an illegally filled wetland. Roberge had a buyer for the land, but when he learned of the Corps' accusation, the buyer backed off.

Roberge spent $50,000 on consultants to apply for an "after the fact" permit that would have allowed him to develop the lot. Three years later he got his reply: it was denied. Roberge then filed suit, alleging a temporary taking of his property.

Eventually, it was discovered that the Corps had never adequately surveyed Roberge's property, and that their motive wasn't really the protection of the wetland after all. They just wanted to discourage and frighten off other potential developers. Corps official Jay Clement had written, "Roberge would be a good one to squash and set an example—Old Orchard is heating up these days."[8]

---

[7] *Robert Layton's testimony before the Sub-Committee on National Economic Growth, National Resources and Regulatory Affairs on February 9, 1996*

[8] *Jonathan Adler "Property Rights, Regulatory Takings, and Environmental Protection" published by the Competitive Enterprise Institute in April 1996*

Regina Gonzalez, a sales engineer from Coral Springs, Florida, paid $ 60,000 for two lots in the Florida Keys nine years ago intending to build one house for herself and another for her parents. But then her lots were declared a "salt marsh" even though the lots are completely landlocked and seemingly bone dry. Although she is prohibited from building and her land is absolutely worthless, Gonzalez still has to make $688 monthly mortgage payments. The worst part is that Gonzalez says that her plots are directly across the street "from a $ 500,000 home with a tennis court and swimming pool." [9]

"Milo Folley purchased 50 acres of land in Pennellsville, New York 44 years ago as a retirement investment. He wanted to build houses on the wooded ridges and sell them, but since then the land has been declared a wetland. The 82 year-old retired architect is stuck with a piece of worthless land, but he still pays the taxes on the land as if it had full value. "If the government feels that my land is important, then buy it. I have invested my savings and the efforts of my retirement. I will expect to be paid the cost of the purchase, the loss of expected income and the cost of expenditures for taxes paid including the loss of investment income."[10]

In December 1997 Stephen Tvedten got an interesting letter in the mail. The Michigan Department of Environmental Quality (DEQ) threatened sanctions against him for building dams without a permit. David Price, District Representative of the DEQ's Land and Water Management Division wrote to Tvedten that "The Department has been informed that one or both of the dams partially failed during a recent rain event, causing debris and flooding at downstream locations." Price went on to say that "We find that dams of this nature are inherently hazardous and cannot be permitted. The Department therefore orders you to cease and desist all unauthorized activities at this location and to restore the stream to free-flow

---

[9] *Sean Paige in the article "Almost Paradise" contained in the April 6, 1998 edition of Insight*

[10] *Carol LaGrasse "The Property Owner's Experience"*

condition by removing all wood and brush forming the dams from the strewn channel." Tvedten was stunned. He had nothing to do with the dams. Had DEQ officials bothered to look at the dams in question, they would have realized that *beavers*, not Tvedten, had built them.[11]

In 1995, the residents of Ogden Dunes, Indiana were worried. The beach in front of some residents' houses was eroding at an alarming rate, and the water was creeping toward their homes.

When a heavy storm swept away what was left of the beach in front of one man's house, the waves crashed against the $30,000 steel wall he had built to try to save his property from destruction. Another resident had to build a flight of stairs from his house down to the beach and only two weeks after he had built it, the bottom step was dangling five feet above the sand

Who or what is responsible for the erosion of the beach in Ogden Dunes? The ones who are supposed to be protecting the beaches from erosion: the United States Army of Corps of Engineers. A series of break walls, constructed by the Corps at the mouth of a nearby waterway, block the normal flow of sand, which in turn causes the erosion of Ogden Dunes' beaches.[12]

Allegheny, New York City Councilman Thomas Allen, whose family has operated oil wells in the area for more than 100 years has seen times get harder and harder for the independent oil producer. An avalanche of regulation has crushed them. The state Department of Environmental Conservation (DEC) blames low market prices. But the state required bonds and permits make it too expensive to drill new wells. Independent producers have to adhere to costly regulations that seem ridiculous. The DEC regulations require them to use expensive high-pressure pipe when the pressure in New York's oil fields is low. Also, they require that all independent producers store all water that comes up in during the

---

[11] *National Directory of Environmental and Regulatory Victims*

[12] *Joyce Russell "Residents Prepared to File Lawsuit" contained in the Ogden Dunes, Indiana Times on November 13, 1995*

drilling process with the oil in storage tanks instead of being able to dispose of it. The cost of storing and hauling this water to a special site is too high for many small producers. Producers are also required to permanently plug inactive wells, which is expensive as well. Ironically, the state owns over 70 abandoned oil wells in Allegheny State Park but has never bothered to have them plugged.[13]

## Endangered Species

Most Americans are saddened to see the bald eagle threatened, or the carrier pigeon lost forever. However, the government is utilizing this concern to declare war upon the rights of the American people. Every educated person knows that species are created and die out as part of the natural order. Some protection is warranted, but in this next segment, I am sure you will be able to see how the governmental intrusion has become over-zealous and unconstitutional.

Years ago Doug Bernd purchased some land as a retirement investment. The city of Poway, California had different plans for Bernd's land: the city decided to make it into a home for endangered species. Of course, as such, no improvements or developments could be made to the property.

The city of Poway, along with the California Department of Fish and Game, told Bernd that he could use only 10% of his total acreage. This 10% covers everything he wanted to do with the property, from driveways and vegetable gardens to a home. The worst part is that the road already on his land takes up more than 10% of the acreage. The city and the Department of Fish and Game also informed Bernd that for every two acres of his own land that he wanted to use above the specified 10%, he would have to give four acres of his land to Poway or purchase another four acres and give it to the city.

"I spent two years in the service of this country, came home, got married and lived the American Dream," Bernd said. "I wanted to have kids and work and then retire with my

---

[13] *Carol LaGrasse in "The Property Owner's Experience":*

grandkids. Now this has taken away all my hopes and dreams. . . . A local environmentalist told me that I'm selfish for wanting to use my land and I should give it to the creatures."[14]

We elect a draft-dodging, immoral man to the White House and place Al Gore, a man who loves the environment more than the people, in the vice presidency. Meanwhile, a man who fought for his country and earned a decent living is thrown into poverty. He is called selfish, while Al Gore is hailed a hero for creating this type of eco-terroristic attitude in the United States and throughout the world. The whole situation makes me ill, but it also motivates me to continue spreading the truth. Regrettably, it can get worse. I implore you to not wait until it is your family they are destroying and your dreams their crushing before you take action. If you are not convinced, read on.

In January 1993, the city of Temecula, California was hit with over $10 million in damages from a flood because federal regulators, concerned more with protecting an endangered bird, refused to allow maintenance of the flood control system. The Last Bell's Vireo bird lived just downstream from the Murrietta Creek flood control facility. Eager to expand its habitat, the United States Fish and Wildlife Service refused to allow the Riverside County Flood and Water Conservation District to remove branches and other debris that were clogging the channels. The United States Fish and Wildlife Service wanted to use the flooded channel to make a nice home for the bird. They got more than they bargained for. Riverside County Commissioners and county engineers testified before Congress that being denied permission to remove the debris led to a clogging of the channel and subsequent flooding that seriously damaged businesses and homes. Ken Edwards, the chief engineer of the flood control agency, said "Ironically, after the flooding, federal authorities allowed the maintenance to take place."[15]

---

[14] *National Center for Public Policy Research*
[15] *"Field Hearing of the U.S. House of Representatives Committee on Natural Resources" on April 26, 1995. Reprinted in the 1998 National Directory of Environmental and Regulatory Victims*

Jay Montfort owns a gravel mine in Fishkill, New York. He has been trying for eight years to get permission to expand it. For three hundred years, his forefathers were businessmen and farmers in the area, and Montfort today owns a company that produces concrete blocks for building material.

Montfort owned property that could supply the additional gravel he needed for his business. The town of Fishkill decided that Montfort was in compliance with its zoning requirements and approved the expansion of his gravel company. Then state Department of Environmental Conservation (DEC) stepped in.

As soon as he filed for his permit application with the DEC, Montfort was enveloped in a complicated and tedious process that has yet to end. His draft Environmental Impact Statement (EIS) was rejected as incomplete nearly six months after the state was legally required to issue an opinion.

Montfort resubmitted his EIS, the DEC approved it two years later in 1995. But then the DEC, in league with local conservation groups, stopped him once again. The DEC informed Montfort he would have to start the process over again from the beginning because a den of rattlesnakes was discovered on an adjoining property owned by a conservationist group.

The snakes were not even on Montfort's land. He had already addressed this issue in his previous impact statements, outlining the potential impacts his mine would have on the snakes that everybody knew already existed in the area. Still, the DEC told Montfort there would need to be several years of studying the snakes before a decision could be made on his proposed expansion.

Montfort says that the motivation for all he has endured from the DEC appears to be that the state and the local conservationist group, Scenic Hudson, wants to acquire his property for land trust. Montfort is still fighting it out. In January 1998, he filed a lawsuit demanding that the state issue a final decision based on his original permit application. The permit process itself has already cost Montfort more than $2 million.[16]

---

[16] *Carol LaGrasse in "The Property Owner's Experience"*

Patty and Findley Ricard have run a flourishing nursery business on Big Pine Key in the Florida Keys for more than seventeen years. One year, they found that the hungry Key Deer were damaging their business, so the Ricards built a fence around a three-acre tract.

Then the state's Department of Community Affairs informed the Richards that they could not have a fence, and that it must come down. When the Ricards asked why, the DCA said that the fence blocked the roaming of the Key Deer and caused increased auto traffic on the adjoining road. The Ricards were asked by the state to move to a less "environmentally sensitive" location. But, no one wanted to buy their property. Due to the excessive land regulation in the Keys, their property was worthless. Anyone who bought it would pay more out in taxes than he could ever make from the land.

Protracted negotiations and threats of condemnation of their property dragged on. Findley had a heart attack and the Ricards gave up. They ended up selling the property to the state for half of what they had originally paid for it. Ironically, the United States Fish and Wildlife Service took over their property but never bothered to tear down the fence.[17]

In California flood control barriers were in a state of disrepair for environmental reasons, with disastrous results. This incidence of over-regulation caused three deaths and forced 32,000 people to flee from their homes.

For *six years* prior to the 1997 flood, local flood control officials, and even the Army Corps of Engineers had warned that the levee in the town of Arboga badly needed repairs. The Corps report flatly stated that the "Loss of human life is expected under existing conditions (without remedial repairs) for major flood events."

Despite this warning, the United States Fish and Wildlife Service insisted that lengthy studies had to be done to determine the impact repair work would have on the Valley Elderberry Longhorn Beetle- a protected species.

---

[17] *Sean Paige in the article "Almost Paradise" published by Insight in April 1998*

The Valley Elderberry Longhorn Beetle lives in elderberry bushes. Since 43 bushes would be cleared away on the levee, federal regulators decided to force local officials to spend $10 million replanting *seven thousand five hundred* elderberry stems on an 80-acre site.

In addition, the local flood control authority complained it was prevented from performing simple, but necessary maintenance tasks such as clearing brush and controlling rodents that burrow in the levees because of ESA regulations. They also objected to the requirement that they build a wetland within 600 feet of the levee even though there were serious concerns that water from the 17-foot-deep pond would seep into the levee and weaken it.

The levee broke on January 2, 1997. Twenty-five square miles of property and habitat were flooded, destroying too, ironically enough, the 80-acre plot of newly planted elderberry bushes. County officials and local congressman said that the ESA red tape that delayed the vital repair work for so long contributed to the collapse of the levee.[18]

The Molycorp Company operates a mine in a Southern California desert. In September of 1996, federal agents conducted a tactical raid on their headquarters based on an allegation that they had violated endangered species regulations. This was not the normal service of an arrest warrant or a fine; it was a full-blown assault by federal authorities.

What was Molycorp's violation? Months earlier, one of the waste water pipes at the factory had accidentally burst during maintenance pouring thousands of gallons of fresh water into the desert. It seems that this water was allegedly threatening the environment of the endangered Desert Tortoise.

Susan Messler, an employee of Molycorp, reported that heavily armed federal agents assaulted the mine's property, with guns drawn and flak jackets on, to inform the owners that the spilled water was considered a *toxic waste*.

---

[18] *Testimony given by Rep. Wally Herger before the U.S. House of Representatives Committee on Resources on April 10, 1997, published in the 1998 National Directory of Environmental and Regulatory Victims.*

A few weeks later, a dead tortoise was discovered on the mine's property. All 300 workers at Molycorp attended a compulsory "Desert Tortoise worker education class" in an attempt to educate them on the intricate workings of the Desert Tortoise, even though it was never proven that any action of a Molycorp employee had resulted in the death of the tortoise.

An ounce of prevention means a ton of regulation. Federal authorities first ordered that employees drive no faster than 15 miles an hour and maintain a 100-foot distance from any tortoise that they see. Then they also halted all use of heavy equipment unless an authorized governmental biologist was present to make sure that no tortoises would be harmed.

Finally, on top of all of that, the government assessed over $6.2 million dollars in fines against Molycorp. As a result, the mine was forced to lay off one-third of its employees and they may have to let more go because $6.2 million is more than the companies' 5-year gross earnings.[19]

Lake Koocanusa is a large reservoir in northwestern Montana built in the 1970's, for fishing and tourism. After a while, salmon and other fish species thrived in the lake. As it gradually became a tourist attraction, the lake started generating significant income for the town nearby, which it desperately needed due to the collapse of the mining and timber industry, mostly due to Endangered Species and Clean Water regulations.

In 1992 the salmon were listed as a protected species. The United States Fish and Wildlife Service and the National Marine Fisheries Service decided to conduct a 50-year study, releasing large amounts of water upstream and increasing the volume of the Columbia River. They wanted to know if the increased water volume would help the salmon in their spawning migration.

These water releases included Libby and Lake Koocanusa 800 miles away from the Columbia. Now, during the height of the tourist season in summer, so much water is released from Lake Koocanusa that the shoreline ends 300 feet from the docks. Much of the lake is reduced to a thick mud, and with the

---

[19] *"American Investigator" published by America's Voice*

irony typical of US Fish and Wildlife tales, this reduction in water leaves the spawning grounds of the salmon and other fish exposed.

The tourism industry has taken a plunge since no one wants to fish, swim or boat in a mudflat. In another ironic twist, it seems the federal government's efforts to save the salmon are threatening the White Sturgeon, another protected species, which dwells below Lake Koocanusa.

Libby resident Bruce Vincent says this tragedy is an all-too-typical result of federal environmental policy. "They suffer from a serious tunnel vision in which they take one species at a time. What they fail to realize is that species don't exist in a vacuum. What you do to help one species will invariably impact another." Vincent says that since nobody, human or fish, can use the lake anymore, the bumper stickers around town now refer to it as "Lake Who-Can-Use-It".[20]

## Miscellaneous Stories Involving Environmental Regulatory Horrors

Part of the natural process in growing Bluegrass is to burn the fields each year. This tends to invigorate seed development and growth. In 1998, this practice came under fire from environmentalists in Washington State who claimed that the Bluegrass growers were harming the environment.

Residents of Spokane and those in the surrounding areas complained about the burning of the grass because they did not like the smell. Then, the EPA moved in and began to impose extremely strict regulations on just how growers could burn their fields.

These rules became so outlandish that growers had only 7 days to burn their fields each year, much less time than needed. However, this narrowed window of opportunity was not enough

---

[20] *Bruce Vincent, 1998 National Directory of Environmental and Regulatory Victims*

for the EPA. Along with the American Lung Association, the EPA filed several lawsuits that ended up compelling the states to ban outside burning.

It was a death knell to the Bluegrass growers' businesses. This is sad enough, but, as always, there are a tremendous number of ironies in this particular situation. For example, the United States Soil and Conservation Service had praised the production of Bluegrass when it started 50 years ago. It seems that the burning process actually replenished the topsoil at a rate of about one inch every ten years. Compare this to other farming methods that only replace one inch of topsoil every hundred years.

The worst part of this situation is that the United States Department of the Interior has declared that it plans to burn one million acres of trees in the same area in order to avoid a serious forest fire.[21]

On August 23, 1991, eighteen armed Environmental Protection Agency agents raided Higman Sand and Gravel. For 53 years the owners had run the business legitimately and had a spotless record. The agents burst into the room like storm troopers, waving guns and screaming "Don't move!"

What had happened here? This was not a drug bust or a search for known killers. It turns out that a paid informant had told the EPA that Higman was illegally storing hazardous waste. After a thorough search of the property, the EPA agents did find a small quantity of paint thinner spilled on the property. The EPA felt the need to file charges and send the case to a Federal Court in Sioux City.

During the course of the trial, however, it was discovered that the EPA's paid informant had actually planted the paint thinner on Higman Sand and Gravel's property. If the company had been convicted of the charges, the informant stood to profit handsomely: He was promised $24,000, plus the $2,000 he had already received, for tipping off the EPA.[22]

---

[21] *National Center for Public Policy Research*

[22] *1998 National Directory of Environmental and Regulatory Victims*

The Beggerly family, long time residents of Horn Island, Mississippi had a nasty surprise in store for them in the early 80's. The federal government stormed in and seized their land because the U.S. Department of the Interior wanted to finish constructing a sea- shore park and needed their land to complete the project.

The Beggerly family asked for just compensation for the value of their land. Astonishingly, the Department of the Interior refused, claiming that the government had owned the property ever since the Louisiana Purchase in 1803. The government finally did offer the Beggerly's $200 an acre for their land, despite the fact that it was valued at over $6,000 an acre.

The Beggerly's hired a genealogist to trace the ownership of the land back as far as possible to try to disprove the government's claim. It was discovered that the land was privately owned at the time of the Louisiana Purchase and therefore, the government had no claim to it.

Despite this, the U.S. Department of the Interior refused to recognize the legal rights of the Beggerly's. Suing the government in the Fifth Circuit Court of Appeals, the Beggerly family won and the government was ordered to pay damages. The government then appealed to the Supreme Court and they overturned the decision of the appellate court. Worse than that, they chillingly asserted that no one has the right to second-guess the federal government in these matters. Not even the courts have the authority to control government regulatory actions.[23]

In 1993 Coors Brewing Company officials discovered that fumes from spilled beer were actually more potent and harmful to the environment than originally believed.

Trying to be an environmentally responsible as possible, the Coors Brewing Company voluntarily spent over $1.5 million to analyze the situation. They then turned over an in-depth report to the Colorado Department of Health and Environment so that brewers could learn from it and fix potential problems. They were thanked by the government for their honesty and their

---

[23] *Defenders of Property Rights*

thorough report, then slapped with $1.05 million fine for violating the emissions standards of the Clean Air Act.

Seeing this, it would be highly unlikely that any corporation that discovers a problem will come forward voluntarily. In the end, Coors paid over $2.5 million for a problem they could have kept quiet about.[24]

Clinton and Gore are two of the people most responsible for these injustices. Working together with the multitude of regulatory agencies, the federal government has set the goals of regulatory actions and numerous state agencies are simply following their direction. All of this is nothing more than an Enviro-Scare tactic that will make it easier to create the new "One World Order".

Already, Al Gore has traveled to other countries and forced them, utilizing the strong economic forces of the United States, to accept the insane environmental regulations that the Clinton Administration endorses. All these regulations add up to little more than a bigger government with extremely socialistic tendencies.

Think back to when I told you about the necessary elements for the creation of a socialist society. Three of the most important aspects are:

1) A large federal government that asserts its control over nearly every single facet of daily life
2) The governmental control of all land and resources
3) The erosion of the right to keep and bear arms

Do not doubt for one minute that each day we, the people, allow men like Al Gore to operate this country under the maniacal, socialistic principles of environmentalism, we will slowly lose our freedom. The New World Order is nothing more than a One World, Socialist Order where peoples' homes are taken, destroyed and devalued for the sake of a bird. The New

---

[24] *Washington Times on March 18, 1997*

World Order is the end of America. It will not be long until the Constitution becomes a meaningless document because the government has utilized Enviro-Scare tactics to manipulate everyone into giving up their rights.

In order for this to be successful, men like Al Gore and Bill Clinton, have to slowly assert governmental control over all private land. If this sounds like an outlandish conspiracy theory, maybe these following stories will open up your eyes.

Take for example the Billion Dollar Land Grab proposed by House Resources Chairman Don Young and supported by Frank Murkowski. Basically, this bill (CARA- Conservation and Reinvestment Act- HR701/S25) is designed to set up a Land and Water Conservation Fund. These billion dollars each year would be utilized to purchase privately owned land for governmental control and use. Many times, federal agents conceal themselves as private citizens and use funds from this trust to purchase plots from unsuspecting citizens. Furthermore, this billion dollars becomes a war chest for environmental agencies to fight landowners who stand in the way of government land ownership.

This bill will take our tax dollars and use the money to purchase land for government-only use and control. Regrettably, a lot of Representatives who are usually supportive of landowner's rights are supporting this measure that will most likely pass. The fact is, the representatives are being enticed by large "pork barrel" spending proposals that accompany this bill. Therefore, our politicians are not looking at the big picture, rather they are "back scratching" and "wheeling and dealing" away the rights of landowners.

For those of you who consider one billion "chump change", I must bring to your attention another bill (HR798/S446) that is currently making its way through congress. The Miller-Boxer Land Acquisition Trust is highly endorsed by Al Gore because it gives another 900 million dollars to environmental agencies to purchase private land. This is a 900 million dollar a year appropriation.

However, that is not enough for Al Gore. He has announced his program of "Partnership for America's Resources". In the end, he wants to supply over 10 billion dollars a year to the Land and Water Conservation Fund and force the taxpayers to support the destruction of private land ownership. This is a significant amount of money that leads some to draw only one conclusion: Al Gore's number one agenda is the transfer of privately owned land to government ownership and control.

Regrettably, "pork barrel" spending projects are how Al Gore and Bill Clinton are manipulating our representatives. Trying to look out for the best interests of their constituency, our representatives are being fooled and thus missing the big picture. Take for example the Omnibus Parks Bill that is slipping its way through Congress. In the end, it will appropriate over $200 million for the federalization of privately owned land. This is how it happens, little bits here and there add up to the 10 billion Al Gore wants.

This $200 million is being spent on small projects that gain the support of House Republicans who are normally loyal to the rights of private landowners. Representatives Chris Cannon and Robert Bennett, normally loyal supporters of private ownership, are pushing for the "San Rafael Swell National Heritage Area" in Utah. This program will effectively convert millions of acres of wilderness into federally owned land. The short-term benefits are there, but the long-term loss in economic power and resources are staggering. How about the "Baca Ranch Purchase" in New Mexico where Senator Pete Domenici is supporting the bill that would utilize $150 million of our tax dollars for the federal purchasing of 95,000 acres? This money will assist small oil well owners in the short term, but will turn over 95,000 acres of land to the government. This is land the people will never get back.

These small "pork barrel" tactics are how Al Gore will finally get his 10 billion dollars in appropriations. However, I am sure he will not stop there. At the rate he would like to go, 75% of this country's land will be federally owned by 2020. This is truly part of the One World Order.

In all of their speeches, Clinton and his sidekick Al, make promises of a better tomorrow. All of their plans seem so good for the environment and for the society. Furthermore, they constantly attempt to lull Americans into believing that if we just hand over our lives to the "New World Order" everything will be all right. Well, I don't buy it and neither should you.

Let's quickly examine one of Clinton-Gore's great plans for the environment and our country- The Interior Columbia Basin Ecosystem Management Project. This effort was designed to "save" the environment in the Northwest as well as to create thousands of jobs. Pushed into existence by Bruce Babbitt (Secretary of the Interior) and Al Gore, this project has done little more than increase governmental power, destroy thousands of free enterprise jobs and diminish the rights of every American.

The plan was to take 144 million acres of land and turn it over to federal control by placing severe restrictions on grazing, mining, logging and private property usage. The federal government already owned only 72 million of those acres. The total area in the end is only slightly smaller than the thirteen original colonies. Ironic isn't it?

Already this project has destroyed the economies of countless small towns by over-regulating those who own the land. If this program is allowed to continue, the end result will be a total destruction of the logging, mining and cattle industries throughout the region. The most sickening fact about this project is the basic philosophy under which it operates.

Twenty federal agencies are expected to increase their efforts to accomplish the goals of this program, which is guided by the following principles:

- All ecosystem management activities should consider human beings as a biological resource. That's right folks, humans are the same as a beetle, an ant or a cow. In order for this project to work fully, the citizens of the United States must be dehumanized and placed on the same level as mosquitoes. This sounds so much like the doctrine of the Nazi's that it scares me. Don't forget that hiding fascist tendencies behind environmentalism is no different than hiding them behind racism.

- Ecological, rather than political boundaries will

be used. Say goodbye to the sovereign nation of the United States if Al gets his way. How can we even consider electing a president that considers political boundaries 2nd to environmental boundaries? This project is little more than the destruction of state sovereignty. This would be the final blow necessary to create a totally dominant federal system. State government would lose all power as interstate boundaries broke down and federal regulations ruled supreme with no state recourse.

- A federal policy would be developed that accounts for ecological values equally with economic values. Thus, your job, retirement, children's future and financial security are just as important as a school of salmon attempting to spawn. If it were necessary, Al Gore would sacrifice the lives of thousands of Americans (as he did with the flood in California) to save a single elderberry beetle. This is just sickening.

- The EPA must make ecosystem protection a primary goal of the agency on par with human health. Finally, we should let our children die and suffer from illness. We should stop testing drugs, or conducting experiments to save human lives because they effect the natural balance of a rat. Al Gore wants humans to become nothing more than a bug on this planet.

This is Bill and Al's plan for our future. Their promises and speeches are nothing more than lies utilized to cover up their true intentions and lead the American people into a ruined future. I have said it before, and I will say it again. I am all for protecting our environment, but I draw the line when it come to treating men, women and children like roaches and destroying the future livelihood of millions for the sake of a few.

These are all facts, not something that I made up. Those

stories I put throughout this book involve actual citizens of this country. There is only one conclusion that can be drawn from this wealth of knowledge: that the New World Order is actually an attempt by men like Bill Clinton and Al Gore to socialize our country and use Eco-Scare tactics to compel Americans to hand over their property and their rights to the federal government.

In this grand scheme to federalize private property, one of the greatest sufferers is the American farmer. Arguably no one in this country is more closely tied to the land than the farmer. Despite this fact, it seems that farmers are on the top ten hit list of the Clinton-Gore administration.

Take for example the "Woolsey Farmland Condemnation Act". Politicians call it HR1995. This act is designed to federalize 38,000 acres of land in the Pt. Reyes area. This seizure will subsequently cause 90 historically significant farm families to lose their land. No one is saved from this onslaught.

In the end, after the land is taken from the people, the federal government will be able to control our lives like puppets in a show. Giving and taking away resources that land provides will give the federal government total control over the economy of this society. Furthermore, the rights that they have to trample on in order to accomplish this goal will make the Constitution obsolete.

At the drop of a hat, the government could cut off access to public land and restrict people from earning their livings. This is best demonstrated by the moratorium proposed by the United States Forest Service in all National Forests. Michale Dombeck, Chief of the USFS, has said the agency "will aggressively decommission old, unneeded and unused roads". What he fails to mention is that most of these roads are neither unneeded or unused, although they may be old.

Originally constructed for lumber or recreational uses, these roads have become vital to the economies of the surrounding towns throughout this nation that lie adjacent to National Parks. By cutting of access to these roads, resources will become scarce, land will become inaccessible and tourism will plummet from the loss of recreational activities. In other words, at the whim of some governmental agency, the lives of millions of people will be upset. I thought this was a government for the people, not for the forest.

All in all, these actions are part of a trend towards the end to capitalism and freedom in America. If men like Bill Clinton and Al Gore continue to have support (most of it comprised of ill-informed people just being spoon fed lies) then the sovereign nation of the United States will no longer exist.

There will truly be a New World Order and it will be the One World Order of a socialist government. No more freedom, no more control over our lives, only the failing economy that socialistic bureaucracies create. But, what does it matter after all? According to Al Gore, we're only as important as a flea.

## Criticism: The Backlash Begins

I am sure many of you have not heard of these atrocities committed against our fellow citizens. However, do not believe for one instant that this has gone unnoticed by all of us. Despite years of criticism, the EPA, the White House and other governmental agencies continue on their rampage to destroy the 5th amendment. This erosion of our civil liberties is done in the name of regulations that have never been proven to protect the environment.

Property owners from around the country have long been criticizing the intrusion of government into the homes of private citizens. David Langford, a rancher who leads the 3,500 member Texas Wildlife Association, understands the importance of keeping up the land. He, however, takes issue with what he calls "pesky bureaucrats" scraping around trying to secure their jobs and gain money for their agencies by harassing free, law-abiding citizens. He criticizes the government for overlooking the rights of property owners in their fight to preserve the landscape. He, as well as myself, also takes issue with the fact that the government does not recognize how landowners want to preserve the environment as well.

Members of the Texas Wildlife Association, as well as other groups like them, believe that environmental laws are laden with burdensome, costly and unnecessary regulations. Bureaucrats from Washington D.C., who understand little about the local communities and turn a blind eye to the financial woes they create for landowners, then enforce these regulations.

Overzealous wetland and endangered species regulations have devalued too much land to the point where some people are not able to make a living anymore. In exchange, the government has made absolutely no effort to compensate these people for their loss. Furthermore, too many people are being placed in prison and fined exorbitant amounts of money for violations of vague laws that are unknown to over 99.9% of the population.

Meanwhile, Bill and boys in the White House are protecting individuals who are truly harming our society, because they give fat contributions to the Democratic National Committee.

Examine the following five cases that were reported in 1993 by the Washington Times in which corporations that were truly harming the environment walked away with little more than a slap on the wrist.

- PureGro Company Inc. in Pasco, Wash, was indicted for illegally disposing, storing and transporting hazardous wastes and for knowingly endangering the lives of people who lived near the dumpsite. The firm later pleaded guilty to a misdemeanor and paid a $15,000 fine.

- Weyerhauser Forest products Inc. in Aberdeen Wash., accused of dumping oil based paint waste into area storm drains. The Environmental Protection Agency sought a 39-count criminal indictment, but later changed their minds when the campaign contribution check cleared. They were allowed to plead guilty to five misdemeanors and pay a nominal fine.

- Thermex Inc. in Dallas, accused of dumping chemicals and hazardous waste water. Allegations of criminal misconduct were mysteriously dropped by the Justice Department and never pursued. This, despite the obvious danger to both the environment and the people.

- Chemical Waste Management Inc. in Baton Rouge, LA, accused of illegally dumping and transporting hazardous waste. Convictions of corporate leaders were overturned and charges dropped in full. Probably after their check cleared as well.

- Hawaiian Western Steel Ltd. in Ewa Beach, Hawaii, accused of illegally storing and disposing of hazardous wastes. Criminal charges were first brought, but then they were promptly dropped after pressure from the White House came to bear. The fact is, Western Steel was a significant contributor to the political campaigns of those who reside in the White House.

All of these cases involved serious violations but they were quickly disposed of. The environment in the areas of these companies was damaged and the lives of American citizens were put at risk. However, because these were big money corporations, they walked away with little or no punishment. Meanwhile, Ms. Kenny has to pay 1.5 million because she built her house where a chicken coop used to be.

As early as 1995, the EPA was highly criticized for their overzealous and misguided tactics. A report filed in Congress in April 1995 said that,

"The Environmental Protection Agency should radically change the way it does business by giving states and even private companies and citizens the responsibility for pollution control."

The reports called for the destruction of the EPA as it is known, and the funneling of the monies spent currently at the federal level down to the state level. As Senator Barbara

Mikulski said,

> "As I travel around the state of Maryland, I hear from small businesses and local elected officials that they are confronted by a growing number of EPA mandates that just don't make sense."

For example, the state of Ohio is required each year to test its water for a pesticide only used in the production of pineapples. This, along with tests for 84 other substances that are never used in the state, makes it very expensive for the state to regulate its water supply. This report given to Congress in 1995, said that control should be given back to the states so they can develop pollution measures that are better suited to the demographics and composition of their particular region.

Despite this fact, in 1995 the EPA continues to grow in its size and stature. In a time when government should be shrinking, the EPA has grown about 58% in the years between 1995 and 1998, according to the General Accounting Office reports on government. This is three years after a report was released into Congress that called for a "radical change".

It is not hard to imagine why this happened, when you have someone like Bill Clinton or Al Gore running the show. Despite facts proving that excessive regulation is harmful to local economies and unconstitutional, the government continues in its over-regulation of privately owned land.

In that same month in 1995, landowners in Memphis Tennessee where engaged in a battle to receive some compensation for the amount of money they were forced to spend to develop a 3-acre plot of prime commercial real estate located in the middle of the city. This company has been forced to spend 28% over budget and is still facing fines from federal regulators because they did not dot all the I's and cross the T's on the forms they were forced to turn in. Incidents like these have caused many reasonable citizens to demand change. Thus, in 1995, the Shuster Bill was announced in Congress.

The Shuster Bill was designed to scale back the wetland regulations by modifying the 1972 Clean Water Act and clarifying exactly what was constituted as a wetland. Bill and the boys killed this bill in Congress because they claimed it was going to hurt the environment. In reality, this bill was only designed to scale down big government, and put common sense back into how the EPA could handle wetland cases.

Even those who follow the rules (the ones they know of) in regards to wetland regulations are handicapped by the extensive regulations and overwhelming red tape. For example, Robert Kuras set out to build a golf course in 1986, and he scrupulously followed both Michigan State and federal guidelines to design his course around protected wetlands. After thousands of dollars in architecture, filing costs and fees he was delayed almost a decade in production.

On the other hand, Donald Moon, who built a golf course nearby without following a single guideline, was fined only $1,000 dollars and given 33 hours community service. His golf course is open for business while Kuras is forced to pay taxes on land he cannot utilize. The absurd bureaucracy has forced normally law-abiding men to break the law just to accomplish reasonable goals.

Those who want to follow the rules get caught up in a bureaucratic nightmare that leads them to just decide to pay the fine and be done with it. In reality, the wetland laws are designed so moronically that someone who violates the rules without ever obtaining a permit is punished far less than someone who goes through the proper channels and then makes an error in violation of the agreement.

Therefore, the government encourages individuals to break the rules, and punishes those who try to follow them. Even after an administrative law judge recommended Mr. Kuras be allowed to develop his land, the EPA blocked the effort. They still wanted more paperwork filed. It was only after the governor intervened that Mr. Kuras was allowed to build his golf course. The end result was hundreds of thousands of dollars in lost revenue, legal fees and property taxes.

With each new regulation put out by the EPA, the plot thickens. It seems that each time the EPA wants to make a new rule, they do so at the cost of the American people. Of course, each new rule they make also insures them a new branch of enforcement, increased appropriations and more job security.

Take for example the air quality rules that were proposed by the EPA back in 1997. Here is an example of rules that were simply designed to justify the intrusion of the EPA into more sectors of the economy. In other words, they were trying to put white sand in the sugar again.

As Tom Delay released in a press conference back in 1997:

> "What they're trying to do is seemingly noble, but it needs to be looked at in a cost benefits way and the EPA is not very good at that. They tend to shoot first and ask questions later."

The EPA just makes up rules without ever thinking about the impact they will have on the society. They are exercising something to the likes of "groupthink" This is a psychological phenomena that occurs when members of an organization began to think alike and make decisions based only on the needs of their particular organization. The EPA comes up with an idea and then quickly tries to implement it, even if the cost would be to increase our utility rates by almost 400%, which is what this action would have accomplished if allowed to go into full swing.

Therefore, the criticism of the EPA does not only come from individual citizens or corporations who have been ruined by their overzealous and illegal activities. Politicians who can keep a clear picture of the needs of the American people can also see that all the EPA wants to do is spend taxpayer's money on projects that are unreasonable and self-serving.

Some say that the EPA never had to rear its ugly head into the public arena. Some critics assert that the environment was never in any danger. Growing in size over the years, the EPA has actually hindered individuals who long supported environmental protection efforts. Take for example Tom Tyler in Baltimore Maryland. He has long been an advocate for protecting the wildlife and environmental landscape and has done so successfully with his 1,000 square miles of forest and wetlands along the Chesapeake shore.

His company has been grudgingly called a "first-class

operation" by many conservationists. Sadly, that has not stopped the EPA from getting involved and forcing him to fill out mounds of paperwork and deal with loads of regulations. Mr. Tyler was quoted saying in 1995 that:

> "Look, we were environmentally sensitive at Chesapeake a long time before it began to get chic. Because we were already doing it, it flat out offended me when some of these environmental rules and regulations (regarding forestry practices) came out; and yes, some of it was brought on by the way the damn idiots in our own industry operate. But, for a company out there to make a profit, they do what they can to protect the environment."

Mr. Tyler was forced to go through the bureaucratic nonsense, even though he was already in compliance. This waste of taxpayer money by regulatory agency self aggrandization is absurd, and it should be stopped. Some people have gone further than just criticizing and they deserve some lip service.


## Fighting Back: Freedom Lovers

The destruction of the 5th amendment has begun to be more than some can bear. The sad thing is that individual citizens have to pay more of their hard earned tax dollars to fight the EPA and other governmental agencies that seek to rob them of their 5th amendment rights. This does not make any sense to me.

The EPA, and the green movement, are able to use the government in their efforts to take away property rights, whereas decent law-abiding Americans have to fight the battle with their own money, while funding the enemy with their tax dollars.

The green movement, as well as the EPA and other governmental regulatory agencies, are lavishly funded by U.S. tax dollars and billions in corporate donations (Rockefellers, Carnegies, Mellons and others). They receive White House endorsements and tax breaks because they are governmental and (supposedly) non-profit organizations.

Despite their "non-profit" status, they receive funding from the sales of everything from T-shirts to world cruises. The American taxpayers fund environmentalists while their opponents must fund themselves. With this money, they can buy off the news media, politicians like Clinton, and greed-driven scientists. With these powers they can manipulate the minds of the American people to make them believe that increased governmental interference at the federal level is best for society.

It is true that the environmental movement and the EPA once served a very important purpose. In the 60's our lakes and rivers had become polluted. Our air was dirty, and we needed someone to quell the interests of greedy corporations who were willing to sacrifice the good of the people and the environment for their healthy bottom line. However, this movement has become too big for its britches. That is why people have begun to fight back, and it's just not those who have been directly effected by the illegal actions of the government.

The property rights movement has begun and is gaining strength each day. However, the longer the delay, the more powerful the EPA and its other minions become. The longer the fight is drawn out, the more people are converted over to the alarmist environmental movement that seeks to destroy the basis of freedom in this country.

The property rights movement acknowledges the fact that there have always been reasonable limitations on how a person can utilize their land. Ownership of property does not give one the right to store nuclear waste, or turn your backyard into a landfill. The fact is, the only thing the property rights movement wants is clear, defined rules that are handled on the local level.

Most groups just want the federal government out of there. Keith and Diane Monti of Florida are two key players in the civil liberties fight in that region. They believe that the environmental movement has become nothing more than excuse utilized by the government to rob Americans of their constitutional rights. Florida is on the front lines in the battle over wetlands because the state there has declared a state of emergency and has clamped down on wetlands more vigorously than any other.

The Florida government, fully supported and encouraged by the EPA, has launched a campaign to make everyone in the state believe that, without government, the world is doomed and the water supply will be irreparably damaged. Keith and Diane disagree with this view and have started a weekly publication to spread anti-propagandist truth to the people.

Keith and Diane believe they are conservationists and shudder at the notion of being called environmentalists. They believe that the land should be preserved but not at the cost of the 5th amendment. They hold that the government has always attempted to hide oppressive doctrines behind legitimate goals. They don't see the issue as obtusely as the government does. They do not believe the answer is more government regulation; rather they believe awareness, education and partnership will accomplish far more, for less money.

They have a little prayer they give out to others which emphasizes their point that a new way of thinking is the best way to deal with the crisis:

"Our father,
Eternal Source of all supply,
Help me to realize
That there is no lack of any needed resource,
At any time or any place,
Except as I create that lack
through my own wrong or limited thinking."

The limited thinking they refer to is that governmental control is the answer to every problem.

The backlash is growing, but not quickly enough. The EPA still wages its war, with the consent of the government not the governed, to seize control of your property and make you foot the bill.

J.W. Lunsford in Tampa Florida, a property rights activist and victim of bureaucratic nonsense said that,

"Any time you buy and sacrifice and pay for a piece

of property, and a rat or a bird's got more right to it than you, then something's wrong."

He purchased the oasis marina 30 years ago and is now facing bankruptcy because his business is in the path of the Kissimmee River revitalization. This revitalization includes putting him out of business with absolutely no compensation.

Property rights groups many times carry patriotic names, and are located throughout the 50 states. However, those in the media who play up the alarmist point-of-view to get ratings have downplayed them. Most of these groups only ask for two things:

1) The end of federal intrusion into their lives.

2) A more education-based system that encourages a team approach to environmentalism, operated at the local level so those involved can understand the economic and social ramifications of conservation efforts. They also call for the end to big government in an attempt to prevent the United States from becoming a socialist country.

The result of these battles is a day in court for property rights activists. Legislators have begun to turn their attention to this issue, albeit slowly. For example, in Maine, a bill sponsored by Rep. Henry Joy would require municipalities and the state to pay landowners if governmental regulation leads to the devaluation or seizure of their land. In other words, those who choose to play by the rules will not be financially ruined because of environmental regulations.

This is true also in Oregon, Washington, Texas and many other states that are independently pulling the reigns back on government regulation.

Sadly, however, the federal government is still controlled by Al Gore wannabes who quash any attempt to limit the power of the EPA and hold the government responsible for financial loss incurred due to governmental regulation. As long as this goes unchecked by the people, and as long as the green movement gains popularity, there is little hope that Big Sister will cease rearing her ugly head and destroying the 5th amendment rights of decent, law-abiding citizens.

## Un-American Politicians

Some organizations in this country strive to protect the rights of every property owner. However, a handful of people cannot do the job for the entire country. Each day, individual citizens have their rights trampled on by governmental agents. The very principles upon which this country was founded are not being upheld.

So many times, the reference to "bad government" is lost in a sea of anonymity. In other words, no one really knows who is at fault for the negative actions of our federal government. Luckily, this is still a democracy and the voting records of every federal Congressman are maintained so that the people may examine them.

I have gathered some information in order to help those of you out there who truly wish to keep America free and preserve the rights of all landowners, including yourself. Examining the issues voted on in 1997 (this was the best data I could locate and analyze in time for this book) I have compiled a list of Representatives and Senators who routinely vote against the rights of individual landowners.

You can withdraw your support from these men and women. You can also call and write them in order to express your dissatisfaction with their actions (please see appendix A for a complete list of your federal elected representatives as well as the information necessary to contact them). Finally, you can vote for other candidates who make promises (and keep those promises) to support the rights of landowners. No matter what you do, I implore you to take some action. Apathetic responses to the facts laid before you so far in this book can only be construed as a desire to throw away the freedom that so many have died to preserve.

For you to truly be an informed voter, I will explain how I determined who was not supporting the rights of landowners.

As I am sure you already know, the U.S. Congress is divided up into the House of Representatives and the U.S. Senate. In order for a bill to become a law it must pass through, in some way, both houses. There are a lot of intricate details in this process, but the basic premise holds true. First the bill must be approved by the House and then by the Senate.

I examined the voting records of the 105$^{th}$ Congress because all of the information was complete. For the House of Representatives, I isolated 12 bills that were uniquely tied into to the rights of property owners. For the Senate, I located 7 bills that dealt with private property rights.

Below, I will describe each bill and then indicate which vote (yes or no) was supporting property rights. Let's start with the House Bills:

### 1.   Endangered Species Act Flood Waivers

This was an attempt by Rep. Sherwood Boehlert (R-NY) to water down the ESA flood waivers bill with a substitute amendment to provide project exemption limitations to waivers of the Endangered Species Act consultation regulations for repair or replacement of flood control projects in counties declared federal disaster areas through 1998. It also waived the requirements for repairs to any project that presents a substantial threat to human lives and property.

In another section of this book, I am sure you read how people have lost their lives because federal regulators would not allow them to properly maintain flood control systems if endangered species were in the area. When this attachment was announced, a bill reducing the rights of the government to stop local authorities from protecting their people was being considered. This attachment would weaken that bill.

It passed because of a threat by House Democrats

and the White House to halt all future environmental votes in the 105th Congress.

Those who supported property rights would have voted "No" on this issue.

## 2. Funding For World Heritage/Biosphere Programs

This was a second and separate vote on the State Department Appropriations Bill at the request of Rep. Jose Serrano (D-NY) on the amendment by Rep. Tom Coburn (R-OK) to prohibit funding for the World Heritage Program or the Man and the Biosphere Program administered by the United Nations Educational, Scientific, and Cultural Organizations and through the State Department and Natural Park Service in the United States

Needless funding would have been pumped into meaningless environmental programs that would have strengthened the National Park Service that is a major supporter of federalizing publicly owned land.

It narrowly passed and the measure succeeded in blocking funding. However, just ten votes the other way and the government's environmental shock troops would have gotten stronger.

## 3. Funding For Forest Service Logging Roads

This vote was on an amendment by Rep. Norm Dicks (D-WA) to the amendment by Rep John Porter (D-IL). The Porter amendment would have slashed forest road construction funds. The Dicks amendment was offered as a compromise to only cut funds for new timber logging roads by $5.6 million. The amendment also reduces funding from $50 million to $25 million for the Purchaser Credit program, which gave timber credits to companies as payments for building new forest roads. Private property owners, hunters, tourists and miners use these roads.

A vote of "yes" would have been pro-property rights. Thankfully the measure passed by a one-vote margin. The funding cuts described in the above section (and defeated in part by this bill) are the ways the U.S. government is trying to stop citizens from accessing publicly owned land. These measures will succeed in the future unless we act now to stop them.

4.  **Biosphere and World Heritage- Interior Appropriations**

This amendment by Rep. Tom, Coburn (R-OK) was to prohibit the use of Interior Department funds in the bill for the U.S. Man and Biosphere Program or the World Heritage Program administered by the United Nations Educational, Scientific and Cultural Organization.

A vote of "yes" signified support of private property owner's rights. You see, pro-environmentalists and supporters of the New World Socialist Order can find many ways to get funding for their wasteful programs. By prohibiting these people from utilizing governmental funds, our own tax dollars will not be used against us in the fight for 5$^{th}$ amendment protection.

Once again the pro-property rights forces narrowly won this battle. Only 10 more votes would be necessary to swing the pendulum to the other side. Most of these issues are like this. Thus, it is vital to contact our representatives and tell them to not let the Enviro-Scare fanatics receive funding from back door methods.

5. **National Monument Designation- Congressional Consent**

An amendment by Rep. Bruce Vento (D-MN) to strike the bill's provision to require the President to obtain congressional approval for proposed national monuments in excess of 50,000 acres. The amendment would have instead established a one-year delay from the time the President announces a monument designation to when the designation actually would take effect.

This was an attempt by the Democrats to allow the President to have carte blanche in seizing privately owned land. This would have created a loophole where the President could declare an area a national monument and then force the people off their land without first requesting the permission of Congress. Enviro-scare supporters would have loved this because it would give the Clinton-Gore clan free reign.

Luckily, enough people voted "no", the pro-property vote, and the measure failed by a very narrow margin.

6. **National Monument Designation- Final Passing**

This was the final bill that allowed the President to designate a monument of 50,000+ acres, but required the approval of Congress or the designation would become null and void. Thus, somebody is still watching the President.

The vote for property rights was "yes" and the measure was passed. The President would be able to designate a National Monument but he needed Congress' approval.

## 7. United Nations Land Designation- RMSAR Convention Exemption

This bill, if passed, would have given the United Nations the right to designate important wetlands in the United States. Then, the U.S. government would be designated as the protector of those wetlands. A vote for this measure would have been a vote for the New World Order of Socialism where political borders became unimportant and the whims of other nations could be thrust upon Americans

The measure was barely defeated, which was lucky for private property rights activists. However, only 13 more converts to the New World Order would have been necessary to gain enough "yes" votes and begin to dismantle political boundaries for the sake of environmentalism.

## 8. United Nations Land Designation- Biosphere Reserves Termination

This amendment would have released the land set aside for the U.N. Biospheres in the United States. This was another back-door attempt by the Democrats to hand over U.S. land to United Nations control.

The good vote was a "no" vote and once again property rights narrowly won.

## 9. United Nations Land Designation- Passage

This bill would require congressional consent before any federal official could nominate U.S. land for protection under the United Nations. This bill also was going to end U.S. involvement in the

Biosphere project and insure that land inside the borders of the United States remained under our control.

The measure passed and the sovereign rights of all U.S. citizens were upheld. However, too many, 191, of our Representatives were willing to turn over U.S. land to the United Nations.

## 10. Private Property Rights- Local Land Use Decision Appeals

This amendment, introduced by Sherwood Boehlert (R-NY) would have prevented private landowners from appealing local land restriction actions to Federal Court. This would have stopped landowners from seeking redress in federal courts from illegal governmental activities.

It was defeated soundly, but 178 representatives were willing to vote "yes" and accelerate the deterioration of private property rights.

## 11. Private Property Rights- Passages

This bill was designed to strengthen the rights of landowners and insure that they would have 5th amendment standing in federal court when the government seized their land. This bill was designed to make it easier for private landowners, wronged by the government, to sue the federal government and receive just compensation for their land.

Supported by 248 representatives, the vote passed and the first step towards protecting privately owned land was taken. What was disheartening however, was the 178 representatives who felt it necessary to stop individual landowners from fighting unconstitutional governmental actions. Apparently, these 178 members of Congress forgot that it was there job to uphold the Constitution, not dismantle it.

## 12. Grazing Fees and Rangeland Management-Passage

This bill was designed to reduce grazing fees for sheep and goats on federally owned land. Currently, fees are so high to use federal land that some ranchers cannot stay in business. The government first seizes all the land around and then charges them exorbitant fees to use the land.

This bill was passed and despite the efforts of 182 representatives to restrict free access to public land, property rights were upheld.

I am sure you have noticed that most of these measures were won in favor of private property rights. However, the abuses still continue and tougher legislation is needed to stop people like Al Gore from federalizing all private property.

The margins of victory in many of these cases were very small and if those who support big government continue to gain power, then it will not be long until the votes begin to sway back the other way.

Study the list of representatives (listed after the next section on the Senate bills concerning private property legislative issues) who openly voted against the rights of property owners and the sovereignty of the United States in these 12 examples. Let's get them out of office before they can do more damage.

Now, on to the Senate. In the Senate there were only 7 votes that related to private property rights. Let's take a look at them in more detail.

## 1. Rights of Way on Federal Lands

An Interior Department Directive holds that individual states cannot claim right of way on federal owned land. Senate Republicans introduced a 1997 Interior Appropriations bill that would, in part, repeal that directive. Senator Bumpers (D-AR) attempted to stop that by attaching an amendment that would strike that part of the Appropriations bill. This particular vote here was on a motion made by Senator Stevens (R-AK) that would stop the Bumpers Amendment from watering down the bill.

Very narrowly, the motion passed (51 to 49). A vote in favor of this motion was a vote in favor of property rights. The Democrats are attempting to give federal regulatory agencies supreme rule over everything. If they had their way, the states would have absolutely no power. Only one more Senator would have been necessary to deadlock the Senate and force a "tie-breaking" vote by Al Gore. We all know how he would have voted.

## 2. Repeal the "Depletion Allowance" for Hardrock Mining Companies

Senator Dale Bumpers (D-AR) attempted to withdraw an important tax break for mining companies all around the United States. This tax break is a "depletion allowance" that doesn't penalize companies for the expensive cost of decommissioning depleted mines. Frank Murkowski (R-AK) fought back and claimed that Bumpers amendment violated a budgetary technicality. (I am sure he was just trying to find a way to stop this type of amendment). Once Sen. Murkowski made this claim, a 3/5ths vote was necessary to allow the Bumpers amendment to proceed despite its budgetary violations.

63 Senators voted in favor of property rights when they said "no" to allowing Bumpers to violate budgetary rules and make his amendment. This was a solid victory for property rights.

## 3. Jurisdiction of the Ninth Circuit Court of

### Appeals

Do you recall all of the stories about how American Citizens have no redress in the federal courts when their land is illegally taken? I was just as stunned and awed as you were when I continually heard of landowners losing in court when it was clear that federal agents violated their constitutional rights. Well, it turns out this is made possible by Senators like Diane Feinstein (D-CA) who attempt, such as in this case, to reorganize the Circuit Courts of Appeals at the federal level and stop them from ruling against the government in cases of illegal land seizures.

Divided totally down party lines , 45(D)-Yes, 55(R)-No, this attempt to hurt the rights of property owners was defeated. Once again, only 5 votes were needed to send it to a tiebreaker where Al Gore would have been able massacre the virtues in the Constitution and prevent anyone from questioning his policies.

### 4. Funding For Forest Service Logging Roads

You may recall a vote similar to this one in the House. Senator Bryan (D-NV) attempted the same thing in the Senate. He attempted to reduce spending by $10 million and stop tax credits for companies that build roads using their own funds.

This measure, an attempt to stop citizens from having access to federal land, was barely defeated. 51 Senators voted "no" and the amendment was stopped. The vote was too close for comfort.

### 5. Interior Appropriations- American Heritage Rivers

President Clinton wanted to implement the American Heritage Rivers Initiative without the approval of Congress. Technically, via executive order, he can do this. The end result would have been the illegal seizure of thousands of acres of privately owned land. Senator Tim Hutchinson (R-AR) attempted to enter an amendment that would have required Clinton to seek Congressional approval before he could go ahead with this project. Alfonse D'Amato called for a vote to table this amendment.

Property rights were set back when 57 Senators voted "yes" and tabled the Hutchinson Amendment. In other words, the President would be allowed to issue an executive order and seize thousands of acres of land without the approval of Congress. There would be no way to stop the Clinton-Gore team from illegally seizing privately owned land.

6. **Interior Appropriations- Mining and Royalty Fees**

Senator Slade Gorton (R-WA) was forced to call for a vote on this motion because Senator Dale Bumpers (D-AR) was at it again. Sen. Bumpers was attempting to increase the fees necessary to mine on publicly owned lands. He was trying to make it so expensive, that few companies would be able to afford the prices and they would be put out of business. In order to accomplish his goals, Senator Bumpers was violating the Constitution by originating a revenue bill in the Senate and breaching the principles of the Supreme Court decision in Buckley vs. Valeo. Apparently, New World Order fanatics will stop at nothing, even in Congress.

Well, Senator Bumper's attempts to destroy freedom were halted once again when Senator Gorton's "point of order" was passed by a vote of 59-39. What is truly sad however, is that 39 Senators were willing to go against the Constitution.

I thought we put them in office to uphold the Constitution.

### 7. Omnibus Property Rights Act

This bill would call for the increased protection of private property. It has not been voted on yet. It was introduced in 105th Congress and for the purposes of this evaluation, those who sponsored the bill received credit for their actions that support the U.S. Constitution and the right to own land.

This bill would force the federal government into paying reasonable amounts of money when they seize privately owned land. Furthermore, it would give individual citizens the chance to fight governmental land grabs in federal court under the guise of the 5th amendment. If passed, this would be a great victory for landowners. However, the Democrats have constantly stalled the bill and it is becoming more doubtful that it will ever be voted upon. Clinton and Gore have made it their goal to quash this bill.

Similar to the circumstances in the House, most of the battles in 105th Senate over property rights were won in the favor of the people. However, the votes were extremely close and the tide could easily turn if the Clinton-Gore group gets more support. Therefore, it is important to speak out on this issue before other members start to believe that this is what the American people want.

The following is a list of all of the Representatives from the various states that voted less than half of the time for the rights of property owners. I have noticed that, in general, the Democrats have the poorest voting record in Congress. That is expected because they are teamed up with Clinton-Gore. Next to the names of the person responsible for the loss of our freedoms, is the number of times out of twelve (or out of 7 for Senators) they **voted for** our rights. You will see that many of them vote totally against the rights of individual landowners (i.e. Snyder and Bumpers of Arkansas).

Each of these politicians are responsible for the slow erosion of our civil liberties. I implore you to utilize Appendix A in the back of this book and get in touch with any or all of these individuals. Only when they hear our collective cry for freedom will they change their ways. As long as this is still a Democracy, we should make it work for the people, not against them.

Furthermore, we need to give support to any representative who supports private property rights. As I have already noted, most of the time the Republicans vote for the rights of the individual landowner. However, there are some that still vote contrary to the rights of the people. The bottom line is that we must constantly watch our representatives. Whether or not they are contained on this list, be sure to write them and tell them that the Constitution is important to you and you will only support a candidate that upholds their oath to protect the Constitution and the rights of the people.

---

| **House of Representatives** | **Senate** |
| --- | --- |
| **Alabama** | |
| None | None |
| **Alaska** | |
| None | None |
| **Arizona** | |
| None | None |
| **Arkansas** | |

| | | | |
|---|---|---|---|
| Snyder- D | 0/12 | Bumpers- D | 0/7[25] |

**California**

| | | | |
|---|---|---|---|
| Becerra-D | 0/12 | Boxer-D | 0/7 |
| Berman-D | 0/12 | | |
| Brown-D | 0/12 | | |
| Capps-D | 0/12 | | |
| Dellums-D | 0/12 | | |
| Dixon-D | 0/12 | | |
| Dooley-D | 5/12 | | |
| Eshoo-D | 0/12 | | |
| Farr-D | 0/12 | | |
| Fazio-D | 3/12 | | |
| Filner-D | 0/12 | | |
| Harman-D | 2/12 | | |
| Horn-R | 4/12 | | |
| Lantos-D | 0/12 | | |
| Lofgren-D | 0/12 | | |
| Martinez-D | 4/12 | | |
| Matsui-D | 0/12 | | |
| McDonald-D | 0/12 | | |
| Miller-D | 0/12 | | |
| Pelosi-D | 0/12 | | |
| Roybal-Alland-D | 0/12 | | |
| Sanchez-D | 1/12 | | |
| Sherman-D | 0/12 | | |
| Torres-D | 0/12 | | |
| Watos-D | 0/12 | | |
| Waxman-D | 0/12 | | |
| Woolsey-D | 0/12 | | |

**Colorado**

| | | | |
|---|---|---|---|
| DeGette-D | 0/12 | None | |
| Skaggs-D | 0/12 | | |

**Connecticut**

---

[25] This figure indicates that Senator Bumpers never voted in favor of property rights

| | | | |
|---|---|---|---|
| DeLauro-D | 0/12 | Dodd-D | 0/7 |
| Gejdenson-D | 1/12 | Liebeman-D | 0/7 |
| Johnson-R | 1/12 | | |
| Kerrelly-D | 1/12 | | |
| Maloney-D | 0/12 | | |
| Shays-R | 1/12 | | |

**Delaware**

| | | | |
|---|---|---|---|
| Castle-R | 2/12 | Biden-D | 0/7 |
| | | Roth-R | 3/7 |

**Florida**

| | | | |
|---|---|---|---|
| Brown-D | 0/12 | Graham-D | 0/7 |
| Davis-D | 0/12 | | |
| Deutsch-D | 2/12 | | |
| Hastings-D | 0/12 | | |
| Meek-D | 0/12 | | |
| Thurman-D | 2/12 | | |
| Wexler  -D | 1/12 | | |

**Georgia**

| | | | |
|---|---|---|---|
| Lewis-D | 1/12 | Cleland-D | 1/7 |
| McKinney-D | 0/12 | | |

**Hawaii**

| | | | |
|---|---|---|---|
| Abercrombie-D | 0/12 | Akaka-D | 0/7 |
| Mink-D | 0/12 | Inoye-D | 3/7 |

**Idaho**

| | | |
|---|---|---|
| None | | None |

**Illinois**

| | | | |
|---|---|---|---|
| Blagojevich-D | 1/12 | Durbin-D | 0/7 |
| Costello-D | 0/12 | Moseley-Brown-D | 0/7 |
| D. Davis-D | 0/12 | | |
| Evans-D | 1/12 | | |
| Fawell-R | 2/12 | | |
| Guitterrez-D | 0/12 | | |
| J. Jackson-D | 0/12 | | |
| Lipinski-D | 2/12 | | |
| Porter-R | 1/12 | | |
| Poshand-D | 0/12 | | |
| Rush-D | 0/12 | | |
| Yates-D | 0/12 | | |

## Indiana

| | | | |
|---|---|---|---|
| Carson-D | 0/12 | None | |
| Hamilton-D | 1/12 | | |
| Roemer-D | 2/12 | | |
| Viclosky-D | 0/12 | | |

## Iowa

| | | | |
|---|---|---|---|
| Leach-R | 2/12 | Harkin-D | 0/7 |

## Kansas

| | | | |
|---|---|---|---|
| None | | None | |

## Kentucky

| | | | |
|---|---|---|---|
| None | | Ford-D | 1/7 |

## Louisiana

| | | | |
|---|---|---|---|
| Jefferson-D | 4/12 | Breaux-D | 3/7 |
| | | Landrieu-D | 1/7 |

## Maine

| | | | |
|---|---|---|---|
| Allen-D | 0/12 | Collins-R | 2/7 |
| Balducci-D | 1/12 | Snowe-D | 2/7 |

## Maryland

| | | | |
|---|---|---|---|
| Cardin-D | 0/12 | Mikulski-D | 1/7 |
| Cummings-D | 0/12 | Sarbanes-D | 0/7 |
| Gilchrest-R | 5/12 | | |
| Hoyer-D | 2/12 | | |
| Morella-R | 0/12 | | |
| Wynn-D | 1/12 | | |

## Massachusetts

| | | | |
|---|---|---|---|
| Delahunt-D | 1/12 | Kennedy-D | 0/7 |
| Frank-D | 0/12 | Kerry-D | 0/7 |
| Kennedy-D | 0/12 | | |
| Markey-D | 0/12 | | |
| McGovern-D | 0/12 | | |
| Meehan-D | 0/12 | | |
| Moakley-D | 0/12 | | |
| Neal-D | 0/12 | | |
| Oliver-D | 0/12 | | |
| Tierney-D | 0/12 | | |

## Michigan

| | | | |
|---|---|---|---|
| Bonior-D | 0/12 | Levin-D | 1/7 |
| Conyers-D | 1/12 | | |
| Dingell-D | 2/12 | | |
| Ehlers-R | 2/12 | | |
| Kildee-D | 0/12 | | |
| Kilpatrick-D | 0/12 | | |
| Levin-D | 0/12 | | |
| Rivers-D | 0/12 | | |
| Staberow-D | 0/12 | | |
| Stupak-D | 3/12 | | |

## Minnesota

| | | | |
|---|---|---|---|
| Luther-D | 0/12 | Wellston-D | 0/7 |
| Minge-D | 1/12 | | |
| Ramstad-R | 1/12 | | |
| Sabo-D | 0/12 | | |
| Vento-D | 0/12 | | |

**Mississippi**

| | | | |
|---|---|---|---|
| Thompson-D | 4/12 | None | |

**Missouri**

| | | | |
|---|---|---|---|
| Clay-D | 0/12 | None | |
| Gephardt-D | 0/12 | | |
| McCarthy-D | 0/12 | | |

**Nebraska**

| | | | |
|---|---|---|---|
| None | | Kerrey-D | 0/7 |

**Nevada**

| | | | |
|---|---|---|---|
| None | | Bryan-D | 3/7 |
| | | Reid-D | 2/7 |

**New Hampshire**

| | | | |
|---|---|---|---|
| None | | Gregg-R | 2/7 |

**New Jersey**

| | | | |
|---|---|---|---|
| Andrews-D | 0/12 | Lautenberg-D | 0/7 |
| Franks-R | 4/12 | Torricelli-D | 0/7 |
| Frelinghuysen-R | 3/12 | | |
| Menendez-D | 0/12 | | |
| Pallone-D | 1/12 | | |
| Pascrell-D | 3/12 | | |
| Payne-D | 0/12 | | |
| Rothman-D | 2/12 | | |
| Rookeman-R | 1/12 | | |
| Saxton-R | 1/12 | | |
| Smith-R | 4/12 | | |

**New Mexico**

None

Bingaman-D    2/7

**New York**

| | | | |
|---|---|---|---|
| Ackerman-D | 0/12 | Moynihan-D | 1/7 |
| Engel-D | 0/12 | | |
| Flake-D | 1/12 | | |
| Forbes-R | 3/12 | | |
| Gilman-R | 2/12 | | |
| Hinchey-D | 0/12 | | |
| Kelly-R | 5/12 | | |
| LaFalce-D | 0/12 | | |
| Lazio-R | 3/12 | | |
| Lowry-D | 0/12 | | |
| Maloney-D | 0/12 | | |
| Manton-D | 1/12 | | |
| McCarthy-D | 0/12 | | |
| McNulty-D | 0/12 | | |
| Nadler-D | 0/12 | | |
| Owens-D | 0/12 | | |
| Rangel-D | 2/12 | | |
| Schumer-D | 0/12 | | |
| Serrano-D | 0/12 | | |
| Slaughter-D | 0/12 | | |
| Towns-D | 0/12 | | |
| Velazquez-D | 0/12 | | |

**North Carolina**

| | | |
|---|---|---|
| Clayton-D | 0/12 | None |
| Etheridge-D | 2/12 | |
| Hefner-D | 2/12 | |
| Price-D | 0/12 | |
| Watt-D | 0/12 | |

**North Dakota**

| | | | |
|---|---|---|---|
| Pomeroy-D | 4/12 | Conrad-D | 3/7 |

**Ohio**

| | | | |
|---|---|---|---|
| Brown-D | 0/12 | DeWine-R | 3/7 |
| Hall-D | 1/12 | | |
| Kaptur-D | 0/12 | | |
| Kucinich-D | 0/12 | | |
| Sawyer-D | 0/12 | | |
| Stokes-D | 0/12 | | |
| Strickland-D | 0/12 | | |

**Oklahoma**

| | | |
|---|---|---|
| None | | None |

**Oregon**

| | | | |
|---|---|---|---|
| Blumenauer-D | 2/12 | Wyden-D | 1/7 |
| DeFazio-D | 1/12 | | |
| Furse-D | 0/12 | | |
| Holley-D | 2/12 | | |

**Pennsylvania**

| | | |
|---|---|---|
| Borski-D | 0/12 | None |
| Coyne-D | 0/12 | |
| English-R | 5/12 | |
| Fattah-D | 0/12 | |
| Foglietta-D | 0/12 | |
| Fox-R | 5/12 | |
| Kanjorski-D | 0/12 | |
| Klink-D | 5/12 | |
| Mascara-D | 3/12 | |
| McHale-D | 0/12 | |
| Murtha-D | 5/12 | |

**Rhode Island**

| | | | |
|---|---|---|---|
| Kennedy-D | 0/12 | Chafee-R | 2/7 |
| Weygand-D | 1/12 | Reed-D | 0/7 |

**South Carolina**

| | | | |
|---|---|---|---|
| Clyburn-D | 1/12 | Hollings-D | 2/7 |
| Sanford-R | 5/12 | | |
| Spratt-D | 0/12 | | |

**South Dakota**

| | | | |
|---|---|---|---|
| None | | Daschle-D | 2/7 |
| | | Johnson-D | 2/7 |

**Tennessee**

| | | | |
|---|---|---|---|
| Clement-D | 2/12 | Frist-R | 3/7 |
| Ford-D | 2/12 | | |
| Gordon-D | 3/12 | | |

**Texas**

| | | |
|---|---|---|
| Bentsen-D | 0/12 | None |
| Doggett-D | 1/12 | |
| Frost-D | 4/12 | |
| Gonzalez-D | 0/12 | |
| Hinojosa-D | 3/12 | |
| B. Johnson-D | 1/12 | |
| Lampson-D | 1/12 | |
| Lee-D | 0/12 | |
| Reyes-D | 1/12 | |
| Rodriguez-D | 3/12 | |

**Utah**

| | |
|---|---|
| None | None |

**Vermont**

| | | | |
|---|---|---|---|
| Sanders-I | 0/12 | Jeffords-R | 1/7 |
| | | Leahy-D | 0/7 |

**Virginia**

| | | | |
|---|---|---|---|
| Boucher-D | 0/12 | Robb-D | 0/7 |
| Moran-D | 0/12 | | |
| Scott-D | 3/12 | | |

**Washington**

| | | | |
|---|---|---|---|
| Dicks-D | 1/12 | Murray-D | 0/7 |
| McDermott-D | 0/12 | | |
| Smith-D | 1/12 | | |

**West Virginia**

| | | | |
|---|---|---|---|
| Mollohan-D | 1/12 | Byrd-D | 3/7 |
| Rahall-D | 2/12 | Rockefeller-D | 1/7 |
| Wise-D | 1/12 | | |

**Wisconsin**

| | | | |
|---|---|---|---|
| Barrett-D | 0/12 | Feingold-D | 0/7 |
| Johnson-D | 2/12 | Kohl-D | 0/7 |
| Kind-D | 0/12 | | |
| Kleczka-D | 1/12 | | |
| Klug-R | 4/12 | | |
| Obey-D | 1/12 | | |

**Wyoming**

| | |
|---|---|
| None | None |

As I already stated, this is a list of un-American politicians who have no qualms about handing away your rights. Due to the fact that a vast majority of Democrats are on this list, it is easy to see that if Al Gore wins the presidency and the democrats seize control of Congress then the One World Order is not far away.

Hiding behind the environment, these men and women will slowly destroy your rights, some of them without even realizing it. Only by contacting them can you put a stop to this.

Furthermore, if they refuse to stop their oppressive acts then removal from office is the only choice. Stand up and be heard America, before it is too late.

## A Recipe for Fascism

All throughout this book I have clearly demonstrated that the government is getting far too large. The fact is, over half of our lives are spent working for the government, and those in control have become corrupt and self-serving.

The politicians in Washington have handed over the control of our lives to large governmental regulatory agencies that act as an unelected representation. These individuals are not accountable to the people, nor do they serve the interests of the people.

The EPA and BATF have become loose cannons in the government, helping those who seek to erode public liberty and destroy the Constitution.

I implore you to carefully consider the following summation of facts:

- The United States federal government is growing at an alarming rate, and already accounts for 1/7th of our nations employed individuals. There is no one keeping the regulatory agencies in check, and those who have the real power, have formed the unelected representation that have the ability to control our daily lives.

- The green movement coupled with the EPA, the Department of Natural Resources, the Department of Ecology, and other Federal and State environmental agencies have utilized thousands of wetland, and other environmental regulations to erode the 5th amendment protection of private property. Property is being seized for public use, over-regulated and devalued by governmental actions with no form of reparation for law-abiding citizens. This is a form of taxation without representation, because the American people have no control over the EPA, or any other regulatory agency, and it has become clear that our tax dollars are being utilized to lobby in congress for increased support of these same regulatory agencies.

- Increased gun control and storm trooper tactics of the BATF and other federal law enforcement agencies are attempting to systematically destroy the 2nd amendment right to keep and bear arms. Over-glamorized crime rates and widespread fear, have compelled Americans to trust government officials who say that disarming the people is the best way to protect them. Tragic incidents are being utilized to curry public opinion, and turn non-committal citizens against those who choose to exercise their right to bear arms. Honest, law-abiding citizens are being arrested, having their property seized and being limited in their right to keep firearms in their possession.

These facts are indisputable, and I argue that the conclusion is inevitable. If these events are not altered, the United States is becoming a melting pot where the recipe calls for fascism. Socialists like Bill Clinton, Al Gore, scores of regulatory agency bureaucrats, and any other politicians who support the same causes, are hell-bent on destroying a nation founded in liberty and dedicated to the principles of freedom.

# <u>Chapter 5</u>

# Restoring Freedom and Preserving the Union

# The Road to Fascism is Rarely Paved with Good Intentions

Throughout this book I have attempted to point out some of the major problems with the federal government today. It is undeniable that problems in the government have also led to problems in our country. Already I have proven that the government has gotten so large, that no one really can tell us all of its functions. In addition, many Americans have been convinced that more governmental intervention is the best thing for the society.

As the federal government has grown, the need for government has increased as well. The bureaucratic nightmare created by so many federal employees has spawned a system, as demonstrated in agencies like the EPA and the BATF, which exists only for the benefit of the government, not the people. We have become the forgotten masses, as our lives have been turned over to an unelected representation.

Our politicians have become corrupted or out of touch with the needs of the average working and middle class citizen. Those of the unelected representation use our tax dollars appropriated to them in order to lobby congress for additional funding and expanded programs.

Many times, as I pointed out with the BATF and the EPA, those tax dollars never benefit the people. They tend to only inflate the prestige of a particular agency or line the pockets of those who wish to usurp the system.

The American people have been put to sleep by the overwhelming hand of the federal government. With one in seven working Americans employed by the federal government, and many others employed by state governments or supported by federal contracts, we have become dependent upon big government. It's hard for many of us to see the negative side of such an inflated government when someone we know is employed within the structure.

This apathetic attitude has allowed an individual like Bill Clinton to float into office aloft a platform of nonsense. It has allowed his immoral actions to go unpunished. Worse yet, if we continue on the same path, someone like Al Gore, who believes that the EPA should be the most powerful government organization, may become the most powerful person in the country.

Our society has lost its principles, especially since we have handed over the responsibility of educating our children to the very government that has caused the problems. Billions each year are spent on bureaucratic nonsense instead of on our children.

Furthermore, God has been eliminated from the public sector and we have lost our moral compass. Whether you believe in God or not there has never been, nor will there ever be, a better set of rules to live by then those written about in the bible. The word of God represents fair play, honesty, truthfulness and care for the common good. For so many years are nation stayed on the path of righteousness, following the rules of the Ten Commandments and the Ten Amendments to the Constitution. It is no surprise then that the deterioration of our moral and social fiber is correlated with the intrusion of government into our personal lives. Our country was fine up and to the point when atheistic, secular principles replaced godly ones and the government began to tread on the Constitution. This is all because we have allowed government to intrude itself upon every part of our lives. Thus, with government, there can be no religion.

The godly principles that our country was founded upon were necessary elements to the maintenance of a free society. Currently, government actions are unfair and unjust and they result in unprincipled behavior. When our government exists in conflict with the very principles upon which our nation was founded it becomes impossible to prevent criminal governments from forming. This opens up the door to socialists and communists who have no idea what the concepts of fair play and justice mean.

This has got to end, and we still have a chance. Once again, I will reiterate my first point in this book. I am not calling for Freedom Fighters. I am calling for Freedom Lovers who are willing to put an end to this governmental growth. The first step is to educate everyone about what is going on and remind them that we are indeed living in a Democracy and that each and every opinion and vote counts. Then, we have to hold our elected officials accountable and force them to start taking out some of these unelected representatives whom we had no say in hiring.

Big government must end, or we are on a fast track to fascism. Look throughout history and you will find that the people are easily subjugated when:

- They lose their ability and/or right to protect themselves

- They lose control of their own property.

- Their government increasingly taxes them and forces them to pay for programs no one wants or needs.

- Their government becomes uncontrollable and asserts its dominance over all facets of daily life

- Their society loses faith in God and the principles of decency that his word creates.

Every one of these phenomena is occurring in the modern United States. As I write this book, the Columbine Initiatives are gaining popularity and gun regulation is becoming very popular in government and among the people. We are being swindled into giving up our 2nd amendment right to protect our freedom.

The EPA, U.S. Department of Agriculture, ATF, DEA, and other governmental organizations are utilizing forfeiture and eminent domain laws to devalue and actually steal away private property from lawful, legitimate landowners. Each of these departments, staffed with the unelected representation, have become self-perpetuating entities free of any control. They have the utmost power in the society and our Congressional

Representatives are too busy squabbling and lining their own pockets to care.

If these departments remain uncontrolled, they will slowly erode property rights to the point that no one will feel safe and secure. Then the government will be able to barge in and take what some of us have worked a lifetime to build. Regrettably, for some Americans, as I have pointed out throughout this book, this has become a reality.

Taxes, in all forms, have become atrocious. As I write (in June 1999) most Americans are just starting to work for themselves. We collectively work at least 5 months out of the year to support those in the federal government. Our tax dollars are wasted each year in programs that never benefit us. In addition, our trusted politicians determine how they will spend our money by listening to other bureaucrats and not the Constitution or the will of the people.

Every facet of our daily lives has become regulated in some way by the government. The food we eat, the clothes we wear, the cars we drive and the schools our children attend are regulated, subsidized or outright controlled by the federal government. What are subsidies anyways? They are nothing more than our tax dollars, collected by the federal government and dispersed back out to specific sectors of the economy. That is, after the wasteful bureaucracy in Washington misappropriates, consumes and steals at least 50% of that money. Furthermore, too often the subsidies do not go to the right people. Many farmers have been assisted by farming subsidies throughout the years. Regrettably however, too many subsidies are paid to large farming conglomerates and corporations. Instead of assisting the family farmer, large, mass producing farms are receiving our tax dollars. These kinds of collective farms need to be kicked out of the system, but few citizens are willing to call for this because they are afraid that this cut in federal funding will somehow effect them. All Americans have become addicted to this large government and fear the harm that will befall them if certain programming is cut. What they fail to realize however is that if this money was just kept in the local communities and given directly to township trustees and local elected officials, everyone could benefit from the extra money without wasting money in a government bureaucracy, teeming with corruption and mismanagement.

Thus, whenever anybody tries to cut down on spending, groups come out of the woodwork to protect their share. Even if they never really see any real benefits from this federal spending. The perception of betterment is keeping them loyal to a big, over-powering government. Furthermore, certain governmental agencies have begun to criminalize the honest, Constitution loving American. Gun owners and landowners are being portrayed and treated like criminals.

Finally, the expanse of government to every daily operation has destroyed God in our society. We have become a society that has turned its back and we can no longer say, "In God We Trust." Regrettably, we have replaced God with the atheistic notions of humanism and socialism, and now, many Americans actually say, "In Bill Clinton We Trust". This is truly frightening.

Without big government in every sector of our private and public lives, God would be allowed back into our children's hearts and minds. This would bring back a principled society that is truly "Under God".

We are a divided people on a slippery slope to fascism. Each day we allow the government to grow larger, we sacrifice another opportunity to bring back the original freedom our founding fathers spoke of.

Regrettably, every thing our government touches it destroys. Furthermore, individuals like Bill Clinton just want to keep on making government bigger. After all that I have told you the EPA has done to destroy our rights, I picked up the paper and read a big headline "Tough New Water Pollution Standards Unveiled by Clinton". He wrote a check for 870 million dollars to the EPA to begin to look for a microbe in local drinking water that "... is suspect in approximately 900 estimated deaths a year."

870 million dollars for a "suspected" pollutant in our water that killed an "estimated" 900 people. Who were those people? Well, we will never know because it is only estimation with no real cases.

So, Bill and the boys have no qualms about spending

nearly a billion dollars, no doubt on the recommendation of the EPA, to investigate a suspected water pollution problem where no identifiable person was brought forth as a victim. This is just one example.

I can personally remember 70-cent corn back before the election of Richard Nixon in the 70's. At this time, all around the country were grain filled bins that the government kept in reserve. The trigger point was around $ 1.10, and when the price of grain hit this level, the government flooded the market with their corn to bring it back down. They intentionally prevented farmers from making a profit off of their corn and following the principles of a capitalistic economy. I can personally remember a farmer who committed suicide because the government bankrupted him and his farm. Although this is not occurring today, it is still an example of how the government continually tries to intrude upon our lives, sometimes with negative ramifications.

We need to do something right now in order to stop these dangerous trends. This chapter is the second reason why I am writing this book. The first pages were designed to educate you; these pages are designed to give some ideas about how to get our America back. The time for criticism is over, and action is now.

## I. Eradicate Governmental Conflict of Interest

All throughout this book I have pointed out how governmental agencies are acting under the flag of conflict of interest. They actually create problems and request funding in order to inflate the prestige and size of their particular organization. The mentality of "spend it, or we will lose it next appropriations" is commonplace in big government.

Agencies find ways to waste money just to avoid cutbacks. Efficiency, in this system, is despised, and anyone who wants to put in a hard days work is told to "slow down, or you will work yourself out of a job".

Would you allow a juror onto a jury if they were the

boyfriend of the accused? Would you allow the victim of a crime to represent the accused in court? Would you allow the other party in a lawsuit to sit in judgment and determine the disposition of your lawsuit? The answer to all of these questions is a big "NO".

So, I ask, why do we allow unelected representatives to testify before congressional hearings (and be the only ones to testify for that matter) in order to determine if spending is appropriate? Why do we allow government employees to serve as Inspector Generals, who, if they determine the department is no longer necessary, will lose their jobs? Why do we allow the EPA to pass on lies about the state of our environment and request additional funds to initiate needless programs? Or, create policies that have no proven benefit. Why do we allow the government, who wants land for a certain purpose, to use another branch of the same governmental body to seize the land and turn it over to governmental control?

These are all conflicts of interest as well. This book has been full of specific, case-by-case examples of this. That is a lot more reliable evidence than you will ever see the BATF or the EPA produce to justify their nazi tactics. Our elected representatives have turned over the control of this country to the millions of bureaucrats in Washington D.C. These unelected representatives suck up our tax dollars and work only to perpetuate their own jobs and promote the stability, security and prestige of their agencies.

Government should be for the people, not the employees of the federal government. Therefore, the only way to end big government is to stop allowing this conflict of interest to continue.

Agency self-aggrandization must end. Whenever the motives of government are not guided by the principles of "betterment of the community as a whole" they should be halted and the tax dollars returned to the American people.

Look at the tragedy in Littleton, CO again. The government is so self-serving; it is using this tragedy to destroy the 2nd amendment. Examine the environmental issue again utilizing the information I have provided in this book. The government is using the people's concern for this matter to take away private property. Reconsider the tobacco lawsuits that are only being used to take away personal responsibility. The government is always trying to serve its own needs and not the needs of the people. Those in government have become so preoccupied with telling us how we should think, live and feel that they forgot that WE, not them, are the ones in control. Maybe, it is all of us who have forgotten that we are in control.

This conflict of interest has gotten out of control and it is one of the major reasons why government has gotten so large. Therefore, the solution to this problem is to hold governmental agencies far more accountable. We can accomplish this in many ways that I will describe next.

## *Lawsuits for Freedom*

Currently, if you have property taken through forfeiture by the ATF, EPA or DEA, you have to put up a $5,000 bond to help cover the legal costs of the government if you want to challenge the seizure. The reality of this should be the exact opposite.

If a judge determines there is cause to believe an individual's constitutional right to own property or a gun has been abridged, then the government should have to foot the legal bill. If it was determined, in a court, that an individual was incorrect and the government was right, then the money should be paid back. However, if the government loses, then they should have to keep the legal bill as well as return the property. Then, that money should come out of the operating budget of the offending agency, not the general governments tax base.

This, in my opinion, would reduce the number of constitutional violations by government agencies. Right now, too many unelected bureaucrats are running around treading on the Constitution with no recourse against them. When a citizen is lucky enough to win a lawsuit, we all end up paying for it from our tax dollars. That agency is not held responsible for their illegal actions.

If we begin to hit those agencies where it hurts, the pocketbook, then they will change their mind. These agencies will have a hard time explaining to Congress how millions of dollars each year are being spent to help citizens re-assert the constitutional rights that these agencies attempted to illegally take away.

In addition, individuals in these agencies should no longer be able to hide behind "the color of law". In other words, if their actions were over-zealous, and resulted in the loss of Constitutional Liberty to a citizen, they should be personally held accountable.

This would cut down on the cowboy attitude of some federal employees like the U.S. Forest Service representative who said that the American people were useless and the trees were more important than they were.

Stiff fines to high-level agents of major governmental bureaucracies should be levied if it has been determined that their minions have been violating constitutional rights. No longer should the "higher ups" hide in ignorance when they are the ones who design the policies and procedures that let loose these shock troops upon the people.

Federal service should be a temporary job, not a way of life. This would discourage people from trying to increase the size and security of their agencies at the price of American freedom.

The A.C.L.U. constantly goes around preventing local communities from exercising their religious beliefs by suing them. I ask you, why can't the godly communities unite together and sue for a return to God in our schools? We have to prove that the Constitution was originally designed to protect religion from government, not vice-versa. How can the principles of the Ten Commandments and the Eight Beatitudes hurt anyone? I remember a story about a little girl who got in trouble for reading the bible out loud on a school bus. We should have all rallied around her and sued the school just like the A.C.L.U. sues a school for not letting a girl where purple and green colored hair.

Lawsuits for freedom should include the unification of the godly and the end to oppressive government tactics that force God out of our schools and our children's hearts. I guarantee that will prevent another Columbine massacre.

## *Proving Cost Effectiveness*

Just like American corporations, government agencies should have to prove the cost effectiveness of their programs. Departments like HUD should not be allowed to get away with going decades without proving their dollars were well spent. Independent counsels could be set up to determine if the programs currently in effect are actually accomplishing the goals they were designed to. If not, they should be scrapped, the agency dismantled and the people compensated for their losses.

Most of the time I think we would learn that these agencies are actually wasting money. That money, if given to the local communities, could better serve the people. The department heads would be accountable for proving that they need every dollar. It will no longer suffice to say, "we spent all of our money last year so we need it again."

Many of you may say this goal is impossible, after all the government is so big this would take forever. Maybe that's the best point I have ever heard. If the government is so big that we cannot hold it accountable then something is definitely wrong, don't you think?

If no one is accountable, and no one believes we could hold any government body accountable, then we are no longer a democracy and the Constitution is worthless. Thus, we must make a way for government to be held accountable for all of its actions.

It may take decades, after all we let it slide for decades, but after we start holding agencies just as accountable as we hold corporate CEO'S, there will be a tremendous change in government. I personally guarantee cutbacks of 50% if we were to successfully accomplish this task. That's trillions of dollars back into the American economy.

## *Firing By the People*

I have no say in who is hired or fired by the government. In fact, none of my elected representatives have direct control over the hiring and firing of governmental employees.

Therefore, individual citizens should have the power to fire governmental employees who have been found to harass, violate or harm a citizen.

That's right, there should be ways a person can civilly sue a governmental employee and make them prove, to the people's standards not the agency's, that they are doing a good job that serves the people. Government employees are forgetting that they work for the people, not an agency.

If you are getting the impression that I am trying to make government service unappealing in some ways, then you have got the right idea. Today, too many people want government jobs because they know they will be easy rides. Good benefits, high pay, job security etc...

I personally do not want my tax dollars supporting individuals who just want to "collect a pay check" and don't give two cares about me. After all, I am paying the bill and when I call up a governmental agency they pretend like I do not matter. Every one of us does matter and we should be careful to remind every government employee of that fact.

Thus, those that serve the people well in the federal government and honestly report findings can be very well compensated, and those who just try to "collect a paycheck" will be weeded out.

This will end the philosophy of "not working yourself out of a job". The regrettable fact is that federal employees are encouraged to not accomplish goals. For, if they accomplish their goals, they will no longer be necessary. If prisoners are rehabilitated we will not need police and prisons. If the environment is OK, we do not need the EPA. If Agriculture is running fine (which it is) we do not need the Department of Agriculture. If our schools are handed back to the communities, we do not need a Federal Department of Education. The list goes on and on and the end result is millions of people working to keep their jobs, not benefit the taxpayer. This must end.

In addition, since depriving citizens of their property and/or rights is just like theft, criminal sanctions should be a consideration for any governmental employee or elected official that commits one or more of these atrocities against the people. Just because our legislators and other elected officials have allowed this to go on does not make it right. There were hundreds of stories contained in this book that were examples of individual citizens losing their property and rights. In each of these cases, the governmental agents that acted in this manner should be removed from their jobs and possibly prosecuted for their activities. Hiding behind their positions in government should no longer be allowed.

This high level of accountability is the only way to ensure that big government will be eradicated for good.

### *Levied Appropriations*

Whenever a department wants to increase its spending; it should be a levy before the American people. This is just like we do for school spending. Let's put control of government agencies into the hands of the people. If the DEA wants more money, ask the American people. If the EPA (although it should just totally be dismantled) wants more money, ask the American people.

Therefore, instead of using our money to lobby in congress, they will have to spend their money proving to the American people they are worthwhile and should continue to receive appropriations.

I doubt a government agent will scoff at any citizen in the future when they call about a problem, if that person knows their job depends on their work performance.

All of these actions can be utilized to break the conflict of interest that currently exists in the federal government. Only by demanding the accountability of our federal employees and agencies can we ever expect to reduce the size of government. Furthermore, it is only by holding government agencies accountable that we can guarantee no agency will step outside the law and trample our civil liberties.

## II. Stop the Cycle of Governmental Dependence

How many of us have heard that welfare makes people

reliant on the government? I believe that big government has become the welfare of all American citizens. We have become so reliant upon the government to provide for us that we have voluntarily given up too many rights. Most of us have forgotten that we control the government, not vice-versa. If we do not want the agents of the government intruding into our personnel lives then all we have to say is "No".

The fact remains that the government has expanded to such a level that every single citizen receives some assistance from its existence. Be it Social Security, farm subsidies, highway funds, disability insurance, deposit insurance, or any of the other thousands of government functions, most Americans are afraid of their share being cut out. This has become a sort of insurance policy for those in government. They know that if everyone has their hand in the cookie jar, no one is going to put the lid on governmental spending.

This is the cycle of dependence that has engulfed our society. This cycle of dependence has created large government bureaucracies that have become too big to be controlled by the people. The average citizen has no way to challenge their credibility, even though we hear countless stories in the news about government corruption and waste. At the same time, each of these governmental agencies have full-time lobbying departments who do not look out for the needs of the people. Instead, they lobby to keep their organization intact.

In order to break this cycle of dependence we must first dispel the belief that "government knows best". From day one in grammar school civics, children are taught deference and respect for the government. This is a good thing, as long as the government is a just one. The problem occurs when we all have been programmed to trust our government, even when they no longer deserve that trust.

Those in governmental agencies have actually become the problem themselves. They have inflated the reality of the danger in the environment, while downplaying truly important issues like principles and God. All people like Bill Clinton and Al Gore talk about are re-inventing government. Well, if their re-invention of government includes the erosion of personal liberty and autonomy, then I want nothing to do with it.

Socialists, like Bill, have already re-invented government. At one time, the people elected citizens to lead them and make decisions. Now, the people elect less than .01% of those employed in the federal government. Those we have elected have handed over the daily operations to people who we have never heard of, and who have the goal of maintaining their position and collecting our tax dollars.

We have to seize the power from those bureaucrats in Washington and return it to the local communities. A system wide dismantling of the centralized federal government would bring more money back into the communities. In Departments like HUD, over half of our tax dollars are eaten up in the bureaucratic paperwork. That money could all be returned to the local communities so that they could use it to their advantage.

Local township trustees and other elected officials will be able to place those funds directly into the hands of those in the community who truly care. I have said it before and I will say it again, I am not advocating the destruction of government as a whole. Rather, I am saying that having such a large bureaucratic central government needlessly drains away precious resources from those in the country that truly need the money. Furthermore, as we increase the workload and funds available to local elected officials, the salaries of these men and women should increase drastically. Those we elected locally (sheriff's, trustees, councilmen and mayors) should receive just as much, or more than those who work for the EPA.

The billions, perhaps trillions of dollars saved from the dismantling of a wasteful central government could be used to create REAL jobs in the private sector. These jobs will be ones that actually produce something valuable and help America re-assert herself as a world economic power.

Most of our tax dollars currently go to pay the wages of people who do little more than file paperwork no one will ever see, or even cares about. Most of that paperwork is so far backlogged that it has lost its meaning. If that money is taken away from the federal government, the jobs lost at the federal level will be replaced by twice as many, more efficient jobs, at the local level. In addition, there will be twice as many jobs created in the pubic sector, with equal pay and benefits, because that money would be more properly utilized in order to make a product that could be sold for a profit.

All of the money returned to the local communities could be funneled into projects that directly benefit those who paid the taxes. Improvements in local parks, trash collection, street repair and other infra-structural improvements, local business investments and local environmental clean-up efforts could all be accomplished more efficiently and for less money. Shooting ranges could be built that teach every citizen about the importance of the $2^{nd}$ amendment and the proper handling and discharging of firearms.

I guarantee that the local townships and cities run far more efficiently than the federal government. Take for example Vinton County in Ohio. Despite a very low population and tax base, the county commissioners and trustees do an excellent job at getting things done because they realize that they answer to the people.

People would become less reliant on the government if it was no longer involved in every little facet of their daily lives. With the local elected officials in control of that extra revenue, industry would flourish and all the functions that the federal government completes will still go on.

I ask you, why is it that we believe the federal government always knows best? Why do we believe that individuals who we do not even know will manage our money better than the man who you have dinner next to in a local restaurant? Each one of them are human, and will be subject to corruption, but at least you have direct control over who runs your local community through direct elections.

None of us, and I repeat, none of us know who is in control of our money in Washington D.C. If you believe that your representative is, then you need some remedial education. We have no control over our money in Washington. That is why it should be returned to the local level where it can be disbursed more efficiently and with better supervision by those who are truly qualified: The American People.

While the EPA and other governmental agencies are busy seizing our land and guns, our country is falling behind. Those in government have tunnel vision and can only see the world through the eyes of governmental control. They do not see the value of the land or the people on it. They treat us like children who cannot responsibly handle the resources of this society without their help.

If we can successfully stop this cycle of dependence on government, it could begin to erode the "cult of personal irresponsibility" that has plagued our society for too long. Too many people want the government to take care of everything. Furthermore, whenever something bad happens, people want to blame someone and try to sue him or her.

Throughout this book, I noted for you many cases that were just the tip of the legalistic iceberg in this society. We have become a society of whiners and crybabies. Gun manufacturers are being sued because some scumbag decides to shoot someone for their "starter" jacket. Tobacco companies are being sued because people ignored the obvious warning labels on the sides of cigarette packs.

This trend will begin to reverse itself if people learn to become more reliant on themselves and break free of the oppressive bond of big government. Breaking the cycle of dependence is one of the most important things we must do in order to reverse the negative trends in our society. We can do this be realizing that we are, indeed, the people and without us this country is meaningless. We must trust in our own abilities and realize that we have the skills, know-how and training to overcome any obstacle without the federal government's help.

## III. End the Socialist Tendencies of Our Country Before it's Too Late

The societal dependence on government, combined with the overwhelming size and uncontrollable power of the federal branch has brought about a system that teeters on the edge of Socialism. Our current president, supported by the big government lovers in the public and Congress, has successfully moved this country closer to Socialism over the past decade. This is truly a frightening thought.

Remember the history lessons explained earlier in this book. Remember the fact that a big government, publicly controlled property and the elimination of a well-regulated people's militia are the warning signs of communism. This cannot be allowed to happen here.

Our situation in the U.S. is even more precarious than other countries. There will not be an open revolution that instills a communistic or fascist form of government. The changes will be so minor and slow that we may not notice the conversion over to socialism until our children's children open their history books and realize it had not always been this way. Our children will then lose the trust and confidence in the United States that is necessary for its survival. There is indeed a silent revolution occurring in this society and if the tide is not turned, we may see the Constitution lose its value.

The United States may fall into the trap of other European countries that have become socialist democracies. The United States will become like countries such as France and the Netherlands where taxes amount to over 60% of your income and unemployment rates soar into the upper twenties. These countries slowly lost their strong capitalistic economies as they were lulled into government reliance and self-indulgence. Now, a French citizen is guaranteed a monthly income whether or not they work. This means that the French people have little desire to succeed or strive to better themselves. They have become reliant on the government. This also means that at anytime, if those in power choose, the people can be quickly subjugated. It is a recipe for disaster. Combine this fact with the worldwide destruction of private ownership of firearms and you have lost the insurance policy of freedom.

Bill Clinton always talks about a "New World Order", and uniting the world under one flag. Now, I am all for peace among men, but I don't believe that giving up our sovereignty is the best way to accomplish this goal. Look were the "New World Order" got Europe. Their economies are collectively failing to the point that forced them to create the new European Union. Thus, countries that have hard-working, free, capitalist citizens are forced to carry the weight of the other socialist countries. The "New World Order" is synonymous with a "One

World Order" where moochers and freeloaders will live off the backs of the hard working. The United States has never been that way and it should never fall into that trap.

How can we possibly trust a man like Bill Clinton who shows such a disdain for morality. Too many Americans trust a man to lead us into a century of "One World Order" who cannot be trusted by his own wife. Furthermore, Bill Clinton has never shown one iota of responsibility, starting from the day he decided to dodge the draft and shirk his patriotic responsibility, and ending when he did not step down after feasting at the table of corruption and wiping his slobbering mouth with the legal system.

Men like Bill Clinton and Al Gore want to destroy that which our forefathers have built. Your parents and mine have collectively worked their hands to the bone in order to get us ahead. Now, Bill and the boys just want to hand that over to anyone who puts out their hands for a donation. Furthermore, they want that to happen in a society where the government has total control over the land and the weapons. With that power, no one will be able to oppose their socialistic tendencies.

This may sound like a conspiracy theory, but it really isn't. I don't believe that Bill or Al are plotting the take over of our society. However, they are beginning to tear down our societal walls of defense against someone who does want to take away our freedom. They are slowly eroding our freedoms to a point that makes them worthless in the face of governmental oppression. Therefore, the actions of myopic men like Bill and Al may lead us into a future of fascism and communistic control.

One of the most important steps in the eradication of this socialistic trend is to destroy the environmental scam that is being perpetrated on the American people. I have not the time to sum it up in total, but take the time to read the book "Eco-Scam: The False Prophets of Ecological Apocalypse" by Ronald Bailey. This is a definitive work that proves that sham scientists who are being bought off by the green movement have scammed the American people. They are trying to convince the American people, and the world, that we must turn over control of all the land to a collective world government.

This government would supposedly ensure the safety of

the environment. In reality, however, this book points out that there is really no cause for major concern. Furthermore, there is certainly no reason for the United States people to give up their constitutional rights and their sovereignty and capitulate to the demands of the green movement.

We all must learn the truth behind the green movement. If the current trends continue, those who wish to usurp our freedom and lead us down the pathway to socialism will hide behind the terrifying falsehood of environmental degradation. Few American citizens have degrees in molecular biology and ecology and they trust the judgment of those that do. But, before you believe another doomsayer, think about these few questions.

- Who is telling you this information?

- Where do they receive their funding? (government perhaps)

- How well do they explain the situation so that you can truly understand the intricacies of the matter?

The truth is, the ozone layer is not depleting to the point of increasing cancer rates. The fresh water supply is not diminishing; in fact it is getting better each year. Indeed there are some species of animals that are becoming extinct, but that is just the natural way of things. In the end, the environment must be protected but handing over our freedom to the government in order to accomplish this goal is inconceivable.

Each time the government gets larger it creates more jobs for itself. If we allow the government to expand its control over the environment, government jobs will only produce more government jobs. On and on the cycle will continue to the point where a majority of Americans will be employed by a bureaucratic system that has become out of control and unable to preserve the constitutional freedoms it was intended to keep.

Remember one very important thing. The Constitution was created to protect the American people from the abuse of government. Do you honestly believe then that the government can be trusted to ensure its agencies are complying with the Constitution? It is our responsibility to hold our leaders accountable and force them out of office when they over-step their lines of power and infringe upon our rights to life, liberty and the pursuit of happiness.

That is how we can stop this trend towards socialism. Let's, for lack of a better term, "throw the bums out". Votes do count. Call your congressman, vote against those who have big government platforms. Politicians respond to the people and will deliver what we want because we are their bosses. Local governments do not go around creating new departments to accomplish the tasks that are necessary, they just roll up their sleeves and do it themselves.

We must re-assert that power and tell philandering, immoral and godless leaders like Clinton to get the hell out! We need a new "Contract with America". We need a contract with some power behind it.

We need to get out and vote and get rid of those representatives who do not vow to eliminate environmental scare tactics, decrease the size of government, and ensure the constitutional freedoms we are guaranteed. In addition, we must be willing to wean ourselves off of this socialist nipple that has made us into governmental dependents. Thus, we cannot punish our representatives who make the hard decisions to cut federal jobs and decrease social spending throughout the country. This is not an easy task, but it must happen if we are to thwart the trend towards socialism in this country. The next presidential election may just be the most vital in the history of this great nation. Our freedom may be lost if we fail to remain vigilant.

Socialism is not just a word. It is a total way of life. It entails handing over the control of your entire life to a large centralized government. Each citizen will have to transfer his or her civil liberties over to the government. Many do not understand the full gravity of this notion. Imagine if you will, losing control of the right to choose your own career, or the particular brand of soap you use in the shower. When a government moves towards socialism, each new step removes more and more freedom of choice. Do you really think the

Cuban people voted for Castro? Their society is totally impoverished and the only reason for this is that they are under communistic rule. Under socialism, you will have to do exactly what the government says. Your children will be told how the rest of their lives will be when they are 14. In short, the road to life, liberty and happiness is not yours to choose any longer. Because we are free in America, we have the choice of giving up our rights, but believe me, you will only get that choice once... and it will be your last choice.

## IV. Protect the Constitution

I have alluded to this next statement throughout this book and especially in the last paragraph, but I must say it again. We are the ones who are responsible for ensuring that the government follows the rules of the Constitution. We cannot possibly expect the government to regulate itself. After all, that would be like asking the criminals to turn themselves in after they break the law.

Protecting the Constitution must become the highest priority of every American citizen. It is a precious product of the blood that has been shed throughout the centuries and if we hand it away we will spit on the graves of the soldiers who died to maintain that freedom.

In order to get back our rights, we must first re-assert the right to own and control private property. Barring actions that directly harm others, a person should be able to utilize their own land to its fullest potential. Any regulations should come from the local level and not from the federal level. There is no way some pencil pusher in Washington understands the value or importance of the land I own.

If we do not re-assert our right to own and control private property, we will lay ourselves open to government oppression.

Forfeiture laws have gotten out of control. When a man owns a piece of land, his rights should protect that land as well. One of the great loopholes that make forfeiture so popular to government agencies is that our property is not protected from the government as strictly as we are. In a court of law, when we are accused of a crime by the state, we must be found guilty beyond "a reasonable doubt". This means that the jury, or judge, must be almost totally certain that we are guilty of the offense before they can punish us.

In a civil court, where land is forfeited and the legal battles are fought, the judge or jury can make a decision based on the preponderance of the evidence presented in the case. In other words, they only have to think that a person had improperly used the property in an illegal way. In addition, the burden of proof rests on the individual to prove that they were not doing anything wrong.

Thus, in order to protect our property, everything we own should be afforded the same constitutional protections as ourselves. If the state cannot prove, beyond a reasonable doubt, that we improperly used our land for illegal purposes, then they have to keep their paws off. The burden of proof should be on their part.

The freedom of an individual person is directly related to the freedom that person has to own and control property, whether it is land or some other object. Denying our property the same protections as our bodies opens American citizens up for a whole new wave of governmental intrusion and persecutory power. In order to enforce the 5th amendment we must give these rights back to property owners.

In addition, the government must be held accountable for its regulatory actions that devalue or destroy a person's land. If the government tells me I cannot develop my own land, or grow some sort of crop there, or cut down my trees, my land loses value. The government should then have to pay me the fair market value of that land, or the depreciated value of that land.

If it is determined that an endangered species resides on that land, and the government wishes to protect that particular animal, they should either have to buy the land at fair market value, or pay the owner of the land rent (equal to the farming profit) to use that property as a reserve. The decisions should be with the landowners, not the government. People will be lining up to find endangered species on their land, and we may learn that they are not as endangered as we once thought.

The government should never have the power to seize our land without just cause and reasonable compensation. Any government that continues down this path is an illegal government and those who represent it should be removed from office and the agencies they created dismantled. This must be done to ensure freedom.

Secondly, we need to maintain the integrity and strength of the 2nd amendment. We cannot allow those who are shortsighted and prone to emotional hysterics destroy our right to keep and bear arms. Regulations of guns should be kept to the minimum necessary to maintain a substantial level of accountability in this society. Fears of guns should be subsided with education programs that teach how important guns have been in the fight for freedom.

Few people believe that we may ever have to fight for freedom again. This I totally disagree with. Our government should fear the people, that's right, fear! For when they stop fearing us, those in power will gladly rob us of our freedom and assert their dominance and control over our daily lives.

We cannot be lulled into believing that everyone in government has good intentions. The truth of the matter is that there are many individuals who would like to see the United States destroyed and a fascist state placed in the ashes of a once great society.

The ownership of guns should be a celebrated fact, not a demonized one. Education programs should be established in the community to teach the history, proper handling and importance of firearms. Each community should have a rifle and pistol range where lessons can be given and people can organize and form the bonds that create a "well-regulated citizens militia".

Revenues from hunting licenses should be utilized to start these programs and landowners should be getting a cut of this money for hunting. The government should not be allowed to seize private land for hunting purposes, nor compel any owners of land to open their farms or lands up to hunters who have not given them proper compensation. 70,000,000 gun owners should no longer be punished for the criminal actions of violent scum who plague our society. We all should not lose our right to protect ourselves because two godless children decided to kill their schoolmates. This tragedy should be viewed for what it is, a sad statement on the youth in a society without principles.

We should expect no less from our children when we allow leaders like Clinton to get away with his unprincipled, immoral and illegal actions. Furthermore, we should not blame guns for the loss of God in our society. We project the disappoint in ourselves for allowing our children to become killers to guns and other implements of violence. Fully forgetting that a gun cannot fire itself. Any person who blames the gun for violence is either foolish or deceitful.

Finally, in order to preserve the Constitution, we must get government out of our children's socialization. They have failed miserably in this endeavor. The first step in accomplishing this goal is removing the control of our children's education from the hands of those in the government. God and the principles he has bestowed upon us can be reasserted into their lives if we give the money collected for school operations back to the people.

Parents want their children to be educated, and they will have to utilize the money returned to them for that purpose. Schools that teach the right things will then receive the funding they deserve, whereas schools that continue teaching godless traditions will dwindle away quickly. The teachers in schools that are currently government controlled, will be able to get pay increases when the Department of Education is totally dismantled. That way, these truly talented people will be properly compensated for the vital work they do. In addition, you will never have to hear another story about a devoted teacher who spends their own money to buy children necessary educational equipment because some pencil pusher in Washington is eating up necessary educational funds.

We can maintain the integrity of the 1st amendment and protect religion from government, rather than protect the government from religion. The 1st amendment, as pointed out earlier, was written to keep government from rearing its ugly head in the affairs of the church. It never said once we should sanitize our public sector so that God could never spread his grace throughout the masses. As long as the government never imposes any restrictions on the peoples' ability to freely worship, there can be no end to the power of God in our society.

We must bring this country "Under God" once again. We have tried to stand on our own too long and we have tested God's love for us. We cannot exist without God and it is time we realize that fact. Without God there are no principles and we will continue to see our country destroyed by those who seek to send us down the pathway of the Devil.

Therefore, government should not be involved in the socialization of our children. Programs like head start, WIC, and AFDC should be eradicated and the money made available to the communities to utilize as they see fit. This money can still be set-aside for children, but it can then be utilized the way a community wants, not the way some atheistic bureaucrat in Washington desires.

By stopping the further decay of our 1st, 2nd and 5th amendment rights, we can begin to work on the damage already caused by government violations. Everyday I see those in government expanding the rights of criminals under the guise of the 4th, 8th and 14th amendments. So I ask, why has there been a blind eye turned towards the rights of decent, law-abiding citizens?

I have no problem with enforcing all of the rules of the Constitution, but I shudder to think that a rapist or murderer has more rights than myself.

Only together can we fight this governmental menace to society. Which leads me to the next ingredient in the recipe for freedom.

## V. Solidarity of the People

It is only united that we stand to face these actions that erode our freedom. We must all take part in educating each other about the abuses of government. We must collectively dispel the apathy that has engulfed our collective psyche.

It is vital that we all begin to hold government

accountable for their actions that infringe upon our guaranteed constitutional rights.

I remember years ago when the "throw the bums out" saying was popular. Everyone began to talk about how their representatives were not doing their jobs. Everyone sat around at home and complained about how bad our government was, and that action was necessary to change the face of our representation. When it came time to vote, only 3 incumbents were removed from office out of 435. Most of the complainers stayed at home and those who were calling for action did not put their money where the mouths were.

As it stands now, the Republican Party offers those who wish to destroy big government the best representation. Despite this, the Republicans need some work themselves. Too many of our representatives are caught up in pork barrel spending, and they cannot downsize the federal government. We must remind these representatives that downsizing the federal government does not mean a loss of jobs. It actually will increase the number of jobs available to the American people at the local level. Representatives who stand by me on this point, and downsize the federal government, will undoubtedly be heralded as great statesmen and heroes by future generations.

We must demand, together, that they develop a new Contract with America that will guarantee the end to big government. We must collectively show our support for candidates who stand up for localized government, reduced governmental powers and a return to the principles of God.

Every two years we can throw out those who do not accomplish the goals we have outlined for them. Without our solidarity, change will never be forthcoming and the country will continue to move in its negative direction towards a total loss of freedom.

If we do not begin to collectively protest the seizure of land illegally and the destruction of our right to bear arms, those in power will never capitulate. If we force people to stand alone against the forces of the federal government, we will not be able to expect support when they come booting down our doors. If we remain a divided people, we will surely fall and be easy prey for individuals who wish to rob us of our freedom.

## VI. The Return of Power to Local Control

The bums we truly have to throw out are the unelected representation that roams the halls of bloated federal regulatory agencies. These people have had too much power for too long. We must demand that our representatives take our tax dollars away from these people and turn them over to our local councils, trustees and elected officials. That way, this money could be used to directly help the economy and social stability of the people.

For too long the unelected representatives of the EPA, ATF, HUD, Department of Agriculture, etc... have gone unchecked by the American people. Our elected representatives have failed to see the enormous conflict of interest that exists when you turn over all the decisions and enforcement making positions to those who rely on those positions of power for their ways of life. I firmly believe that local real estate experts in your community can complete all of the functions of HUD for less money and with absolutely no conflict of interest.

The men and women of the unelected representation have actually displayed a disdain for the needs of the people and act as if we are there to serve them, rather than the opposite. They take their little environmental lies and conspiracies and turn them into witch-hunts and crusades. They firmly believe that they act above the law and have no regard for the Constitution or the protections the American people must have.

These people have sold their souls to the government in exchange for good benefits and wages. They have become wasteful spenders who work only to perpetuate their own jobs, thus never accomplishing any true goal. The only things they do are request and receive more of our tax dollars to inflate the prestige of their department and further their careers. This is totally reprehensible and can no longer be tolerated.

We must compel our elected leaders to dismantle these organizations and turn the power, money and control over to local governments. That way, the bureaucracy will not devour over half of the tax revenues before any benefits can reach the community.

Local trustees should be in control of the regions in which they are elected. These trustees should be making over $50,000 a year. The money necessary to pay them good wages can be obtained from dismantling agencies like the EPA, HUD, U.S. Department of Education and the BATF. Local trustees and other elected officials can take action to protect the environment in their regions. This higher pay will appeal to those who have the ability to properly manage our government and they would thus be encouraged to run for these positions. Furthermore, those who currently hold these positions, who have done an excellent job for so long, will finally be properly compensated for their efforts.

This is the only way to truly have a representative government. The federal and state agencies I have identified as acting illegally and wastefully should be shut down. After the money wasted by agencies like the EPA and the BATF are diverted back to the local communities, our local representatives could put that money to good use. These men and women would be easily accessible to the people and then, when someone acted improperly, they could be corrected or removed from office.

Many of our local townships are operated very efficiently with the few resources that they have. I can only imagine how much good would be accomplished if the vast resources of the federal government were given to the local leaders to manage. All of our roadways would be paved, our parks would be clean, our water and air would be pollution free and our towns would sparkle in the sun.

By placing local officials in charge of environmental conservation efforts, needless regulations for certain regions would be abolished so that valuable resources are not spent on enforcing rules that have no bearing on the functions of the lives of people living in these areas.

Law enforcement funds normally utilized by the BATF to erode our rights to keep and bear arms can be diverted to local sheriff's departments after the BATF is dismantled. This way, locally elected law enforcement officials can use that money to actually combat crime and violence. Instead of creating problems, as the BATF seems to do, that money can be used to stop crime.

The U.S. Department of Education can also be dismantled. If a voucher system is utilized, it will no longer be necessary to have this overarching federal bureaucracy wasting tax dollars. Each citizen of this country will be able to choose the school their child attends. Then, the communities, who I am sure care more about their children's education than some bureaucrat, will make sure the schools are run properly.

The extra money from the dismantling of the Department of Education should be given to local school boards and teachers. Teachers are the ones who are really doing the work, and too many times they do not have adequate pay or supplies. All of that money wasted at the federal level could be used to actually educate. This concept may seem foreign to those in government, but that is because they have become blinded by the cycle of governmental dependence. There are too many people in the federal government today that believe that the American people cannot take care of themselves. In the end, they are simply too scared to turn that money back over to the people because we would only prove that their jobs are totally unnecessary.

Although the process may take some time, it will be worth the effort to bring about this shift from federal to local governmental control. The abuses have become too costly and this change is the only way to ensure that once big government is under control, it will never emerge again.

We do not need any department of government, not controlled at the local level, to take actions that effect our daily lives. Furthermore, no government agency, elected official or employee should deprive a citizen of his or her constitutional rights. Finally, our federal government should never be allowed to change its functioning system (i.e. change from capitalism to socialism) without the consent of the people. For too long, elected officials and unelected representatives that are out of touch with the people have forged the foundations of a socialist society. This would never have happened if our local elected officials were in charge of the majority of our governmental resources.

The federal government is necessary to preserve the

Union, regulate trade, and maintain an army for the protection of the people. The federal government was never intended to be the number one employer of the American people. Nor did our forefathers expect unelected individuals to have tremendous power over our personal rights. This has become an affront to freedom and the only way to end it is to destroy big government and return it to local control.

In addition, too many of the stories I put in this book mentioned the U.S. Army. I was appalled to find out that the U.S. Military was being utilized to enforce federal regulations. This should end immediately. Local law enforcement and elected officials are more than adequate. The army is there to defend the people and uphold the freedom of the Constitution. It is totally illegal and immoral to have the U.S. Army enforcing illegal federal regulations. The practice should end immediately. I don't remember ever giving my elected officials the right to impose martial law.

A very limited number of federal representatives can still oversee the spending of tax dollars, to make sure they do not violate the constitution or the laws derived thereof, but the daily decisions should be left to local elected officials. As long as they are serving the needs of their people, the government should keep its ugly head out of the matters of various communities.

Local communities have proven their ability to protect the environment, control crime and ensure the security of their members throughout time. Take for example the problems with pesticides. Do not believe for one minute that the EPA had anything to do with the eradication of dangerous pesticides.

Sure, the EPA always wants to stick its nose into the farmers business, but any good farmer knows that if you taint your crops with dangerous chemicals and poison the landscape, no one will buy your product and you will lose the means to support yourself.

Today, we have generated "Round-Up" resistant strains of crops that allow us to freely use a herbicide that effectively controls weeds and is not traceable after 10 days. The EPA had nothing to do with this. Free enterprise created all of this because farmers knew what was best. Furthermore, without the help of the EPA, farm containers that hold dangerous chemicals are being picked up, stored and disposed of in a safe and environmentally friendly manner. The fact is, the EPA has done nothing but hinder this progress with their constant bureaucratic bull.

Farmers want to maintain the integrity of the land and increase future crop yields. No farmer will destroy his own land for just a year or two of crops. Thus, the EPA is only hindering this process with their overzealous regulation. Given to itself, the free market, along with the enterprise it creates, will solve many of the problems that plague our society.

Our individual communities are best suited to determine what is necessary. All the local government would have to do is say, "pesticides or herbicides are hurting the environment and may reduce future crop yields." If this is true, farmers will rally to change the current practices and ensure safe and plentiful crop yields well into the future.

Take for example another case where federal meddling in local affairs had deleterious effects. Throughout the 80's the EPA ordered many gas station throughout the Midwest closed, despite the fact that these gas stations had been around since the dawn of motor vehicles. These sites were then declared hazardous areas and the old tanks were pulled up out of the ground. These tanks had leaked some gasoline into the soil, so that soil was dug up and hauled away to another area.

These "other areas" became dumping grounds for millions of yards of contaminated dirt. Thus, they endangered that area because of a high concentration of contaminated dirt. The EPA made a small problem in little communities a gigantic problem for a few others. Each one of those communities could have conducted their own clean-up project. This would have ensured that all communities would be free of hazardous materials.

The worse part is that after screwing everything up, the EPA charged the owners of the gas stations the exorbitant amount of money it took to ship the dirt across the state, or even the nation. Bare in mind that these small businessmen had to pay the bill instead of the EPA that is given billions a year and actually made the rule that forced this change. If this had been handled locally, the cost would have been nominal. Instead, a person who had never done anything wrong was forced to fit the bill of federal incompetence.

For a final example, let's examine the wetlands issue. This whole issue has become a farce and has been utilized by the EPA to further their own agenda. It remains a terrible conflict of interest. The real problem is not with wetlands, but it is with the lack of water in some places and an abundance in others.

The fact that we rely on the federal government has blinded our leaders to obvious solutions to this problem.

Whereas some regions have an abundance of water, some to the point where terrible floods destroy billions of dollars of property a year, other areas have little fresh water. Working together at the community level and building a canal system like the ones built in Ohio in the 1800's could solve this problem.

These canals could help funnel water into more arid regions and other areas where freshwater is hard to come by. Wetlands would not be as vital then, because there would be plenty of watersheds from those other regions to properly irrigate and moisten the land. Furthermore, a source of fresh drinking water would no longer be a problem as well.

Over the years, local communities have made efforts to do this and the problem with the fresh water supply has almost been eradicated. Realizing this, the EPA had to create the "problem" of the wetlands so that they would be able to continue operating.

The EPA does not want us solving problems on our own. They want the American people to believe that the only way for us to protect our land, is to hand it over to their control. I don't buy this con, and you should not either. If we return control to our local communities, you can be rest assured that all of the problems will be handled much better then the federal government ever could have dreamed. Furthermore, they will be handled at a fraction of the cost.

Since the EPA believes that it is so just to march in and seize our land with no recourse, they must have no regard for individual rights. Therefore, unless their hypocrites, they should have no problem when we dismantle their offices and buildings and throw them out of their jobs. The EPA seems to think it is reasonable to subject American citizens to excessive fines and other forms of cruel and unusual punishment. Thus, they will not take it so hard when they no longer have jobs and are held accountable for their criminal actions.

We must compel our government to trust the people. Write your congressman and tell them to return the control of your land, your guns, your children, your religion and your money to the local governments. Enforcement and supervision is always important, but it should not come at the price of freedom. Only by administering government at the local level can we insure that politicians and government bureaucrats will never act unconstitutionally. There is no doubt that government agencies, like the EPA, have become totally unnecessary and a full audit of the federal government should be completed in order to determine which parts of each department require downsizing or complete dismantling. This is how we will reassert freedom and protect it for generations to come.

## VII.   Elect Statesmen and Leaders

Instead of electing popular icons and politically correct know-nothings we must begin to elect men and women who resemble our founding fathers. Men like Bill Clinton have been allowed to slither into the White House because we have lowered our standards. Furthermore, the current process by which we elect public officials is flawed.

Bill Clinton would never have won a second term if a third party had not pulled votes away from the Republicans. Worse yet, if Pat Buchanan runs on a third ticket in the 2000 election, vital votes will be pulled away from whomever opposes Al Gore. A third party is a good thing, but not when it allows socialists to seize power. In order to stop the advancement of the socialist agenda, we must prevent Al Gore from getting in the White House. The practice of allowing a third party to disrupt an election must cease.

Mind you, I do not support the elimination of all additional parties. In fact, I believe they are vital to healthy political discourse. However, individuals are afraid to support a third party because they feel as if their vote will not count. In addition, most of the time, precious votes are taken away from candidates who support God, freedom and democracy because individuals choose to vote for third party. Thus, in order to avoid this problem, I believe that we should institute an alternative ballot in all major elections involving multiple candidates from different parties.

An alternate ballot would allow individuals to choose two candidates, their primary choice and a secondary one. After the primary votes are tabulated, any individual who chose a candidate that did not finish in the top 2 would be allowed to transfer over to their secondary vote. This way, no vote would be wasted. Individuals could still show their support for the platforms and ideals of a third party without drawing support away from a major candidate.

This would not only encourage third party participation, but it will also ensure that someone like Al Gore will not be able to slip into the White House because freedom loving American's votes were split among two candidates. Creating this sort of system would ensure that we truly have a representative democracy.

In addition to the alternative ballot, there should be a change in the eligibility requirements to run for public office. The most important of these changes would be preventing draft dodgers form running for public office. Currently, if a person is dishonorably discharged from the military, they cannot own a gun and they have a permanent black mark on their record. I doubt any person dishonorably discharged from the armed forces could ascend to the presidency.

However, we currently have a president that is worse than a dishonorably discharged soldier. At least someone who was dishonorably discharged tried and failed. Bill Clinton, and other draft-dodgers, just shirked their responsibility. They refused to do their patriotic duty because they lacked the courage and conviction to fight for freedom. In order to ensure that we have leaders in the White House, we must make sure that another draft-dodger doesn't slip through the front doors.

Throughout this book I have cited example after example of corrupted politicians. Too many of our federally elected politicians have become corrupt and immoral. They seek to destroy the Constitution rather than uphold it. As a result, corruption has spread like a disease throughout the entire federal system. Tremendous conflict of interest has resulted in corrupted bureaucrats serving their own selfish needs while forgetting their responsibilities to the American people.

If we elect statesmen and leaders instead of draft-dodgers and eco-fanatics, we will have a better nation for our children in the future. We must force our leaders to live principled lives and work for the people, not against them. Only then will we be able to reduce big government, give the money back to the people and stop the deterioration of our civil liberties.

# <u>Conclusion:</u>

## The Constitution- A
## Foundation of Freedom

"No man in the wrong can stand up against a fellow that's in the right and keep on a-comin'"

Texas Ranger Bill
McDonald

". . . You cannot strengthen the weak by weakening the strong . . . you cannot help the wage earner by pulling down the wage payer . . . you cannot further the brotherhood of men by encouraging class hatred . . . you cannot help the poor by discouraging the rich . . . you cannot build character and courage by taking away a man's initiative and independence."

Abraham Lincoln

# The Constitution: The Compass of Freedom and a Guide to Good Government

Throughout this book I have tried to tell you a fraction of the truth that is really out there. I know there has been a lot of anti-government talk in the recent years, but most of that remains around the kitchen table. Few of us are actually taking action to stop the negative trends we all see occurring in government today.

If we are not careful, government agencies, comprised of the unelected representation of our society, will cease to be under our control. This has already happened to a certain extent. There are less than 700 elected individuals in Washington D.C. whom we send there to oversee over two million employees. Furthermore, we have appointed less than 60 Inspector Generals to oversee the various agencies and insure their compliance with federal law and constitutional integrity. The integrity of these Inspectors is even questioned when one considers the enormous conflict of interest they face each day.

These agencies of the over-extended federal government have been allowed to exist despite the enormous conflict of interest they have with the Constitution. The people are losing control over these agencies and no one is taking any action to prevent a further decay of democracy.

Men like Bill Clinton and Al Gore are actively attempting to socialize our society and convince the people that more government is good government. Men like this have a very myopic view of this country and they will eventually destroy the foundations of freedom so many people have died in the past to maintain.

Agencies, especially ones like the EPA and BATF, are absolutely unnecessary. These agencies have realized this fact and have attempted over the years to inflate the prestige of their agency and remain in existence. Instead of serving the people, these agencies have a goal of self-preservation. They commit atrocities that are in direct violation of the Constitution and threaten the liberty of every American.

Our representatives and elected officials have trusted the leaders of these government agencies to respect the laws of the land. Instead of honoring that trust, those in control of these organizations have utilized this trust to expand their governmental empires and infringe upon the rights of millions of Americans.

America is no longer a representative Democracy, and we are slowly starting to realize the folly of our ways. It has become necessary to remedy the mistake of allowing the federal government to get too big. Regrettably, if action is not taken quickly enough, our government will take on a mind of its own and quickly overpower the will of an individual citizen.

There are some truly frightening trends occurring in the United States as you read this book.

- The EPA, supported by the White house and the Green movement, are spreading propagandous lies about the stability of our ecosystem. They are preying upon the ignorance and fear of the American people to execute a campaign with only one goal: The destruction of private property ownership. The EPA is the leader of this campaign and they will not rest until every acre of land is turned over to government control. They have received unprecedented support from the Clinton Administration, who has just this year in 1999, announced plans to "buy out America". The plan, called Agenda 21 is designed to obtain millions of acres of privately owned land by offering the people about one-quarter the true value of the property. Utilizing vaguely drafted environmental policies, the Clinton Administration, at the urging of Al Gore, has initiated a campaign to control as much land as possible. The final result of this action would be the destruction of the 5th amendment and the end to private ownership of land in the United States.

- The BATF has, under the direction of the Clinton Administration, declared war on the Constitution, most specifically the 2nd amendment. In the course of waging their war, they have treaded upon the 4th and 5th amendment rights of those they target for their harassment. Supported by ignorant Americans who allow emotionally charged events to influence them, the Clinton Administration has given us a gigantic nudge down the slippery slope towards total gun control. If unchecked, gun control advocates will slowly open the door for the BATF to harass and intimidate even more law-abiding Americans. Soon, if we do not unite against this injustice, the American people will willingly give up their guns in order to avoid the harassment and persecution of the federal government.

- Too many of our children are being socialized by a secular government that has become wrought with corruption and a loss of morality. By controlling all of the public schools, and enforcing compulsory education, our government subjects our children to more propaganda in the schools. Parents, who wish to exercise their right to have their children taught a certain way, are forced to spend extra money to send their child to a private school. Meanwhile, they still have to pay taxes to support other children going to school, as well as the U.S. Department of Education that does nothing to help any individual child. Those parents who lack the financial ability to pull their children out of atheistic schools are forced to have their children brainwashed and exposed to elements in the schools that seek to destroy good moral foundations.

- Our leaders are no longer being held accountable for their wrongdoings. Immoral behavior has become widely accepted because God has been forced out of the public sector. The 1st amendment to the Constitution was actually designed to protect religion from the government, not vice-versa. Regrettably, government has expanded to such an extent, that every single aspect of our lives falls under government regulation. Therefore, because nearly everything receives governmental support, religion is not allowed to work its magic in the general population. We have turned away from a nation under God, which has caused us to lose the most important guide to a successful life: Faith. Immoral behavior is the result of this loss. Nowadays, the streets, media, and entertainment industry are filled with immoral behavior. Those who wish to usurp the principles of Christian behavior are given a free ticket to say and do whatever they want. Meanwhile, anyone who calls for moral accountability in the community is labeled a "fanatic" and their opinions are disregarded. These phenomena have given evil center stage in our society, and have forced good, law-abiding, moral people into the backstage.

- A loss of principles has led to a loss of community and personal responsibility. Millions of people make their living off the backs of hard working Americans. They sit around, reproduce, use drugs and commit crimes while others are forced to support their immoral habits. The federal government writes people like this a blank check and encourages this behavior. Furthermore, we have lost our sense of community. Nowadays, we sue each other, utilizing the conflictual way of life our secular lifestyle has created. Those in government like it this way because as long as we are fighting each other, we have little time to control those who seek to better secure their stranglehold on our lives.

These are all facts. Sure, there are those out there who choose to deny the truth, but that does not change reality. Our government was not formed so that it could rule every waking moment of our lives. In fact, the exact opposite is true.

It was very difficult in the early years of our society to form a strong union because there was concern about placing trust in any form of a centralized government. Therefore, our founding fathers demanded a small-centralized federal government. Most statesmen were devoted to the notion of strong local and state governments and a weak federal government concerned only with national defense and inter-state trade.

At one time, a Civil War was fought in this country, where the Southern States challenged the dominance of the federal government. Some will still say the war was a fight over slavery, but that is blatantly false. The war was fought because the federal government was attempting to assert its dominance over all the other states. Although it is good that the Union was preserved, it is very disappointing that this victory led to the unfettered support of a big government.

Slowly, but surely, throughout history, Americans have become more and more dependent on a big federal government. Whenever there is a crisis, or even a perceived crisis, instead of relying on our local communities, we run to the federal government for help. Every citizen of the United States has his or her hand in the federal "cookie jar" and it has become very hard for us to remove ourselves from the codependency big government has created.

The fact is, we must do this. We must return our country to the principled society it once was. We must reassert our control over the federal government. We must demand the accountability of anyone whom we pay to employ. We must regain control of our society.

Each day that passes, we lose another opportunity to stop the dangerous trends I have described throughout this book. I caution all of you to realize one important fact: There will come a time when we cannot stop government.

That is right, if we continue to let days, months, years and decades pass on with no action to stop men like Bill Clinton and Al Gore, we will see our precious Republic destroyed.

The myopic planning of men like these is setting us up for disaster. If we disarm the people, dismantle the protections of the Constitution, and turn our backs on God and morality, our society will cease to exist.

I call out to all of you, make your stand in the present. Demand the accountability of those you employ (everyone in the government). Educate yourselves and oppose governmental oppression every chance possible. There are others out there who will join you.

Organizations like the NRA and the People for Property Rights are searching for help. Tell your representatives what you demand through letters, phone calls and personal visits. Go to the voting booths and make our voices heard.

We must re-establish government, but not the way Al Gore wants us to. The Constitution, the supreme law of the land, should be in your thoughts whenever you go to the poles. Furthermore, if you do not go to the polls and cast your vote, then you should ponder the Constitution further and realize the folly of your ways.

You should not have undying faithfulness to any party or candidate, be they Republican, Democrat, Reform or Libertarian. Political parties often change their platforms because they can be infiltrated and affected by unjust and unconstitutional characters with political ambitions and no regard for the good of the people. Candidates should only receive your support when they endorse the Constitution and assist in the dismantling of the EPA, BATF, U.S. Forest Service, HUD, Department of Education or any other federal bureaucracy that could be replaced by local governments. If the candidates do not support the Bill of Rights and the Ten

Commandments, then they do not deserve our support.

We must stop the trend towards socialism and eradicate those who seek to utilize a terrible conflict of interest to advance their own personal agendas.

Only then will we be "one nation under God, indivisible, with liberty and justice for all".

We are the people. Now let's make a government that is truly

## FOR THE PEOPLE!

# Appendix A

On the following pages you will find the names, addresses and phone numbers of every Representative and Senator in the U.S. Congress. As election season comes ever closer, it is vital that these men and women hear what the American people have to say.

I suggest that you use this list to write to them whenever possible. Tell them about what you have learned in this book and demand that they put an end to the illegal practices by government regulatory agencies. Be sure to offer your support to representatives that protect your rights.

I urge all of you to keep a close eye on the news and when you see a major bill being introduced into Congress, speak up and let your voice be heard. The information you need to control your representatives is easily accessible out there via the Internet if you would just take the opportunity to get it. If you are not connected to the Internet, look through your papers, magazines or contact organizations like the National Rifle Association for important information.

This call goes out to all Americans. Just as our Founding Fathers grabbed their muskets when the bells of revolution were rung, we must grab our pens and make our voices heard. I regret that if we wait too long, we may have to grab our muskets again, as long as we still have them.

### Understanding The Table

There are three tables in the next pages for you to use. The first one is an alphabetical listing of every Representative in the United States House of Representatives. For each Representative, his or her state, district and party are given. In addition, their phone number is provided. The area code for all of these numbers is 202, give them a call whenever you see anything going on that grabs your attention. Believe me, they will take notice.

Next, there is the room number for each of their offices

and the building that office is in. In order to write your representative use the following address:

> Honorable John T. Smith, Ohio
> U.S. House of Representatives
> 1001 Longworth HOB
> *(or whatever room and building they are in)*
> Washington, D.C. 20510

Your mail will reach your representative.

For easy reference, I also included a listing of all Representatives sorted by the state they represent. This way, you can quickly look up each of the congressman in your state.

The last section is an entire list of the U.S. Senate in alphabetical order. Included with each Senator is their address, party, phone number and email address. A Senator represents the entire state, so no matter where you live in the state, your Senator should still answer to you as a voter. You can use the same procedures listed above to contact them as well.

Do not waste away the gift of freedom our forefathers gave us. Demand that your representatives return America to the people and re-establish the strength of the United States Constitution. If you do not speak up, who will?

Please note, even if the representatives listed below were removed during their current terms, their successor will be in the same office.

## Table A-1    <u>U.S. House of Representatives Directory</u> (Sorted Alphabetically)

| Name | State | Dist. | Party | Phone | Room | Building |
|------|-------|-------|-------|-------|------|----------|
| Abercrombie, Neil | HI | 1 | Democrat | 225-2726 | 1502 | Longworth |
| Ackerman, Gary L. | NY | 5 | Democrat | 225-2601 | 2243 | Rayburn |
| Aderholt, Robert B. | AL | 4 | Republican | 225-4876 | 1007 | Longworth |
| Allen, Thomas H. | ME | 1 | Democrat | 225-6116 | 1717 | Longworth |
| Andrews, Robert E. | NJ | 1 | Democrat | 225-6501 | 2439 | Rayburn |
| Archer, Bill | TX | 7 | Republican | 225-2571 | 1236 | Longworth |
| Armey, Richard K. | TX | 26 | Republican | 225-7772 | 301 | Cannon |
| Bachus, Spencer | AL | 6 | Republican | 225-4921 | 442 | Cannon |
| Baird, Brian | WA | 3 | Democrat | 225-3536 | 1721 | Longworth |
| Baker, Richard H. | LA | 6 | Republican | 225-3901 | 434 | Cannon |
| Baldacci, John Elias | ME | 2 | Democrat | 225-6306 | 1740 | Longworth |
| Baldwin, Tammy | WI | 2 | Democrat | 225-2906 | 1020 | Longworth |
| Ballenger, Cass | NC | 10 | Republican | 225-2576 | 2182 | Rayburn |
| Barcia, James A. | MI | 5 | Democrat | 225-8171 | 2419 | Rayburn |
| Barr, Bob | GA | 7 | Republican | 225-2931 | 1207 | Longworth |
| Barrett, Bill | NE | 3 | Republican | 225-6435 | 2458 | Rayburn |
| Barrett, Thomas M. | WI | 5 | Democrat | 225-3571 | 1214 | Longworth |
| Bartlett, Roscoe G. | MD | 6 | Republican | 225-2721 | 2412 | Rayburn |
| Barton, Joe | TX | 6 | Republican | 225-2002 | 2264 | Rayburn |
| Bass, Charles F. | NH | 2 | Republican | 225-5206 | 218 | Cannon |
| Bateman, Herbert H. | VA | 1 | Republican | 225-4261 | 2211 | Rayburn |
| Becerra, Xavier | CA | 30 | Democrat | 225-6235 | 1119 | Longworth |
| Bentsen, Ken | TX | 25 | Democrat | 225-7508 | 326 | Cannon |
| Bereuter, Doug | NE | 1 | Republican | 225-4806 | 2184 | Rayburn |
| Berkley, Shelley | NV | 1 | Democrat | 2255965 | 1505 | Longworth |
| Berman, Howard L. | CA | 26 | Democrat | 225-4695 | 2330 | Rayburn |
| Berry, Marion | AR | 1 | Democrat | 225-4076 | 1113 | Longworth |
| Biggert, Judy | IL | 13 | Republican | 225-3515 | 508 | Cannon |
| Bilbray, Brian P. | CA | 49 | Republican | 225-2040 | 1530 | Longworth |
| Bilirakis, Michael | FL | 9 | Republican | 225-5755 | 2369 | Rayburn |
| Bishop, Sanford D. | GA | 2 | Democrat | 225-3631 | 1433 | Longworth |
| Blagojevich, Rod R. | IL | 5 | Democrat | 225-4061 | 331 | Cannon |
| Bliley, Tom | VA | 7 | Republican | 225-2815 | 2409 | Rayburn |
| Blumenauer, Earl | OR | 3 | Democrat | 225-4811 | 1406 | Longworth |
| Blunt, Roy | MO | 7 | Republican | 225-6536 | 217 | Cannon |
| Boehlert, Sherwood | NY | 23 | Republican | 225-3665 | 2246 | Rayburn |

| | | | | | | |
|---|---|---|---|---|---|---|
| Boehner, John A. | OH | 8 | Republican | 225-6205 | 1011 | Longworth |
| Bonilla, Henry | TX | 23 | Republican | 225-4511 | 1427 | Longworth |
| Bonior, David E. | MI | 10 | Democrat | 225-2106 | 2207 | Rayburn |
| Bono, Mary | CA | 44 | Republican | 225-5330 | 516 | Cannon |
| Borski, Robert A. | PA | 3 | Democrat | 225-8251 | 2267 | Rayburn |
| Boswell, Leonard L. | IA | 3 | Democrat | 225-3806 | 1029 | Longworth |
| Boucher, Rick | VA | 9 | Democrat | 225-3861 | 2329 | Rayburn |
| Boyd, Allen | FL | 2 | Democrat | 225-5235 | 107 | Cannon |
| Brady, Kevin | TX | 8 | Republican | 225-4901 | 1531 | Longworth |
| Brady, Robert A. | PA | 1 | Democrat | 225-4731 | 216 | Cannon |
| Brown, Corrine | FL | 3 | Democrat | 225-0123 | 2444 | Rayburn |
| Brown, Sherrod | OH | 13 | Democrat | 225-3401 | 210 | Cannon |
| Bryant, Ed | TN | 7 | Republican | 225-2811 | 408 | Cannon |
| Burr, Richard | NC | 5 | Republican | 225-2071 | 1513 | Longworth |
| Burton, Dan | IN | 6 | Republican | 225-2276 | 2185 | Rayburn |
| Buyer, Steve | IN | 5 | Republican | 225-5037 | 227 | Cannon |
| Callahan, Sonny | AL | 1 | Republican | 225-4931 | 2466 | Rayburn |
| Calvert, Ken | CA | 43 | Republican | 225-1986 | 2201 | Rayburn |
| Camp, Dave | MI | 4 | Republican | 225-3561 | 137 | Cannon |
| Campbell, Tom | CA | 15 | Republican | 225-2631 | 2442 | Rayburn |
| Canady, Charles T. | FL | 12 | Republican | 225-1252 | 2432 | Rayburn |
| Cannon, Chris | UT | 3 | Republican | 225-7751 | 118 | Cannon |
| Capps, Lois | CA | 22 | Democrat | 225-3601 | 1118 | Longworth |
| Capuano, Michale E | MA | 8 | Democrat | 225-5111 | 1232 | Longworth |
| Cardin, Benjamin L. | MD | 3 | Democrat | 225-4016 | 104 | Cannon |
| Carson, Julia | IN | 10 | Democrat | 225-4011 | 1541 | Longworth |
| Castle, Michael N. | DE | A-L | Republican | 225-4165 | 1227 | Longworth |
| Chabot, Steve | OH | 1 | Republican | 225-2216 | 129 | Cannon |
| Chambliss, Saxby | GA | 8 | Republican | 225-6531 | 1019 | Longworth |
| Chenoweth, Helen | ID | 1 | Republican | 225-6611 | 1727 | Longworth |
| Clay, William | MO | 1 | Democrat | 225-2406 | 2306 | Rayburn |
| Clayton, Eva M. | NC | 1 | Democrat | 225-3101 | 2440 | Rayburn |
| Clement, Bob | TN | 5 | Democrat | 225-4311 | 2229 | Rayburn |
| Clyburn, James E. | SC | 6 | Democrat | 225-3315 | 319 | Cannon |
| Coble, Howard | NC | 6 | Republican | 225-3065 | 2468 | Rayburn |
| Coburn, Tom A. | OK | 2 | Republican | 225-2701 | 429 | Cannon |
| Collins, Mac | GA | 3 | Republican | 225-5901 | 1131 | Longworth |
| Combest, Larry | TX | 19 | Republican | 225-4005 | 1026 | Longworth |
| Condit, Gary A. | CA | 18 | Democrat | 225-6131 | 2234 | Rayburn |
| Conyers, John | MI | 14 | Democrat | 225-5126 | 2426 | Rayburn |
| Cook, Merrill | UT | 2 | Republican | 225-3011 | 1431 | Longworth |

| Cooksey, John | LA | 5 | Republican | 225-8490 | 317 | Cannon |
|---|---|---|---|---|---|---|
| Costello, Jerry F. | IL | 12 | Democrat | 225-5661 | 2454 | Rayburn |
| Cox, Christopher | CA | 47 | Republican | 225-5611 | 2402 | Rayburn |
| Coyne, Williams J. | PA | 14 | Democrat | 225-2301 | 2455 | Rayburn |
| Cramer, Robert E. | AL | 5 | Democrat | 225-4801 | 2350 | Rayburn |
| Crane, Phillip M. | IL | 8 | Republican | 225-3711 | 233 | Cannon |
| Crowley, Joseph | NY | 7 | Democrat | 225-3965 | 1517 | Longworth |
| Cubin, Barbara | WY | A-L | Republican | 225-2311 | 1114 | Longworth |
| Cummings, Elijah | MD | 7 | Democrat | 225-4741 | 1632 | Longworth |
| Cunningham, Randy | CA | 51 | Republican | 225-5452 | 2238 | Rayburn |
| Danner, Pat | MO | 6 | Democrat | 225-7041 | 2262 | Rayburn |
| Davis, Danny K. | IL | 7 | Democrat | 225-5006 | 1222 | Longworth |
| Davis, Jim | FL | 11 | Democrat | 225-3376 | 418 | Cannon |
| Davis, Thomas M. | VA | 11 | Republican | 225-1492 | 224 | Cannon |
| Deal, Nathan | GA | 9 | Republican | 225-5211 | 2437 | Rayburn |
| DeFazio, Peter A. | OR | 4 | Democrat | 225-6416 | 2134 | Rayburn |
| DeGette, Diana | CO | 1 | Democrat | 225-4431 | 1339 | Longworth |
| Delahunt, William | MA | 10 | Democrat | 225-3111 | 1317 | Longworth |
| DeLauro, Rosa L. | CT | 3 | Democrat | 225-3661 | 436 | Cannon |
| DeLay, Tom | TX | 22 | Republican | 225-5951 | 341 | Cannon |
| DeMint, Jim | SC | 4 | Republican | 225-6030 | 507 | Cannon |
| Deutsch, Peter | FL | 20 | Democrat | 225-7931 | 204 | Cannon |
| Diaz-Balart, Lincoln | FL | 21 | Republican | 225-4211 | 404 | Cannon |
| Dickey, Jay | AR | 4 | Republican | 225-3771 | 2453 | Rayburn |
| Dicks, Norman D. | WA | 6 | Democrat | 225-5916 | 2467 | Rayburn |
| Dingell, John D. | MI | 16 | Democrat | 225-4071 | 2328 | Rayburn |
| Dixon, Julian C. | CA | 32 | Democrat | 225-7084 | 2252 | Rayburn |
| Doggett, Lloyd | TX | 10 | Democrat | 225-4865 | 328 | Cannon |
| Dooley, Calvin M. | CA | 20 | Democrat | 225-3341 | 1201 | Longworth |
| Doolittle, John T. | CA | 4 | Republican | 225-2511 | 1526 | Longworth |
| Doyle, Michael F. | PA | 18 | Democrat | 225-2135 | 133 | Cannon |
| Dreier, David | CA | 28 | Republican | 225-2305 | 237 | Cannon |
| Duncan, John J. | TN | 2 | Republican | 225-5435 | 2400 | Rayburn |
| Dunn, Jennifer | WA | 8 | Republican | 225-7761 | 432 | Cannon |
| Edwards, Chet | TX | 11 | Democrat | 225-6105 | 2459 | Rayburn |
| Ehlers, Vernon J. | MI | 3 | Republican | 225-3831 | 1714 | Longworth |
| Ehrlich, Robert L. | MD | 2 | Republican | 225-3061 | 315 | Cannon |
| Emerson, Jo Ann | MO | 8 | Republican | 225-4404 | 132 | Cannon |
| Engel, Eliot | NY | 17 | Democrat | 225-2464 | 2303 | Rayburn |
| English, Phil | PA | 21 | Republican | 225-5406 | 1410 | Longworth |
| Eshoo, Anna | CA | 14 | Democrat | 225-8104 | 205 | Cannon |

| Etheridge, Bob | NC | 2 | Democrat | 225-2901 | 2312 | Rayburn |
|---|---|---|---|---|---|---|
| Evans, Lane | IL | 17 | Democrat | 225-5905 | 2335 | Rayburn |
| Everett, Terry | AL | 2 | Republican | 225-2901 | 2312 | Rayburn |
| Ewing, Thomas | IL | 15 | Republican | 225-2371 | 2417 | Rayburn |
| Farr, Sam | CA | 17 | Democrat | 225-2861 | 1221 | Longworth |
| Fattah, Chaka | PA | 2 | Democrat | 225-4001 | 1205 | Longworth |
| Filner, Bob | CA | 50 | Democrat | 225-8045 | 2463 | Rayburn |
| Fletcher, Ernie | KY | 6 | Republican | 225-4706 | 1117 | Longworth |
| Foley, Mark | FL | 16 | Republican | 225-5792 | 113 | Cannon |
| Forbes, Michael | NY | 1 | Democrat | 225-3826 | 125 | Cannon |
| Ford, Harold E. | TN | 9 | Democrat | 225-3265 | 325 | Cannon |
| Fossella, Vito | NY | 13 | Republican | 225-3371 | 431 | Cannon |
| Fowler, Tillie K. | FL | 4 | Republican | 225-2501 | 106 | Cannon |
| Frank, Barney | MA | 4 | Democrat | 225-5931 | 2210 | Rayburn |
| Franks, Bob | NJ | 7 | Republican | 225-5361 | 225 | Cannon |
| Frelinghuysen, R. | NJ | 11 | Republican | 225-5034 | 228 | Cannon |
| Frost, Martin | TX | 24 | Democrat | 225-3605 | 2256 | Rayburn |
| Gallegly, Elton | CA | 23 | Republican | 225-5811 | 2427 | Rayburn |
| Ganske, Greg | IA | 4 | Republican | 225-4426 | 1108 | Longworth |
| Gejdenson, Sam | CT | 2 | Democrat | 225-2076 | 2304 | Rayburn |
| Gekas, George W. | PA | 17 | Republican | 225-4315 | 2410 | Rayburn |
| Gephardt, Richard | MO | 3 | Democrat | 225-2671 | 1226 | Longworth |
| Gibbons, Jim | NV | 2 | Republican | 225-6155 | 100 | Cannon |
| Gilchrest, Wayne T. | MD | 1 | Republican | 225-5311 | 2245 | Rayburn |
| Gilmor, Paul E. | OH | 5 | Republican | 225-6405 | 1203 | Longworth |
| Gilman, Benjamin | NY | 20 | Republican | 225-3776 | 2449 | Rayburn |
| Gonzalez, Charles | TX | 20 | Democrat | 225-3236 | 327 | Cannon |
| Goode, Virgil | VA | 5 | Democrat | 225-4711 | 1520 | Longworth |
| Goodlatte, Bob | VA | 6 | Republican | 225-5431 | 2240 | Rayburn |
| Goodling, William F. | PA | 19 | Republican | 225-5836 | 2107 | Rayburn |
| Gordon, Bart | TN | 6 | Democrat | 225-4231 | 2368 | Rayburn |
| Goss, Porter | FL | 14 | Republican | 225-2536 | 108 | Cannon |
| Graham, Lindsey | SC | 3 | Republican | 225-5301 | 1429 | Longworth |
| Granger, Kay | TX | 12 | Republican | 225-5071 | 435 | Cannon |
| Green, Gene | TX | 29 | Democrat | 225-1688 | 2429 | Rayburn |
| Green, Mark | WI | 8 | Republican | 225-5665 | 1218 | Longworth |
| Greenwood, James | PA | 8 | Republican | 225-4276 | 2436 | Rayburn |
| Guitterez, Luis | IL | 4 | Democrat | 225-8203 | 2438 | Rayburn |
| Gutknecht, Gil | MN | 1 | Republican | 225-2472 | 426 | Cannon |
| Hall, Ralph | TX | 4 | Democrat | 225-6673 | 2221 | Rayburn |
| Hall, Tony | OH | 3 | Democrat | 225-6465 | 1432 | Longworth |

| Hansen, James | UT | 1 | Republican | 225-0453 | 242 | Cannon |
|---|---|---|---|---|---|---|
| Hastert, Dennis | IL | 14 | Republican | 225-2976 | 2263 | Rayburn |
| Hastings, Alcee | FL | 23 | Democrat | 225-1313 | 2235 | Rayburn |
| Hastings, Doc | WA | 4 | Republican | 225-5816 | 1323 | Longworth |
| Hayes, Robin | NC | 8 | Republican | 225-3715 | 130 | Cannon |
| Hayworth, J.D. | AZ | 6 | Republican | 225-2190 | 1023 | Longworth |
| Hefley, Joel | CO | 5 | Republican | 225-4422 | 2230 | Rayburn |
| Herger, Wally | CA | 2 | Republican | 225-3076 | 2433 | Rayburn |
| Hill, Baron | IN | 9 | Democrat | 225-5315 | 1208 | Longworth |
| Hill, Rick | MT | A-L | Republican | 225-3211 | 1609 | Longworth |
| Hilleary, Van | TN | 4 | Republican | 225-6831 | 114 | Cannon |
| Hilliard, Earl | Al | 7 | Democrat | 225-2665 | 1314 | Longworth |
| Hinchey, Maurice | NY | 26 | Democrat | 225-6335 | 2431 | Rayburn |
| Hinojosa, Ruben | TX | 15 | Democrat | 225-2531 | 1032 | Longworth |
| Hobson, David | OH | 7 | Republican | 225-4324 | 1514 | Longworth |
| Hoeffel, Joseph | PA | 13 | Democrat | 225-6111 | 1229 | Longworth |
| Hoekstra, Peter | MI | 2 | Republican | 225-4401 | 1124 | Longworth |
| Holden, Tim | PA | 6 | Democrat | 225-5546 | 121 | Cannon |
| Holt, Rush D. | NJ | 12 | Democrat | 225-5801 | 1630 | Longworth |
| Hooley, Darlene | OR | 5 | Democrat | 225-5711 | 1130 | Longworth |
| Horn, Stephen | CA | 38 | Republican | 225-6676 | 2331 | Rayburn |
| Hostettler, john | IN | 8 | Republican | 225-4636 | 1507 | Longworth |
| Houghton, Amo | NY | 31 | Republican | 225-3161 | 1110 | Longworth |
| Hoyer, Steny | MD | 5 | Democrat | 225-4131 | 1705 | Longworth |
| Hulshof, Kenny | MO | 9 | Republican | 225-2956 | 412 | Cannon |
| Hunter, Duncan | CA | 52 | Republican | 225-5672 | 2265 | Rayburn |
| Hutchinson, Asa | AR | 3 | Republican | 225-4301 | 1535 | Longworth |
| Hyde, Henry | IL | 6 | Republican | 225-4561 | 2110 | Rayburn |
| Inslee, Jay | WA | 1 | Democrat | 225-6311 | 308 | Cannon |
| Isakson, Johnny | GA | 6 | Republican | 225-4501 | 2428 | Rayburn |
| Istook, Ernest | OK | 5 | Republican | 225-2132 | 2404 | Rayburn |
| Jackson, Jesse | IL | 2 | Democrat | 225-0773 | 313 | Cannon |
| Jackson-Lee, S. | TX | 18 | Democrat | 225-3816 | 410 | Cannon |
| Jefferson, William | LA | 2 | Democrat | 225-6636 | 240 | Cannon |
| Jenkins, William | TN | 1 | Republican | 225-6356 | 1708 | Longworth |
| John, Christopher | LA | 7 | Democrat | 225-2031 | 1504 | Longworth |
| Johnson, Eddie | TX | 30 | Democrat | 225-8885 | 1511 | Longworth |
| Johnson, Nancy | CT | 6 | Republican | 225-4476 | 2113 | Rayburn |
| Johnson, Sam | TX | 3 | Republican | 225-4201 | 1030 | Longworth |
| Jones, Stephanie | OH | 11 | Democrat | 225-7032 | 1516 | Longworth |
| Jones, Walter B. | NC | 3 | Republican | 225-3415 | 422 | Cannon |

| Kanjorski, Paul | PA | 11 | Democrat | 225-6511 | 2353 | Rayburn |
|---|---|---|---|---|---|---|
| Kaptur, Marcy | OH | 9 | Democrat | 225-4146 | 2366 | Rayburn |
| Kasich, John | OH | 12 | Republican | 225-5355 | 1111 | Longworth |
| Kelly, Sue | NY | 19 | Republican | 225-5441 | 1122 | Longworth |
| Kennedy, Patrick | RI | 1 | Democrat | 225-4911 | 312 | Cannon |
| Kildee, Dale | MI | 9 | Democrat | 225-3611 | 2187 | Rayburn |
| Kilpatrick, Carolyn | MI | 15 | Democrat | 225-2261 | 503 | Cannon |
| Kind, Ron | WI | 3 | Democrat | 225-5506 | 1713 | Longworth |
| King, Peter | NY | 3 | Republican | 225-7896 | 403 | Cannon |
| Kingston, Jack | GA | 1 | Republican | 225-5831 | 1034 | Longworth |
| Kleczka, Gerald | WI | 4 | Democrat | 225-4572 | 2301 | Rayburn |
| Klink, Ron | PA | 4 | Democrat | 225-2565 | 2448 | Rayburn |
| Knollenberg, Joe | MI | 11 | Republican | 225-5802 | 2349 | Rayburn |
| Kolbe, Jim | AZ | 5 | Republican | 225-2542 | 2266 | Rayburn |
| Kucinich, Dennis | OH | 10 | Democrat | 225-5871 | 1730 | Longworth |
| Kuykendall, Steven | CA | 36 | Republican | 225-8220 | 512 | Cannon |
| LaFalce, John | NY | 29 | Democrat | 225-3231 | 2310 | Rayburn |
| LaHood, Ray | IL | 18 | Republican | 225-6201 | 329 | Cannon |
| Lampson, Nick | TX | 9 | Democrat | 225-6565 | 417 | Cannon |
| Lantos, Tom | CA | 12 | Democrat | 225-3531 | 2217 | Rayburn |
| Largent, Steve | OK | 1 | Republican | 225-2211 | 426 | Cannon |
| Larson, John B. | CT | 1 | Democrat | 225-2265 | 1419 | Longworth |
| Latham, Tim | IA | 5 | Republican | 225-5476 | 324 | Cannon |
| LaTourrette, Steven | OH | 19 | Republican | 225-5731 | 1224 | Longworth |
| Lazio, Rick | NY | 2 | Republican | 225-3335 | 2244 | Rayburn |
| Leach, James | IA | 1 | Republican | 225-6576 | 2186 | Rayburn |
| Lee, Barbara | CA | 9 | Democrat | 225-2661 | 414 | Cannon |
| Levin, Sander | MI | 12 | Democrat | 225-4961 | 2268 | Rayburn |
| Lewis, Jerry | CA | 40 | Republican | 225-5861 | 2112 | Rayburn |
| Lewis, John | GA | 5 | Democrat | 225-3801 | 343 | Cannon |
| Lewis, Ron | KY | 2 | Republican | 225-3501 | 223 | Cannon |
| Linder, John | GA | 11 | Republican | 225-4272 | 2447 | Rayburn |
| Lipinski, Williams | IL | 3 | Democrat | 225-5701 | 1501 | Longworth |
| LoBiondo, Frank | NJ | 2 | Republican | 225-6572 | 222 | Cannon |
| Lofgren, Zoe | CA | 16 | Democrat | 225-3072 | 318 | Cannon |
| Lowey, Nita | NY | 18 | Democrat | 225-6506 | 2421 | Rayburn |
| Lucas, Frank | OK | 6 | Republican | 225-5565 | 438 | Cannon |
| Lucas, Ken | KY | 4 | Democrat | 225-3465 | 1237 | Longworth |
| Luther, Bill | MN | 6 | Democrat | 225-2271 | 117 | Cannon |
| McCarthy, Carolyn | NY | 4 | Democrat | 225-5516 | 1725 | Longworth |
| McCarthy, Karen | MO | 5 | Democrat | 225-4535 | 1330 | Longworth |

| McCollum, Bill | FL | 8 | Republican | 225-2176 | 2109 | Rayburn |
|---|---|---|---|---|---|---|
| McCrery, Jim | LA | 4 | Republican | 225-2777 | 2104 | Rayburn |
| McDermott, Jim | WA | 7 | Democrat | 225-3106 | 1035 | Longworth |
| McGovern, James | MA | 3 | Democrat | 225-6101 | 416 | Cannon |
| McHugh, John | NY | 24 | Republican | 225-4611 | 2441 | Rayburn |
| McInnis, Scott | CO | 3 | Republican | 225-4761 | 320 | Cannon |
| McIntosh, David | IN | 2 | Republican | 225-3021 | 1610 | Longworth |
| McIntyre, Mike | NC | 7 | Democrat | 225-2731 | 1605 | Longworth |
| McKeon, Howard | CA | 25 | Republican | 225-1956 | 2242 | Rayburn |
| McKinney, Cynthia | GA | 4 | Democrat | 225-1605 | 124 | Cannon |
| McNulty, Michael | NY | 21 | Democrat | 225-5076 | 2161 | Rayburn |
| Maloney, Carolyn | NY | 14 | Democrat | 225-7944 | 2430 | Rayburn |
| Maloney, James | CT | 5 | Democrat | 225-3822 | 1213 | Longworth |
| Manzullo, Donald | IL | 16 | Republican | 225-5676 | 409 | Cannon |
| Markey, Edward | MA | 7 | Democrat | 225-2836 | 2108 | Rayburn |
| Martinez, Matthew | CA | 31 | Democrat | 225-5464 | 2269 | Rayburn |
| Mascara, Frank | PA | 20 | Democrat | 225-4665 | 314 | Cannon |
| Matsui, Robert | CA | 5 | Democrat | 225-7163 | 2308 | Rayburn |
| Meehan, Martin | MA | 5 | Democrat | 225-3411 | 2434 | Rayburn |
| Meek, Carrie | FL | 17 | Democrat | 225-4506 | 401 | Cannon |
| Meeks, Gregory | NY | 6 | Democrat | 225-3461 | 1710 | Longworth |
| Menendez, Robert | NJ | 13 | Democrat | 225-7919 | 405 | Cannon |
| Metcalf, Jack | WA | 2 | Republican | 225-2605 | 1510 | Longworth |
| Mica, John | FL | 7 | Republican | 225-4035 | 2445 | Rayburn |
| Millender, Juanita | CA | 37 | Democrat | 225-7924 | 419 | Cannon |
| Miller, Dan | FL | 13 | Republican | 225-5015 | 102 | Cannon |
| Miller, Gary | CA | 41 | Republican | 225-3201 | 1037 | Longworth |
| Miller, George | CA | 7 | Democrat | 225-2095 | 2205 | Rayburn |
| Minge, David | MN | 2 | Democrat | 225-2331 | 1415 | Longworth |
| Mink, Patsy | HI | 2 | Democrat | 225-4906 | 2135 | Rayburn |
| Moakley, John J. | MA | 9 | Democrat | 225-8273 | 235 | Cannon |
| Mollohan, Alan | WV | 1 | Democrat | 225-4172 | 2346 | Rayburn |
| Moore, Dennis | KS | 3 | Democrat | 225-2865 | 506 | Cannon |
| Moran, James | VA | 8 | Democrat | 225-4376 | 2239 | Rayburn |
| Moran, Terry | KS | 1 | Republican | 225-2715 | 1519 | Longworth |
| Morella, Constance | MD | 8 | Republican | 225-5341 | 2228 | Rayburn |
| Murtha, John | PA | 12 | Democrat | 225-2065 | 2423 | Rayburn |
| Myrick, Sue | NC | 9 | Republican | 225-1976 | 230 | Cannon |
| Nadler, Jerrold | NY | 8 | Democrat | 225-5635 | 2334 | Rayburn |
| Napolitano, Grace | CA | 34 | Democrat | 225-5256 | 1407 | Longworth |
| Neal, Richard | MA | 2 | Democrat | 225-5601 | 2236 | Rayburn |

| Nethercutt, George | WA | 5 | Republican | 225-2006 | 1527 | Longworth |
|---|---|---|---|---|---|---|
| Ney, Robert | OH | 18 | Republican | 225-6265 | 1024 | Longworth |
| Northup, Anne | KY | 3 | Republican | 225-5401 | 1004 | Longworth |
| Norton, Eleanor | DC | NA | Republican | 225-8050 | 1424 | Longworth |
| Norwood, Charlie | GA | 10 | Republican | 225-4101 | 1707 | Longworth |
| Nussle, Jim | IA | 2 | Republican | 225-2911 | 303 | Cannon |
| Oberstar, James | MN | 8 | Democrat | 225-6211 | 2365 | Rayburn |
| Obey, David | WI | 7 | Democrat | 225-3365 | 2314 | Rayburn |
| Olver, John | MA | 1 | Democrat | 225-5335 | 1027 | Longworth |
| Ortiz, Solomon | TX | 27 | Democrat | 225-7742 | 2136 | Rayburn |
| Ose, Doug | CA | 3 | Republican | 225-5716 | 1508 | Longworth |
| Owens, Major | NY | 11 | Democrat | 225-6231 | 2305 | Rayburn |
| Oxley, Michael | OH | 4 | Republican | 225-2676 | 2233 | Rayburn |
| Packard, Ron | CA | 48 | Republican | 225-3906 | 2372 | Rayburn |
| Pallone, Frank | NJ | 6 | Democrat | 225-4671 | 420 | Cannon |
| Pascrell, Bill | NJ | 8 | Democrat | 225-5751 | 1722 | Longworth |
| Pastor, Ed | AZ | 2 | Democrat | 225-4065 | 2465 | Rayburn |
| Paul, Ron | TX | 14 | Republican | 225-2831 | 203 | Cannon |
| Payne, Donald | NJ | 10 | Democrat | 225-3436 | 2209 | Rayburn |
| Pease, Edward | IN | 7 | Republican | 225-5805 | 119 | Cannon |
| Pelosi, Nancy | CA | 8 | Democrat | 225-4965 | 2457 | Rayburn |
| Peterson, Collin | MN | 7 | Democrat | 225-2165 | 2159 | Rayburn |
| Peterson, John | PA | 5 | Republican | 225-5121 | 307 | Cannon |
| Petri, Thomas | WI | 6 | Republican | 225-2476 | 2462 | Rayburn |
| Phelps, David | IL | 19 | Democrat | 225-5201 | 1523 | Longworth |
| Pickering, Charles | MS | 3 | Republican | 225-5301 | 427 | Cannon |
| Pickett, Owen | VA | 2 | Democrat | 225-4215 | 2133 | Rayburn |
| Pitts, Joseph | PA | 16 | Republican | 225-2411 | 504 | Cannon |
| Pombo, Richard | CA | 11 | Republican | 225-1947 | 2411 | Rayburn |
| Pomeroy, Earl | ND | A-L | Democrat | 225-2611 | 1533 | Longworth |
| Porter, John | IL | 10 | Republican | 225-4835 | 2373 | Rayburn |
| Portman, Rob | OH | 2 | Republican | 225-3164 | 238 | Cannon |
| Price, David | NC | 4 | Democrat | 225-1784 | 2162 | Rayburn |
| Pryce, Deborah | OH | 15 | Republican | 225-2015 | 221 | Cannon |
| Quinn, Jack | NY | 30 | Republican | 225-3306 | 229 | Cannon |
| Radanovich, G. | CA | 19 | Republican | 225-4540 | 123 | Cannon |
| Rahall, Nick | WV | 3 | Democrat | 225-3452 | 2307 | Rayburn |
| Ramstad, Kim | MN | 3 | Republican | 225-2871 | 103 | Cannon |
| Rangel, Charles | NY | 15 | Democrat | 225-4365 | 2354 | Rayburn |
| Regula, Ralph | OH | 16 | Republican | 225-3876 | 2309 | Rayburn |
| Reyes, Silvestre | TX | 16 | Democrat | 225-4831 | 514 | Cannon |

| Reynolds, Thomas | NY | 27 | Republican | 225-5265 | 413 | Cannon |
|---|---|---|---|---|---|---|
| Riley, Bob | AL | 3 | Republican | 225-3261 | 322 | Cannon |
| Rivers, Lynn | MI | 13 | Democrat | 225-6261 | 1724 | Longworth |
| Rodriguez, Ciro | TX | 28 | Democrat | 225-1640 | 323 | Cannon |
| Roemer, Tim | IN | 3 | Democrat | 225-3915 | 2352 | Rayburn |
| Rogan, James | CA | 27 | Republican | 225-4176 | 126 | Cannon |
| Rogers, Harold | KY | 5 | Republican | 225-4601 | 2470 | Rayburn |
| Rohrabacher, Dana | CA | 45 | Republican | 225-2415 | 2338 | Rayburn |
| Romero-Barce, C. | PR | R-C | Republican | 225-2615 | 2443 | Rayburn |
| Ros-Lehtinen, I. | FL | 18 | Republican | 225-3931 | 2160 | Rayburn |
| Rothman, Steven | NJ | 9 | Democrat | 225-5061 | 1607 | Longworth |
| Roukema, Marge | NJ | 5 | Republican | 225-4465 | 2469 | Rayburn |
| Roybal-Allard, L. | CA | 33 | Democrat | 225-1766 | 2435 | Rayburn |
| Royce, Edward | CA | 39 | Republican | 225-4111 | 1133 | Longworth |
| Rush, Bobby | IL | 1 | Democrat | 225-4372 | 2416 | Rayburn |
| Ryan, Paul | WI | 1 | Republican | 225-3031 | 1217 | Longworth |
| Ryun, Jim | KS | 2 | Republican | 225-6601 | 330 | Cannon |
| Salmon, Matt | AZ | 1 | Republican | 225-2635 | 115 | Cannon |
| Sanchez, Loretta | CA | 46 | Democrat | 225-2965 | 1529 | Longworth |
| Sanders, Bernard | VT | A-L | Republican | 225-4115 | 2202 | Rayburn |
| Sandlin, Max | TX | 1 | Democrat | 225-3035 | 214 | Cannon |
| Sanford, Marshall | SC | 1 | Republican | 225-3176 | 1233 | Longworth |
| Sawyer, Tom | OH | 14 | Democrat | 225-5231 | 1414 | Longworth |
| Saxton, Jim | NJ | 3 | Republican | 225-4765 | 339 | Cannon |
| Scarborough, Joe | FL | 1 | Republican | 225-4136 | 127 | Cannon |
| Schaffer, Bob | CO | 4 | Republican | 225-4676 | 212 | Cannon |
| Schakowsky, J. | IL | 9 | Democrat | 225-2111 | 515 | Cannon |
| Scott, Robert | VA | 3 | Democrat | 225-8351 | 2464 | Rayburn |
| Sensenbrenner, J. | WI | 9 | Republican | 225-5101 | 2332 | Rayburn |
| Serrano, Jose | NY | 16 | Democrat | 225-4361 | 2342 | Rayburn |
| Sessions, Pete | TX | 5 | Republican | 225-2231 | 1318 | Longworth |
| Shadegg, John | AZ | 4 | Republican | 225-3361 | 430 | Cannon |
| Shaw, Clay | FL | 22 | Republican | 225-3026 | 2408 | Rayburn |
| Shays, Christopher | CT | 4 | Republican | 225-5541 | 1126 | Longworth |
| Sherman, Brad | CA | 24 | Democrat | 225-5911 | 1524 | Longworth |
| Sherwood, Don | PA | 10 | Republican | 225-3731 | 1223 | Longworth |
| Shimkus, John | IL | 20 | Republican | 225-5271 | 513 | Cannon |
| Shows, Ronnie | MS | 4 | Democrat | 225-5865 | 509 | Cannon |
| Shuster, Bud | PA | 9 | Republican | 225-2431 | 2188 | Rayburn |
| Simpson, Michael | ID | 2 | Republican | 225-5531 | 1440 | Longworth |
| Sisisky, Norman | VA | 4 | Democrat | 225-6365 | 2371 | Rayburn |

| Skeen, Joe | NM | 2 | Republican | 225-2365 | 2302 | Rayburn |
|---|---|---|---|---|---|---|
| Skelton, Ike | MO | 4 | Democrat | 225-2876 | 2206 | Rayburn |
| Slaughter, Louise | NY | 28 | Democrat | 225-3615 | 2347 | Rayburn |
| Smith, Adam | WA | 9 | Democrat | 225-8901 | 116 | Cannon |
| Smith, Christopher | NJ | 4 | Republican | 225-3765 | 2370 | Rayburn |
| Smith, Lamar | TX | 21 | Republican | 225-4236 | 2231 | Rayburn |
| Smith, Nick | MI | 7 | Republican | 225-6276 | 306 | Cannon |
| Snyder, Vic | AR | 2 | Democrat | 225-2506 | 1319 | Longworth |
| Souder, Mark | IN | 4 | Republican | 225-4436 | 109 | Cannon |
| Spence, Floyd | SC | 2 | Republican | 225-2452 | 2405 | Rayburn |
| Spratt, John | SC | 5 | Democrat | 225-5501 | 1536 | Longworth |
| Stabenow, Debbie | MI | 8 | Democrat | 225-4872 | 1039 | Longworth |
| Stark, Fortney | CA | 13 | Democrat | 225-5065 | 239 | Cannon |
| Stearns, Cliff | FL | 6 | Republican | 225-5744 | 2227 | Rayburn |
| Stenholm, Charles | TX | 17 | Democrat | 225-6605 | 1211 | Longworth |
| Strickland, Ted | OH | 6 | Democrat | 225-5705 | 336 | Cannon |
| Stupak, Bart | MI | 1 | Democrat | 225-4735 | 2348 | Rayburn |
| Sununu, John | NH | 1 | Republican | 225-5456 | 316 | Cannon |
| Sweeney, John | NY | 22 | Republican | 225-5614 | 437 | Cannon |
| Talent, James | MO | 2 | Republican | 225-2561 | 1022 | Longworth |
| Tancredo, Thomas | CO | 6 | Republican | 225-7882 | 1123 | Longworth |
| Tanner, John | TN | 8 | Democrat | 225-4714 | 1127 | Longworth |
| Tausher, Ellen | CA | 10 | Democrat | 225-1880 | 1239 | Longworth |
| Tauzin, W.J. | LA | 3 | Republican | 225-4031 | 2183 | Rayburn |
| Taylor, Charles | NC | 11 | Republican | 225-6401 | 231 | Cannon |
| Taylor, Gene | MS | 5 | Democrat | 225-5772 | 2311 | Rayburn |
| Terry, Lee | NE | 2 | Republican | 225-4155 | 1728 | Longworth |
| Thomas, William | CA | 21 | Republican | 225-2915 | 2208 | Rayburn |
| Thompson, Bennie | MS | 2 | Democrat | 225-5876 | 1408 | Longworth |
| Thompson, Mike | CA | 1 | Democrat | 225-3311 | 415 | Cannon |
| Thornberry, Mac | TX | 13 | Republican | 225-3706 | 131 | Cannon |
| Thune, John | SD | A-L | Republican | 225-2801 | 1005 | Longworth |
| Thurman, Karen | FL | 5 | Democrat | 225-1002 | 440 | Cannon |
| Tiahrt, Todd | KS | 4 | Republican | 225-6216 | 428 | Cannon |
| Tierney, John | MA | 6 | Democrat | 225-8020 | 120 | Cannon |
| Toomey, Patrick | PA | 15 | Republican | 225-6411 | 511 | Cannon |
| Towns, Edolphus | NY | 10 | Democrat | 225-5936 | 2232 | Rayburn |
| Traficant, James | OH | 17 | Democrat | 225-5261 | 2446 | Rayburn |
| Turner, Jim | TX | 2 | Democrat | 225-2401 | 208 | Cannon |
| Udall, Mark | CO | 2 | Democrat | 225-2161 | 128 | Cannon |
| Udall, Tom | NM | 3 | Democrat | 225-6190 | 502 | Cannon |

| | | | | | | |
|---|---|---|---|---|---|---|
| Upton, Fred | MI | 6 | Republican | 225-3761 | 2333 | Rayburn |
| Velazquez, Nydia | NY | 12 | Democrat | 225-2361 | 2241 | Rayburn |
| Vento, Bruce | MN | 4 | Democrat | 225-6631 | 2413 | Rayburn |
| Visclosky, Peter | IN | 1 | Democrat | 225-2461 | 2313 | Rayburn |
| Vitter, David | LA | 1 | Republican | 225-3015 | 2406 | Rayburn |
| Walden, Greg | OR | 2 | Republican | 225-6730 | 1404 | Longworth |
| Walsh, James | NY | 25 | Republican | 225-3701 | 2351 | Rayburn |
| Wamp, Zach | TN | 3 | Republican | 225-3271 | 423 | Cannon |
| Waters, Maxine | CA | 35 | Democrat | 225-2201 | 2344 | Rayburn |
| Watkins, Wes | OK | 3 | Republican | 225-4565 | 1401 | Longworth |
| Watt, Melvin L. | NC | 12 | Democrat | 225-1510 | 1230 | Longworth |
| Watts, J.C. | OK | 4 | Republican | 225-6165 | 1210 | Longworth |
| Waxman, Henry | CA | 29 | Democrat | 225-3976 | 2204 | Rayburn |
| Weiner, Anthony | NY | 9 | Democrat | 225-6616 | 501 | Cannon |
| Weldon, Curt | PA | 7 | Republican | 225-2011 | 2452 | Rayburn |
| Weldon, Dave | FL | 15 | Republican | 225-3671 | 332 | Cannon |
| Weller, Jerry | IL | 11 | Republican | 225-3635 | 424 | Cannon |
| Wexler, Robert | FL | 19 | Democrat | 225-3001 | 213 | Cannon |
| Weygand, Robert | RI | 2 | Democrat | 225-2735 | 215 | Cannon |
| Whitfield, Ed | KY | 1 | Republican | 225-3115 | 236 | Cannon |
| Wicker, Roger | MS | 1 | Republican | 225-4306 | 206 | Cannon |
| Wilson, Heather | MN | 1 | Republican | 225-6316 | 226 | Cannon |
| Wise, Robert | WV | 2 | Democrat | 225-2711 | 2367 | Rayburn |
| Wolf, Frank | VA | 10 | Republican | 225-5136 | 241 | Cannon |
| Woolsey, Lynn | CA | 6 | Democrat | 225-5161 | 439 | Cannon |
| Wu, David | OR | 1 | Democrat | 225-0855 | 510 | Cannon |
| Wynn, Albert | MD | 4 | Democrat | 225-8699 | 407 | Cannon |
| Young, C.W. | FL | 10 | Republican | 225-5961 | 2407 | Rayburn |
| Young, Don | AK | A-L | Republican | 225-5765 | 2111 | Rayburn |

# Table A-2    U.S. House of Representatives Directory
## (Sorted by State)

| State | Name | Dist. | Party | Phone | Room | Building |
|-------|------|-------|-------|-------|------|----------|
| AK | Young, Don | A-L | Republican | 225-5765 | 2111 | Rayburn |
| AL | Aderholt, Robert | 4 | Republican | 225-4876 | 1007 | Longworth |
| AL | Bachus, Spencer | 6 | Republican | 225-4921 | 442 | Cannon |
| AL | Callahan, Sonny | 1 | Republican | 225-4931 | 2466 | Rayburn |
| AL | Cramer, Robert E. | 5 | Democrat | 225-4801 | 2350 | Rayburn |
| AL | Everett, Terry | 2 | Republican | 225-2901 | 2312 | Rayburn |
| AL | Hilliard, Earl | 7 | Democrat | 225-2665 | 1314 | Longworth |
| AL | Riley, Bob | 3 | Republican | 225-3261 | 322 | Cannon |
| AR | Berry, Marion | 1 | Democrat | 225-4076 | 1113 | Longworth |
| AR | Dickey, Jay | 4 | Republican | 225-3771 | 2453 | Rayburn |
| AR | Hutchinson, Asa | 3 | Republican | 225-4301 | 1535 | Longworth |
| AR | Snyder, Vic | 2 | Democrat | 225-2506 | 1319 | Longworth |
| AZ | Hayworth, J.D. | 6 | Republican | 225-2190 | 1023 | Longworth |
| AZ | Kolbe, Jim | 5 | Republican | 225-2542 | 2266 | Rayburn |
| AZ | Pastor, Ed | 2 | Democrat | 225-4065 | 2465 | Rayburn |
| AZ | Salmon, Matt | 1 | Republican | 225-2635 | 115 | Cannon |
| AZ | Shadegg, John | 4 | Republican | 225-3361 | 430 | Cannon |
| CA | Becerra, Xavier | 30 | Democrat | 225-6235 | 1119 | Longworth |
| CA | Berman, Howard L. | 26 | Democrat | 225-4695 | 2330 | Rayburn |
| CA | Bilbray, Brian P. | 49 | Republican | 225-2040 | 1530 | Longworth |
| CA | Bono, Mary | 44 | Republican | 225-5330 | 516 | Cannon |
| CA | Calvert, Ken | 43 | Republican | 225-1986 | 2201 | Rayburn |
| CA | Campbell, Tom | 15 | Republican | 225-2631 | 2442 | Rayburn |
| CA | Capps, Lois | 22 | Democrat | 225-3601 | 1118 | Longworth |
| CA | Condit, Gary A. | 18 | Democrat | 225-6131 | 2234 | Rayburn |
| CA | Cox, Christopher | 47 | Republican | 225-5611 | 2402 | Rayburn |
| CA | Cunningham, R. | 51 | Republican | 225-5452 | 2238 | Rayburn |
| CA | Dixon, Julian C. | 32 | Democrat | 225-7084 | 2252 | Rayburn |
| CA | Dooley, Calvin M. | 20 | Democrat | 225-3341 | 1201 | Longworth |
| CA | Doolittle, John T. | 4 | Republican | 225-2511 | 1526 | Longworth |
| CA | Dreier, David | 28 | Republican | 225-2305 | 237 | Cannon |
| CA | Eshoo, Anna | 14 | Democrat | 225-8104 | 205 | Cannon |

| CA | Farr, Sam | 17 | Democrat | 225-2861 | 1221 | Longworth |
|----|-----------|----|----|----|----|----|
| CA | Filner, Bob | 50 | Democrat | 225-8045 | 2463 | Rayburn |
| CA | Gallegly, Elton | 23 | Republican | 225-5811 | 2427 | Rayburn |
| CA | Herger, Wally | 2 | Republican | 225-3076 | 2433 | Rayburn |
| CA | Horn, Stephen | 38 | Republican | 225-6676 | 2331 | Rayburn |
| CA | Hunter, Duncan | 52 | Republican | 225-5672 | 2265 | Rayburn |
| CA | Kuykendall, Steven | 36 | Republican | 225-8220 | 512 | Cannon |
| CA | Lantos, Tom | 12 | Democrat | 225-3531 | 2217 | Rayburn |
| CA | Lee, Barbara | 9 | Democrat | 225-2661 | 414 | Cannon |
| CA | Lewis, Jerry | 40 | Republican | 225-5861 | 2112 | Rayburn |
| CA | Lofgren, Zoe | 16 | Democrat | 225-3072 | 318 | Cannon |
| CA | McKeon, Howard | 25 | Republican | 225-1956 | 2242 | Rayburn |
| CA | Martinez, Matthew | 31 | Democrat | 225-5464 | 2269 | Rayburn |
| CA | Matsui, Robert | 5 | Democrat | 225-7163 | 2308 | Rayburn |
| CA | Millender, Juanita | 37 | Democrat | 225-7924 | 419 | Cannon |
| CA | Miller, Gary | 41 | Republican | 225-3201 | 1037 | Longworth |
| CA | Miller, George | 7 | Democrat | 225-2095 | 2205 | Rayburn |
| CA | Napolitano, Grace | 34 | Democrat | 225-5256 | 1407 | Longworth |
| CA | Ose, Doug | 3 | Republican | 225-5716 | 1508 | Longworth |
| CA | Packard, Ron | 48 | Republican | 225-3906 | 2372 | Rayburn |
| CA | Pelosi, Nancy | 8 | Democrat | 225-4965 | 2457 | Rayburn |
| CA | Pombo, Richard | 11 | Republican | 225-1947 | 2411 | Rayburn |
| CA | Radanovich, George | 19 | Republican | 225-4540 | 123 | Cannon |
| CA | Rogan, James | 27 | Republican | 225-4176 | 126 | Cannon |
| CA | Rohrabacher, Dana | 45 | Republican | 225-2415 | 2338 | Rayburn |
| CA | Roybal-Allard, L. | 33 | Democrat | 225-1766 | 2435 | Rayburn |
| CA | Royce, Edward | 39 | Republican | 225-4111 | 1133 | Longworth |
| CA | Sanchez, Loretta | 46 | Democrat | 225-2965 | 1529 | Longworth |
| CA | Sherman, Brad | 24 | Democrat | 225-5911 | 1524 | Longworth |
| CA | Stark, Fortney | 13 | Democrat | 225-5065 | 239 | Cannon |
| CA | Tausher, Ellen | 10 | Democrat | 225-1880 | 1239 | Longworth |
| CA | Thomas, William | 21 | Republican | 225-2915 | 2208 | Rayburn |
| CA | Thompson, Mike | 1 | Democrat | 225-3311 | 415 | Cannon |
| CA | Waters, Maxine | 35 | Democrat | 225-2201 | 2344 | Rayburn |
| CA | Waxman, Henry | 29 | Democrat | 225-3976 | 2204 | Rayburn |
| CA | Woolsey, Lynn | 6 | Democrat | 225-5161 | 439 | Cannon |
| | | | | | | |
| CO | DeGette, Diana | 1 | Democrat | 225-4431 | 1339 | Longworth |
| CO | Hefley, Joel | 5 | Republican | 225-4422 | 2230 | Rayburn |
| CO | McInnis, Scott | 3 | Republican | 225-4761 | 320 | Cannon |

| CO | Schaffer, Bob | 4 | Republican | 225-4676 | 212 | Cannon |
|----|----|----|----|----|----|----|
| CO | Tancredo, Thomas | 6 | Republican | 225-7882 | 1123 | Longworth |
| CO | Udall, Mark | 2 | Democrat | 225-2161 | 128 | Cannon |
| CT | DeLauro, Rosa L. | 3 | Democrat | 225-3661 | 436 | Cannon |
| CT | Gejdenson, Sam | 2 | Democrat | 225-2076 | 2304 | Rayburn |
| CT | Johnson, Nancy | 6 | Republican | 225-4476 | 2113 | Rayburn |
| CT | Larson, John B. | 1 | Democrat | 225-2265 | 1419 | Longworth |
| CT | Maloney, James | 5 | Democrat | 225-3822 | 1213 | Longworth |
| CT | Shays, Christopher | 4 | Republican | 225-5541 | 1126 | Longworth |
| DC | Norton, Eleanor | NA | Republican | 225-8050 | 1424 | Longworth |
| DE | Castle, Michael N. | A-L | Republican | 225-4165 | 1227 | Longworth |
| FL | Meek, Carrie | 17 | Democrat | 225-4506 | 401 | Cannon |
| FL | Bilirakis, Michael | 9 | Republican | 225-5755 | 2369 | Rayburn |
| FL | Boyd, Allen | 2 | Democrat | 225-5235 | 107 | Cannon |
| FL | Brown, Corrine | 3 | Democrat | 225-0123 | 2444 | Rayburn |
| FL | Canady, Charles T. | 12 | Republican | 225-1252 | 2432 | Rayburn |
| FL | Davis, Jim | 11 | Democrat | 225-3376 | 418 | Cannon |
| FL | Deutsch, Peter | 20 | Democrat | 225-7931 | 204 | Cannon |
| FL | Diaz-Balart, Lincoln | 21 | Republican | 225-4211 | 404 | Cannon |
| FL | Foley, Mark | 16 | Republican | 225-5792 | 113 | Cannon |
| FL | Fowler, Tillie K. | 4 | Republican | 225-2501 | 106 | Cannon |
| FL | Goss, Porter | 14 | Republican | 225-2536 | 108 | Cannon |
| FL | Hastings, Alcee | 23 | Democrat | 225-1313 | 2235 | Rayburn |
| FL | McCollum, Bill | 8 | Republican | 225-2176 | 2109 | Rayburn |
| FL | Mica, John | 7 | Republican | 225-4035 | 2445 | Rayburn |
| FL | Miller, Dan | 13 | Republican | 225-5015 | 102 | Cannon |
| FL | Ros-Lehtinen, I. | 18 | Republican | 225-3931 | 2160 | Rayburn |
| FL | Scarborough, Joe | 1 | Republican | 225-4136 | 127 | Cannon |
| FL | Shaw, Clay | 22 | Republican | 225-3026 | 2408 | Rayburn |
| FL | Stearns, Cliff | 6 | Republican | 225-5744 | 2227 | Rayburn |
| FL | Thurman, Karen | 5 | Democrat | 225-1002 | 440 | Cannon |
| FL | Weldon, Dave | 15 | Republican | 225-3671 | 332 | Cannon |
| FL | Wexler, Robert | 19 | Democrat | 225-3001 | 213 | Cannon |
| FL | Young, C.W. | 10 | Republican | 225-5961 | 2407 | Rayburn |

| GA | Barr, Bob | 7 | Republican | 225-2931 | 1207 | Longworth |
|----|-----------|---|------------|----------|------|-----------|
| GA | Bishop, Sanford D. | 2 | Democrat | 225-3631 | 1433 | Longworth |
| GA | Chambliss, Saxby | 8 | Republican | 225-6531 | 1019 | Longworth |
| GA | Collins, Mac | 3 | Republican | 225-5901 | 1131 | Longworth |
| GA | Deal, Nathan | 9 | Republican | 225-5211 | 2437 | Rayburn |
| GA | Isakson, Johnny | 6 | Republican | 225-4501 | 2428 | Rayburn |
| GA | Kingston, Jack | 1 | Republican | 225-5831 | 1034 | Longworth |
| GA | Lewis, John | 5 | Democrat | 225-3801 | 343 | Cannon H |
| GA | Linder, John | 11 | Republican | 225-4272 | 2447 | Rayburn |
| GA | McKinney, Cynthia | 4 | Democrat | 225-1605 | 124 | Cannon |
| GA | Norwood, Charlie | 10 | Republican | 225-4101 | 1707 | Longworth |
| | | | | | | |
| HI | Abercrombie, Neil | 1 | Democrat | 225-2726 | 1502 | Longworth |
| HI | Mink, Patsy | 2 | Democrat | 225-4906 | 2135 | Rayburn |
| | | | | | | |
| IA | Boswell, Leonard L. | 3 | Democrat | 225-3806 | 1029 | Longworth |
| IA | Ganske, Greg | 4 | Republican | 225-4426 | 1108 | Longworth |
| IA | Latham, Tim | 5 | Republican | 225-5476 | 324 | Cannon |
| IA | Leach, James | 1 | Republican | 225-6576 | 2186 | Rayburn |
| IA | Nussle, Jim | 2 | Republican | 225-2911 | 303 | Cannon |
| | | | | | | |
| ID | Chenoweth, Helen | 1 | Republican | 225-6611 | 1727 | Longworth |
| ID | Simpson, Michael | 2 | Republican | 225-5531 | 1440 | Longworth |
| | | | | | | |
| IL | Biggert, Judy | 13 | Republican | 225-3515 | 508 | Cannon |
| IL | Blagojevich, Rod R. | 5 | Democrat | 225-4061 | 331 | Cannon |
| IL | Costello, Jerry F. | 12 | Democrat | 225-5661 | 2454 | Rayburn |
| IL | Crane, Phillip M. | 8 | Republican | 225-3711 | 233 | Cannon |
| IL | Davis, Danny K. | 7 | Democrat | 225-5006 | 1222 | Longworth |
| IL | Evans, Lane | 17 | Democrat | 225-5905 | 2335 | Rayburn |
| IL | Ewing, Thomas | 15 | Republican | 225-2371 | 2417 | Rayburn |
| IL | Guitterez, Luis | 4 | Democrat | 225-8203 | 2438 | Rayburn |
| IL | Hastert, Dennis | 14 | Republican | 225-2976 | 2263 | Rayburn |
| IL | Hyde, Henry | 6 | Republican | 225-4561 | 2110 | Rayburn |
| IL | Jackson, Jesse | 2 | Democrat | 225-0773 | 313 | Cannon |
| IL | LaHood, Ray | 18 | Republican | 225-6201 | 329 | Cannon |

| IL | Lipinski, Williams | 3 | Democrat | 225-5701 | 1501 | Longworth |
|----|----|----|----|----|----|----|
| IL | Manzullo, Donald | 16 | Republican | 225-5676 | 409 | Cannon |
| IL | Phelps, David | 19 | Democrat | 225-5201 | 1523 | Longworth |
| IL | Porter, John | 10 | Republican | 225-4835 | 2373 | Rayburn |
| IL | Rush, Bobby | 1 | Democrat | 225-4372 | 2416 | Rayburn |
| IL | Schakowsky, Janice | 9 | Democrat | 225-2111 | 515 | Cannon |
| IL | Shimkus, John | 20 | Republican | 225-5271 | 513 | Cannon |
| IL | Weller, Jerry | 11 | Republican | 225-3635 | 424 | Cannon |
| | | | | | | |
| IN | Burton, Dan | 6 | Republican | 225-2276 | 2185 | Rayburn |
| IN | Buyer, Steve | 5 | Republican | 225-5037 | 227 | Cannon |
| IN | Carson, Julia | 10 | Democrat | 225-4011 | 1541 | Longworth |
| IN | Hill, Baron | 9 | Democrat | 225-5315 | 1208 | Longworth |
| IN | Hostettler, John | 8 | Republican | 225-4636 | 1507 | Longworth |
| IN | McIntosh, David | 2 | Republican | 225-3021 | 1610 | Longworth |
| IN | Pease, Edward | 7 | Republican | 225-5805 | 119 | Cannon |
| IN | Roemer, Tim | 3 | Democrat | 225-3915 | 2352 | Rayburn |
| IN | Souder, Mark | 4 | Republican | 225-4436 | 109 | Cannon |
| IN | Visclosky, Peter | 1 | Democrat | 225-2461 | 2313 | Rayburn |
| | | | | | | |
| KS | Moore, Dennis | 3 | Democrat | 225-2865 | 506 | Cannon |
| KS | Moran, Terry | 1 | Republican | 225-2715 | 1519 | Longworth |
| KS | Ryun, Jim | 2 | Republican | 225-6601 | 330 | Cannon |
| KS | Tiahrt, Todd | 4 | Republican | 225-6216 | 428 | Cannon |
| | | | | | | |
| KY | Fletcher, Ernie | 6 | Republican | 225-4706 | 1117 | Longworth |
| KY | Lewis, Ron | 2 | Republican | 225-3501 | 223 | Cannon |
| KY | Lucas, Ken | 4 | Democrat | 225-3465 | 1237 | Longworth |
| KY | Northup, Anne | 3 | Republican | 225-5401 | 1004 | Longworth |
| KY | Rogers, Harold | 5 | Republican | 225-4601 | 2470 | Rayburn |
| KY | Whitfield, Ed | 1 | Republican | 225-3115 | 236 | Cannon |
| | | | | | | |
| LA | Baker, Richard H. | 6 | Republican | 225-3901 | 434 | Cannon |
| LA | Cooksey, John | 5 | Republican | 225-8490 | 317 | Cannon |
| LA | Jefferson, William | 2 | Democrat | 225-6636 | 240 | Cannon |
| LA | John, Christopher | 7 | Democrat | 225-2031 | 1504 | Longworth |
| LA | McCrery, Jim | 4 | Republican | 225-2777 | 2104 | Rayburn |
| LA | Tauzin, W.J. | 3 | Republican | 225-4031 | 2183 | Rayburn |
| LA | Vitter, David | 1 | Republican | 225-3015 | 2406 | Rayburn |

| MA | Capuano, Michale E. | 8 | Democrat | 225-5111 | 1232 | Longworth |
|----|---------------------|----|----------|----------|------|-----------|
| MA | Delahunt, William | 10 | Democrat | 225-3111 | 1317 | Longworth |
| MA | Frank, Barney | 4 | Democrat | 225-5931 | 2210 | Rayburn |
| MA | McGovern, James | 3 | Democrat | 225-6101 | 416 | Cannon |
| MA | Markey, Edward | 7 | Democrat | 225-2836 | 2108 | Rayburn |
| MA | Meehan, Martin | 5 | Democrat | 225-3411 | 2434 | Rayburn |
| MA | Moakley, John Joe | 9 | Democrat | 225-8273 | 235 | Cannon |
| MA | Neal, Richard | 2 | Democrat | 225-5601 | 2236 | Rayburn |
| MA | Olver, John | 1 | Democrat | 225-5335 | 1027 | Longworth |
| MA | Tierney, John | 6 | Democrat | 225-8020 | 120 | Cannon |
| | | | | | | |
| MD | Bartlett, Roscoe G. | 6 | Republican | 225-2721 | 2412 | Rayburn |
| MD | Cardin, Benjamin L. | 3 | Democrat | 225-4016 | 104 | Cannon |
| MD | Cummings, Elijah | 7 | Democrat | 225-4741 | 1632 | Longworth |
| MD | Ehrlich, Robert L. | 2 | Republican | 225-3061 | 315 | Cannon |
| MD | Gilchrest, Wayne T. | 1 | Republican | 225-5311 | 2245 | Rayburn |
| MD | Hoyer, Steny | 5 | Democrat | 225-4131 | 1705 | Longworth |
| MD | Morella, Constance | 8 | Republican | 225-5341 | 2228 | Rayburn |
| MD | Wynn, Albert | 4 | Democrat | 225-8699 | 407 | Cannon |
| | | | | | | |
| ME | Allen, Thomas H. | 1 | Democrat | 225-6116 | 1717 | Longworth |
| ME | Baldacci, John Elias | 2 | Democrat | 225-6306 | 1740 | Longworth |
| | | | | | | |
| MI | Barcia, James A. | 5 | Democrat | 225-8171 | 2419 | Rayburn |
| MI | Bonior, David E. | 10 | Democrat | 225-2106 | 2207 | Rayburn |
| MI | Camp, Dave | 4 | Republican | 225-3561 | 137 | Cannon |
| MI | Conyers, John | 14 | Democrat | 225-5126 | 2426 | Rayburn |
| MI | Dingell, John D. | 16 | Democrat | 225-4071 | 2328 | Rayburn |
| MI | Ehlers, Vernon J. | 3 | Republican | 225-3831 | 1714 | Longworth |
| MI | Hoekstra, Peter | 2 | Republican | 225-4401 | 1124 | Longworth |
| MI | Kildee, Dale | 9 | Democrat | 225-3611 | 2187 | Rayburn |
| MI | Kilpatrick, Carolyn | 15 | Democrat | 225-2261 | 503 | Cannon |
| MI | Knollenberg, Joe | 11 | Republican | 225-5802 | 2349 | Rayburn |
| MI | Levin, Sander | 12 | Democrat | 225-4961 | 2268 | Rayburn |
| MI | Rivers, Lynn | 13 | Democrat | 225-6261 | 1724 | Longworth |
| MI | Smith, Nick | 7 | Republican | 225-6276 | 306 | Cannon |

| MI | Stabenow, Debbie | 8 | Democrat | 225-4872 | 1039 | Longworth |
| MI | Stupak, Bart | 1 | Democrat | 225-4735 | 2348 | Rayburn |
| MI | Upton, Fred | 6 | Republican | 225-3761 | 2333 | Rayburn |
| | | | | | | |
| MN | Gutknecht, Gil | 1 | Republican | 225-2472 | 426 | Cannon |
| MN | Luther, Bill | 6 | Democrat | 225-2271 | 117 | Cannon |
| MN | Minge, David | 2 | Democrat | 225-2331 | 1415 | Longworth |
| MN | Oberstar, James | 8 | Democrat | 225-6211 | 2365 | Rayburn |
| MN | Peterson, Collin | 7 | Democrat | 225-2165 | 2159 | Rayburn |
| MN | Ramstad, Kim | 3 | Republican | 225-2871 | 103 | Cannon |
| MN | Vento, Bruce | 4 | Democrat | 225-6631 | 2413 | Rayburn |
| MN | Wilson, Heather | 1 | Republican | 225-6316 | 226 | Cannon |
| | | | | | | |
| MO | Blunt, Roy | 7 | Republican | 225-6536 | 217 | Cannon |
| MO | Clay, William | 1 | Democrat | 225-2406 | 2306 | Rayburn |
| MO | Danner, Pat | 6 | Democrat | 225-7041 | 2262 | Rayburn |
| MO | Emerson, Jo Ann | 8 | Republican | 225-4404 | 132 | Cannon |
| MO | Gephardt, Richard | 3 | Democrat | 225-2671 | 1226 | Longworth |
| MO | Hulshof, Kenny | 9 | Republican | 225-2956 | 412 | Cannon |
| MO | McCarthy, Karen | 5 | Democrat | 225-4535 | 1330 | Longworth |
| MO | Skelton, Ike | 4 | Democrat | 225-2876 | 2206 | Rayburn |
| MO | Talent, James | 2 | Republican | 225-2561 | 1022 | Longworth |
| | | | | | | |
| MS | Pickering, Charles | 3 | Republican | 225-5301 | 427 | Cannon |
| MS | Shows, Ronnie | 4 | Democrat | 225-5865 | 509 | Cannon |
| MS | Taylor, Gene | 5 | Democrat | 225-5772 | 2311 | Rayburn |
| MS | Thompson, Bennie | 2 | Democrat | 225-5876 | 1408 | Longworth |
| MS | Wicker, Roger | 1 | Republican | 225-4306 | 206 | Cannon |
| | | | | | | |
| MT | Hill, Rick | A-L | Republican | 225-3211 | 1609 | Longworth |
| | | | | | | |
| NC | Ballenger, Cass | 10 | Republican | 225-2576 | 2182 | Rayburn |
| NC | Burr, Richard | 5 | Republican | 225-2071 | 1513 | Longworth |
| NC | Clayton, Eva M. | 1 | Democrat | 225-3101 | 2440 | Rayburn |
| NC | Coble, Howard | 6 | Republican | 225-3065 | 2468 | Rayburn |
| NC | Etheridge, Bob | 2 | Democrat | 225-2901 | 2312 | Rayburn |
| NC | Hayes, Robin | 8 | Republican | 225-3715 | 130 | Cannon |
| NC | Jones, Walter B. | 3 | Republican | 225-3415 | 422 | Cannon |

| NC | McIntyre, Mike | 7 | Democrat | 225-2731 | 1605 | Longworth |
|----|----------------|---|----------|----------|------|-----------|
| NC | Myrick, Sue | 9 | Republican | 225-1976 | 230 | Cannon |
| NC | Price, David | 4 | Democrat | 225-1784 | 2162 | Rayburn |
| NC | Taylor, Charles | 11 | Republican | 225-6401 | 231 | Cannon |
| NC | Watt, Melvin L. | 12 | Democrat | 225-1510 | 1230 | Longworth |
| ND | Pomeroy, Earl | A-L | Democrat | 225-2611 | 1533 | Longworth |
| NE | Barrett, Bill | 3 | Republican | 225-6435 | 2458 | Rayburn |
| NE | Bereuter, Doug | 1 | Republican | 225-4806 | 2184 | Rayburn |
| NE | Terry, Lee | 2 | Republican | 225-4155 | 1728 | Longworth |
| NH | Bass, Charles F. | 2 | Republican | 225-5206 | 218 | Cannon |
| NH | Sununu, John | 1 | Republican | 225-5456 | 316 | Cannon |
| NJ | Andrews, Robert E. | 1 | Democrat | 225-6501 | 2439 | Rayburn |
| NJ | Franks, Bob | 7 | Republican | 225-5361 | 225 | Cannon |
| NJ | Frelinghuysen, Rod | 11 | Republican | 225-5034 | 228 | Cannon |
| NJ | Holt, Rush D. | 12 | Democrat | 225-5801 | 1630 | Longworth |
| NJ | LoBiondo, Frank | 2 | Republican | 225-6572 | 222 | Cannon |
| NJ | Menendez, Robert | 13 | Democrat | 225-7919 | 405 | Cannon |
| NJ | Pallone, Frank | 6 | Democrat | 225-4671 | 420 | Cannon |
| NJ | Pascrell, Bill | 8 | Democrat | 225-5751 | 1722 | Longworth |
| NJ | Payne, Donald | 10 | Democrat | 225-3436 | 2209 | Rayburn |
| NJ | Rothman, Steven | 9 | Democrat | 225-5061 | 1607 | Longworth |
| NJ | Roukema, Marge | 5 | Republican | 225-4465 | 2469 | Rayburn |
| NJ | Saxton, Jim | 3 | Republican | 225-4765 | 339 | Cannon |
| NJ | Smith, Christopher | 4 | Republican | 225-3765 | 2370 | Rayburn |
| NM | Skeen, Joe | 2 | Republican | 225-2365 | 2302 | Rayburn |
| NM | Udall, Tom | 3 | Democrat | 225-6190 | 502 | Cannon |
| NV | Berkley, Shelley | 1 | Democrat | 2255965 | 1505 | Longworth |
| NV | Gibbons, Jim | 2 | Republican | 225-6155 | 100 | Cannon |
| NY | Ackerman, Gary L. | 5 | Democrat | 225-2601 | 2243 | Rayburn |
| NY | Boehlert, Sherwood | 23 | Republican | 225-3665 | 2246 | Rayburn |

| | | | | | | |
|----|-----|---|---|---|---|---|
| NY | Crowley, Joseph | 7 | Democrat | 225-3965 | 1517 | Longworth |
| NY | Engel, Eliot | 17 | Democrat | 225-2464 | 2303 | Rayburn |
| NY | Forbes, Michael | 1 | Democrat | 225-3826 | 125 | Cannon |
| NY | Fossella, Vito | 13 | Republican | 225-3371 | 431 | Cannon |
| NY | Gilman, Benjamin | 20 | Republican | 225-3776 | 2449 | Rayburn |
| NY | Hinchey, Maurice | 26 | Democrat | 225-6335 | 2431 | Rayburn |
| NY | Houghton, Amo | 31 | Republican | 225-3161 | 1110 | Longworth |
| NY | Kelly, Sue | 19 | Republican | 225-5441 | 1122 | Longworth |
| NY | King, Peter | 3 | Republican | 225-7896 | 403 | Cannon |
| NY | LaFalce, John | 29 | Democrat | 225-3231 | 2310 | Rayburn |
| NY | Lazio, Rick | 2 | Republican | 225-3335 | 2244 | Rayburn |
| NY | Lowey, Nita | 18 | Democrat | 225-6506 | 2421 | Rayburn |
| NY | McCarthy, Carolyn | 4 | Democrat | 225-5516 | 1725 | Longworth |
| NY | McHugh, John | 24 | Republican | 225-4611 | 2441 | Rayburn |
| NY | McNulty, Michael | 21 | Democrat | 225-5076 | 2161 | Rayburn |
| NY | Maloney, Carolyn | 14 | Democrat | 225-7944 | 2430 | Rayburn |
| NY | Meeks, Gregory | 6 | Democrat | 225-3461 | 1710 | Longworth |
| NY | Nadler, Jerrold | 8 | Democrat | 225-5635 | 2334 | Rayburn |
| NY | Owens, Major | 11 | Democrat | 225-6231 | 2305 | Rayburn |
| NY | Quinn, Jack | 30 | Republican | 225-3306 | 229 | Cannon |
| NY | Rangel, Charles | 15 | Democrat | 225-4365 | 2354 | Rayburn |
| NY | Reynolds, Thomas | 27 | Republican | 225-5265 | 413 | Cannon |
| NY | Serrano, Jose | 16 | Democrat | 225-4361 | 2342 | Rayburn |
| NY | Slaughter, Louise | 28 | Democrat | 225-3615 | 2347 | Rayburn |
| NY | Sweeney, John | 22 | Republican | 225-5614 | 437 | Cannon |
| NY | Towns, Edolphus | 10 | Democrat | 225-5936 | 2232 | Rayburn |
| NY | Velazquez, Nydia | 12 | Democrat | 225-2361 | 2241 | Rayburn |
| NY | Walsh, James | 25 | Republican | 225-3701 | 2351 | Rayburn |
| NY | Weiner, Anthony | 9 | Democrat | 225-6616 | 501 | Cannon |
| | | | | | | |
| OH | Boehner, John A. | 8 | Republican | 225-6205 | 1011 | Longworth |
| OH | Brown, Sherrod | 13 | Democrat | 225-3401 | 210 | Cannon |
| OH | Chabot, Steve | 1 | Republican | 225-2216 | 129 | Cannon |
| OH | Gilmor, Paul E. | 5 | Republican | 225-6405 | 1203 | Longworth |
| OH | Hall, Tony | 3 | Democrat | 225-6465 | 1432 | Longworth |
| OH | Hobson, David | 7 | Republican | 225-4324 | 1514 | Longworth |
| OH | Jones, Stephanie | 11 | Democrat | 225-7032 | 1516 | Longworth |
| OH | Kaptur, Marcy | 9 | Democrat | 225-4146 | 2366 | Rayburn |
| OH | Kasich, John | 12 | Republican | 225-5355 | 1111 | Longworth |
| OH | Kucinich, Dennis | 10 | Democrat | 225-5871 | 1730 | Longworth |

| | | | | | | |
|---|---|---|---|---|---|---|
| OH | LaTourrette, Steven | 19 | Republican | 225-5731 | 1224 | Longworth |
| OH | Ney, Robert | 18 | Republican | 225-6265 | 1024 | Longworth |
| OH | Oxley, Michael | 4 | Republican | 225-2676 | 2233 | Rayburn |
| OH | Portman, Rob | 2 | Republican | 225-3164 | 238 | Cannon |
| OH | Pryce, Deborah | 15 | Republican | 225-2015 | 221 | Cannon |
| OH | Regula, Ralph | 16 | Republican | 225-3876 | 2309 | Rayburn |
| OH | Sawyer, Tom | 14 | Democrat | 225-5231 | 1414 | Longworth |
| OH | Strickland, Ted | 6 | Democrat | 225-5705 | 336 | Cannon |
| OH | Traficant, James | 17 | Democrat | 225-5261 | 2446 | Rayburn |
| | | | | | | |
| OK | Coburn, Tom A. | 2 | Republican | 225-2701 | 429 | Cannon |
| OK | Istook, Ernest | 5 | Republican | 225-2132 | 2404 | Rayburn |
| OK | Largent, Steve | 1 | Republican | 225-2211 | 426 | Cannon |
| OK | Lucas, Frank | 6 | Republican | 225-5565 | 438 | Cannon |
| OK | Watkins, Wes | 3 | Republican | 225-4565 | 1401 | Longworth |
| OK | Watts, J.C. | 4 | Republican | 225-6165 | 1210 | Longworth |
| | | | | | | |
| OR | Blumenauer, Earl | 3 | Democrat | 225-4811 | 1406 | Longworth |
| OR | DeFazio, Peter A. | 4 | Democrat | 225-6416 | 2134 | Rayburn |
| OR | Hooley, Darlene | 5 | Democrat | 225-5711 | 1130 | Longworth |
| OR | Walden, Greg | 2 | Republican | 225-6730 | 1404 | Longworth |
| OR | Wu, David | 1 | Democrat | 225-0855 | 510 | Cannon |
| | | | | | | |
| PA | Borski, Robert A. | 3 | Democrat | 225-8251 | 2267 | Rayburn |
| PA | Brady, Robert A. | 1 | Democrat | 225-4731 | 216 | Cannon |
| PA | Coyne, Williams J. | 14 | Democrat | 225-2301 | 2455 | Rayburn |
| PA | Doyle, Michael F. | 18 | Democrat | 225-2135 | 133 | Cannon |
| PA | English, Phil | 21 | Republican | 225-5406 | 1410 | Longworth |
| PA | Fattah, Chaka | 2 | Democrat | 225-4001 | 1205 | Longworth |
| PA | Gekas, George W. | 17 | Republican | 225-4315 | 2410 | Rayburn |
| PA | Goodling, William F. | 19 | Republican | 225-5836 | 2107 | Rayburn |
| PA | Greenwood, James | 8 | Republican | 225-4276 | 2436 | Rayburn |
| PA | Hoeffel, Joseph | 13 | Democrat | 225-6111 | 1229 | Longworth |
| PA | Holden, Tim | 6 | Democrat | 225-5546 | 121 | Cannon |
| PA | Kanjorski, Paul | 11 | Democrat | 225-6511 | 2353 | Rayburn |
| PA | Klink, Ron | 4 | Democrat | 225-2565 | 2448 | Rayburn |
| PA | Mascara, Frank | 20 | Democrat | 225-4665 | 314 | Cannon |
| PA | Murtha, John | 12 | Democrat | 225-2065 | 2423 | Rayburn |
| PA | Peterson, John | 5 | Republican | 225-5121 | 307 | Cannon |

| PA | Pitts, Joseph | 16 | Republican | 225-2411 | 504 | Cannon |
| PA | Sherwood, Don | 10 | Republican | 225-3731 | 1223 | Longworth |
| PA | Shuster, Bud | 9 | Republican | 225-2431 | 2188 | Rayburn |
| PA | Toomey, Patrick | 15 | Republican | 225-6411 | 511 | Cannon |
| PA | Weldon, Curt | 7 | Republican | 225-2011 | 2452 | Rayburn |
| PR | Romero-Bar, Carlos | R-C | Republican | 225-2615 | 2443 | Rayburn |
| RI | Kennedy, Patrick | 1 | Democrat | 225-4911 | 312 | Cannon |
| RI | Weygand, Robert | 2 | Democrat | 225-2735 | 215 | Cannon |
| SC | Clyburn, James E. | 6 | Democrat | 225-3315 | 319 | Cannon |
| SC | DeMint, Jim | 4 | Republican | 225-6030 | 507 | Cannon |
| SC | Graham, Lindsey | 3 | Republican | 225-5301 | 1429 | Longworth |
| SC | Sanford, Marshall | 1 | Republican | 225-3176 | 1233 | Longworth |
| SC | Spence, Floyd | 2 | Republican | 225-2452 | 2405 | Rayburn |
| SC | Spratt, John | 5 | Democrat | 225-5501 | 1536 | Longworth |
| SD | Thune, John | A-L | Republican | 225-2801 | 1005 | Longworth |
| TN | Bryant, Ed | 7 | Republican | 225-2811 | 408 | Cannon |
| TN | Clement, Bob | 5 | Democrat | 225-4311 | 2229 | Rayburn |
| TN | Duncan, John J. | 2 | Republican | 225-5435 | 2400 | Rayburn |
| TN | Ford, Harold E. | 9 | Democrat | 225-3265 | 325 | Cannon |
| TN | Gordon, Bart | 6 | Democrat | 225-4231 | 2368 | Rayburn |
| TN | Hilleary, Van | 4 | Republican | 225-6831 | 114 | Cannon |
| TN | Jenkins, William | 1 | Republican | 225-6356 | 1708 | Longworth |
| TN | Tanner, John | 8 | Democrat | 225-4714 | 1127 | Longworth |
| TN | Wamp, Zach | 3 | Republican | 225-3271 | 423 | Cannon |
| TX | Archer, Bill | 7 | Republican | 225-2571 | 1236 | Longworth |
| TX | Armey, Richard K. | 26 | Republican | 225-7772 | 301 | Cannon |
| TX | Barton, Joe | 6 | Republican | 225-2002 | 2264 | Rayburn |
| TX | Bentsen, Ken | 25 | Democrat | 225-7508 | 326 | Cannon |
| TX | Bonilla, Henry | 23 | Republican | 225-4511 | 1427 | Longworth |
| TX | Brady, Kevin | 8 | Republican | 225-4901 | 1531 | Longworth |
| TX | Combest, Larry | 19 | Republican | 225-4005 | 1026 | Longworth |

| | | | | | | |
|---|---|---|---|---|---|---|
| TX | DeLay, Tom | 22 | Republican | 225-5951 | 341 | Cannon |
| TX | Doggett, Lloyd | 10 | Democrat | 225-4865 | 328 | Cannon |
| TX | Edwards, Chet | 11 | Democrat | 225-6105 | 2459 | Rayburn |
| TX | Frost, Martin | 24 | Democrat | 225-3605 | 2256 | Rayburn |
| TX | Gonzalez, Charles | 20 | Democrat | 225-3236 | 327 | Cannon |
| TX | Granger, Kay | 12 | Republican | 225-5071 | 435 | Cannon |
| TX | Green, Gene | 29 | Democrat | 225-1688 | 2429 | Rayburn |
| TX | Hall, Ralph | 4 | Democrat | 225-6673 | 2221 | Rayburn |
| TX | Hinojosa, Ruben | 15 | Democrat | 225-2531 | 1032 | Longworth |
| TX | Jackson-Lee, Sheila | 18 | Democrat | 225-3816 | 410 | Cannon |
| TX | Johnson, Eddie | 30 | Democrat | 225-8885 | 1511 | Longworth |
| TX | Johnson, Sam | 3 | Republican | 225-4201 | 1030 | Longworth |
| TX | Lampson, Nick | 9 | Democrat | 225-6565 | 417 | Cannon |
| TX | Ortiz, Solomon | 27 | Democrat | 225-7742 | 2136 | Rayburn |
| TX | Paul, Ron | 14 | Republican | 225-2831 | 203 | Cannon |
| TX | Reyes, Silvestre | 16 | Democrat | 225-4831 | 514 | Cannon |
| TX | Rodriguez, Ciro | 28 | Democrat | 225-1640 | 323 | Cannon |
| TX | Sandlin, Max | 1 | Democrat | 225-3035 | 214 | Cannon H |
| TX | Sessions, Pete | 5 | Republican | 225-2231 | 1318 | Longworth |
| TX | Smith, Lamar | 21 | Republican | 225-4236 | 2231 | Rayburn |
| TX | Stenholm, Charles | 17 | Democrat | 225-6605 | 1211 | Longworth |
| TX | Thornberry, Mac | 13 | Republican | 225-3706 | 131 | Cannon |
| TX | Turner, Jim | 2 | Democrat | 225-2401 | 208 | Cannon |
| | | | | | | |
| UT | Cannon, Chris | 3 | Republican | 225-7751 | 118 | Cannon |
| UT | Cook, Merrill | 2 | Republican | 225-3011 | 1431 | Longworth |
| UT | Hansen, James | 1 | Republican | 225-0453 | 242 | Cannon |
| | | | | | | |
| VA | Bateman, Herbert | 1 | Republican | 225-4261 | 2211 | Rayburn |
| VA | Bliley, Tom | 7 | Republican | 225-2815 | 2409 | Rayburn |
| VA | Boucher, Rick | 9 | Democrat | 225-3861 | 2329 | Rayburn |
| VA | Davis, Thomas M. | 11 | Republican | 225-1492 | 224 | Cannon |
| VA | Goode, Virgil | 5 | Democrat | 225-4711 | 1520 | Longworth |
| VA | Goodlatte, Bob | 6 | Republican | 225-5431 | 2240 | Rayburn |
| VA | Moran, James | 8 | Democrat | 225-4376 | 2239 | Rayburn |
| VA | Pickett, Owen | 2 | Democrat | 225-4215 | 2133 | Rayburn |
| VA | Scott, Robert | 3 | Democrat | 225-8351 | 2464 | Rayburn |
| VA | Sisisky, Norman | 4 | Democrat | 225-6365 | 2371 | Rayburn |
| VA | Wolf, Frank | 10 | Republican | 225-5136 | 241 | Cannon |

| State | Name | District | Party | Phone | Room | Building |
|-------|------|----------|-------|-------|------|----------|
| VT | Sanders, Bernard | A-L | Republican | 225-4115 | 2202 | Rayburn |
| WA | Baird, Brian | 3 | Democrat | 225-3536 | 1721 | Longworth |
| WA | Dicks, Norman D. | 6 | Democrat | 225-5916 | 2467 | Rayburn |
| WA | Dunn, Jennifer | 8 | Republican | 225-7761 | 432 | Cannon |
| WA | Hastings, Doc | 4 | Republican | 225-5816 | 1323 | Longworth |
| WA | Inslee, Jay | 1 | Democrat | 225-6311 | 308 | Cannon |
| WA | McDermott, Jim | 7 | Democrat | 225-3106 | 1035 | Longworth |
| WA | Metcalf, Jack | 2 | Republican | 225-2605 | 1510 | Longworth |
| WA | Nethercutt, George | 5 | Republican | 225-2006 | 1527 | Longworth |
| WA | Smith, Adam | 9 | Democrat | 225-8901 | 116 | Cannon |
| WI | Baldwin, Tammy | 2 | Democrat | 225-2906 | 1020 | Longworth |
| WI | Barrett, Thomas M. | 5 | Democrat | 225-3571 | 1214 | Longworth |
| WI | Green, Mark | 8 | Republican | 225-5665 | 1218 | Longworth |
| WI | Kind, Ron | 3 | Democrat | 225-5506 | 1713 | Longworth |
| WI | Kleczka, Gerald | 4 | Democrat | 225-4572 | 2301 | Rayburn |
| WI | Obey, David | 7 | Democrat | 225-3365 | 2314 | Rayburn |
| WI | Petri, Thomas | 6 | Republican | 225-2476 | 2462 | Rayburn |
| WI | Ryan, Paul | 1 | Republican | 225-3031 | 1217 | Longworth |
| WI | Sensenbrenner, Jim | 9 | Republican | 225-5101 | 2332 | Rayburn |
| WV | Mollohan, Alan | 1 | Democrat | 225-4172 | 2346 | Rayburn |
| WV | Rahall, Nick | 3 | Democrat | 225-3452 | 2307 | Rayburn |
| WV | Wise, Robert | 2 | Democrat | 225-2711 | 2367 | Rayburn |
| WY | Cubin, Barbara | A-L | Republican | 225-2311 | 1114 | Longworth |

## Table A.3    Senators of the 106th Congress
### (Sorted Alphabetically)

# A

Abraham, Spencer  (R - MI)
329 DIRKSEN SENATE OFFICE BUILDING
WASHINGTON DC 20510
(202) 224-4822
michigan@abraham.senate.gov

Akaka, Daniel  (D - HI)
720 HART SENATE OFFICE BUILDING
WASHINGTON DC 20510
(202) 224-6361
senator@akaka.senate.gov

Allard, Wayne  (R - CO)
513 HART SENATE OFFICE BUILDING
WASHINGTON DC 20510
(202) 224-5941
http://www.senate.gov/~allard/webform.html

Ashcroft, John  (R - MO)
316 HART SENATE OFFICE BUILDING
WASHINGTON DC 20510
(202) 224-6154
john_ashcroft@ashcroft.senate.gov

# B

Baucus, Max  (D - MT)
511 HART SENATE OFFICE BUILDING
WASHINGTON DC 20510
(202) 224-2651
http://www.senate.gov/~baucus/EmailMax.htm

Bayh, Evan  (D - IN)
B40-2 DIRKSEN SENATE OFFICE BUILDING
WASHINGTON DC 20510
(202) 224-5623
http://bayh.senate.gov/WebMail.html


Bennett, Robert  (R - UT)
431 DIRKSEN SENATE OFFICE BUILDING
WASHINGTON DC 20510
(202) 224-5444
senator@bennett.senate.gov


Biden Jr, Joseph  (D - DE)
221 RUSSELL SENATE OFFICE BUILDING
WASHINGTON DC 20510
(202) 224-5042
senator@biden.senate.gov


Bingaman, Jeff  (D - NM)
703 HART SENATE OFFICE BUILDING
WASHINGTON DC 20510
(202) 224-5521
senator_bingaman@bingaman.senate.gov


Bond, Christopher  (R - MO)
274 RUSSELL SENATE OFFICE BUILDING
WASHINGTON DC 20510
(202) 224-5721
kit_bond@bond.senate.gov


Boxer, Barbara  (D - CA)
112 HART SENATE OFFICE BUILDING
WASHINGTON DC 20510
(202) 224-3553
senator@boxer.senate.gov

Breaux, John  (D - LA)
503 HART SENATE OFFICE BUILDING
WASHINGTON DC 20510
(202) 224-4623
senator@breaux.senate.gov


Brownback, Sam  (R - KS)
303 HART SENATE OFFICE BUILDING
WASHINGTON DC 20510
(202) 224-6521
sam_brownback@brownback.senate.gov


Bryan, Richard  (D - NV)
269 RUSSELL SENATE OFFICE BUILDING
WASHINGTON DC 20510
(202) 224-6244
senator@bryan.senate.gov


Bunning, Jim  (R - KY)
818 HART SENATE OFFICE BUILDING
WASHINGTON DC 20510
(202) 224-4343
jim_bunning@bunning.senate.gov


Burns, Conrad  (R - MT)
187 DIRKSEN SENATE OFFICE BUILDING
WASHINGTON DC 20510
(202) 224-2644
conrad_burns@burns.senate.gov


Byrd, Robert  (D - WV)
311 HART SENATE OFFICE BUILDING
WASHINGTON DC 20510
(202) 224-3954
senator_byrd@byrd.senate.gov

# C

Campbell, Ben Nighthorse  (R - CO)
380 RUSSELL SENATE OFFICE BUILDING
WASHINGTON DC 20510
(202) 224-5852


Chafee, John  (R - RI)
505 DIRKSEN SENATE OFFICE BUILDING
WASHINGTON DC 20510
(202) 224-2921
senator_chafee@chafee.senate.gov


Cleland, Max  (D - GA)
461 DIRKSEN SENATE OFFICE BUILDING
WASHINGTON DC 20510
(202) 224-3521
http://www.senate.gov/~cleland/webform.html


Cochran, Thad  (R - MS)
326 RUSSELL SENATE OFFICE BUILDING
WASHINGTON DC 20510
(202) 224-5054
senator@cochran.senate.gov


Collins, Susan  (R - ME)
172 RUSSELL SENATE OFFICE BUILDING
WASHINGTON DC 20510
(202) 224-2523
senator@collins.senate.gov


Conrad, Kent  (D - ND)
530 HART SENATE OFFICE BUILDING
WASHINGTON DC 20510
(202) 224-2043
homepage@conrad.senate.gov

Coverdell, Paul  (R - GA)
200 RUSSELL SENATE OFFICE BUILDING
WASHINGTON DC 20510
(202) 224-3643
http://www.senate.gov/~coverdell/webform.html

Craig, Larry  (R - ID)
520 HART SENATE OFFICE BUILDING
WASHINGTON DC 20510
(202) 224-2752
http://www.senate.gov/~craig/webform.html

Crapo, Mike  (R - ID)
111 RUSSELL SENATE OFFICE BUILDING
WASHINGTON DC 20510
(202) 224-6142
http://www.senate.gov/~crapo/webform.html

# D

Daschle, Thomas  (D - SD)
509 HART SENATE OFFICE BUILDING
WASHINGTON DC 20510
(202) 224-2321
tom_daschle@daschle.senate.gov

DeWine, Mike  (R - OH)
140 RUSSELL SENATE OFFICE BUILDING
WASHINGTON DC 20510
(202) 224-2315
http://www.senate.gov/~dewine/request_form.html

Dodd, Christopher  (D - CT)
444 RUSSELL SENATE OFFICE BUILDING
WASHINGTON DC 20510
(202) 224-2823
sen_dodd@dodd.senate.gov

Domenici, Pete  (R - NM)
328 HART SENATE OFFICE BUILDING
WASHINGTON DC 20510
(202) 224-6621
senator_domenici@domenici.senate.gov


Dorgan, Byron  (D - ND)
713 HART SENATE OFFICE BUILDING
WASHINGTON DC 20510
(202) 224-2551
senator@dorgan.senate.gov


Durbin, Richard  (D - IL)
364 RUSSELL SENATE OFFICE BUILDING
WASHINGTON DC 20510
(202) 224-2152
dick@durbin.senate.gov


# E


Edwards, John  (D - NC)
825 HART SENATE OFFICE BUILDING
WASHINGTON DC 20510
(202) 224-3154
senator@edwards.senate.gov


Enzi, Mike  (R - WY)
290 RUSSELL SENATE OFFICE BUILDING
WASHINGTON DC 20510
(202) 224-6441
senator@enzi.senate.gov


# F


Feingold, Russell  (D - WI)
716 HART SENATE OFFICE BUILDING
WASHINGTON DC 20510
(202) 224-5323
russell_feingold@feingold.senate.gov

Feinstein, Dianne  (D - CA)
331 HART SENATE OFFICE BUILDING
WASHINGTON DC 20510
(202) 224-3841
senator@feinstein.senate.gov


Fitzgerald, Peter  (R - IL)
555 DIRKSEN SENATE OFFICE BUILDING
WASHINGTON DC 20510
(202) 224-2854
senator_fitzgerald@fitzgerald.senate.gov


Frist, William  (R - TN)
416 RUSSELL SENATE OFFICE BUILDING
WASHINGTON DC 20510
(202) 224-3344
senator_frist@frist.senate.gov


# G


Gorton, Slade  (R - WA)
730 HART SENATE OFFICE BUILDING
WASHINGTON DC 20510
(202) 224-3441
http://www.senate.gov/~gorton/webform.html


Graham, Bob  (D - FL)
524 HART SENATE OFFICE BUILDING
WASHINGTON DC 20510
(202) 224-3041
bob_graham@graham.senate.gov


Gramm, Phil  (R - TX)
370 RUSSELL SENATE OFFICE BUILDING
WASHINGTON DC 20510
(202) 224-2934
phil_gramm@gramm.senate.gov

Grams, Rod  (R - MN)
257 DIRKSEN SENATE OFFICE BUILDING
WASHINGTON DC 20510
(202) 224-3244
mail_grams@grams.senate.gov


Grassley, Chuck  (R - IA)
135 HART SENATE OFFICE BUILDING
WASHINGTON DC 20510
(202) 224-3744
chuck_grassley@grassley.senate.gov


Gregg, Judd  (R - NH)
393 RUSSELL SENATE OFFICE BUILDING
WASHINGTON DC 20510
(202) 224-3324
mailbox@gregg.senate.gov


# H


Hagel, Charles  (R - NE)
346 RUSSELL SENATE OFFICE BUILDING
WASHINGTON DC 20510
(202) 224-4224
chuck_hagel@hagel.senate.gov


Harkin, Tom  (D - IA)
731 HART SENATE OFFICE BUILDING
WASHINGTON DC 20510
(202) 224-3254
tom_harkin@harkin.senate.gov


Hatch, Orrin  (R - UT)
131 DIRKSEN SENATE OFFICE BUILDING
WASHINGTON DC 20510
(202) 224-5251
senator_hatch@hatch.senate.gov

Helms, Jesse  (R - NC)
403 DIRKSEN SENATE OFFICE BUILDING
WASHINGTON DC 20510
(202) 224-6342
http://www.senate.gov/~helms/webform.html


Hollings, Ernest  (D - SC)
125 RUSSELL SENATE OFFICE BUILDING
WASHINGTON DC 20510
(202) 224-6121
http://www.senate.gov/~hollings/webform.html


Hutchinson, Tim  (R - AR)
245 DIRKSEN SENATE OFFICE BUILDING
WASHINGTON DC 20510
(202) 224-2353
senator.hutchinson@hutchinson.senate.gov


Hutchison, Kay Bailey  (R - TX)
284 RUSSELL SENATE OFFICE BUILDING
WASHINGTON DC 20510
(202) 224-5922
senator@hutchison.senate.gov


# I


Inhofe, James  (R - OK)
453 RUSSELL SENATE OFFICE BUILDING
WASHINGTON DC 20510
(202) 224-4721
jim_inhofe@inhofe.senate.gov


Inouye, Daniel  (D - HI)
722 HART SENATE OFFICE BUILDING
WASHINGTON DC 20510
(202) 224-3934
http://www.senate.gov/~inouye/webform.html

# J

Jeffords, James  (R - VT)
728 HART SENATE OFFICE BUILDING
WASHINGTON DC 20510
(202) 224-5141
vermont@jeffords.senate.gov


Johnson, Tim  (D - SD)
502 HART SENATE OFFICE BUILDING
WASHINGTON DC 20510
(202) 224-5842
tim@johnson.senate.gov


# K

Kennedy, Edward  (D - MA)
315 RUSSELL SENATE OFFICE BUILDING
WASHINGTON DC 20510
(202) 224-4543
senator@kennedy.senate.gov


Kerrey, Robert  (D - NE)
141 HART SENATE OFFICE BUILDING
WASHINGTON DC 20510
(202) 224-6551
http://www.senate.gov/~kerrey/pages/webform.html


Kerry, John  (D - MA)
304 RUSSELL SENATE OFFICE BUILDING
WASHINGTON DC 20510
(202) 224-2742
john_kerry@kerry.senate.gov


Kohl, Herb  (D - WI)
330 HART SENATE OFFICE BUILDING
WASHINGTON DC 20510
(202) 224-5653
senator_kohl@kohl.senate.gov

Kyl, Jon  (R - AZ)
724 HART SENATE OFFICE BUILDING
WASHINGTON DC 20510
(202) 224-4521
info@kyl.senate.gov

# L

Landrieu, Mary  (D - LA)
702 HART SENATE OFFICE BUILDING
WASHINGTON DC 20510
(202) 224-5824
senator@landrieu.senate.gov

Lautenberg, Frank  (D - NJ)
506 HART SENATE OFFICE BUILDING
WASHINGTON DC 20510
(202) 224-4744
frank_lautenberg@lautenberg.senate.gov

Leahy, Patrick  (D - VT)
433 RUSSELL SENATE OFFICE BUILDING
WASHINGTON DC 20510
(202) 224-4242
senator_leahy@leahy.senate.gov

Levin, Carl  (D - MI)
459 RUSSELL SENATE OFFICE BUILDING
WASHINGTON DC 20510
(202) 224-6221
senator@levin.senate.gov

Lieberman, Joseph  (D - CT)
706 HART SENATE OFFICE BUILDING
WASHINGTON DC 20510
(202) 224-4041
senator_lieberman@lieberman.senate.gov

Lincoln, Blanche  (D - AR)
708 HART SENATE OFFICE BUILDING
WASHINGTON DC 20510
(202) 224-4843
blanche_lincoln@lincoln.senate.gov


Lott, Trent  (R - MS)
487 RUSSELL SENATE OFFICE BUILDING
WASHINGTON DC 20510
(202) 224-6253
senatorlott@lott.senate.gov


Lugar, Richard  (R - IN)
306 HART SENATE OFFICE BUILDING
WASHINGTON DC 20510
(202) 224-4814
senator_lugar@lugar.senate.gov


# M


Mack, Connie  (R - FL)
517 HART SENATE OFFICE BUILDING
WASHINGTON DC 20510
(202) 224-5274
connie@mack.senate.gov


McCain, John  (R - AZ)
241 RUSSELL SENATE OFFICE BUILDING
WASHINGTON DC 20510
(202) 224-2235
john_mccain@mccain.senate.gov


McConnell, Mitch  (R - KY)
361-A RUSSELL SENATE OFFICE BUILDING
WASHINGTON DC 20510
(202) 224-2541
senator@mcconnell.senate.gov

Mikulski, Barbara (D - MD)
709 HART SENATE OFFICE BUILDING
WASHINGTON DC 20510
(202) 224-4654
senator@mikulski.senate.gov


Moynihan, Daniel (D - NY)
464 RUSSELL SENATE OFFICE BUILDING
WASHINGTON DC 20510
(202) 224-4451
senator@dpm.senate.gov


Murkowski, Frank (R - AK)
322 HART SENATE OFFICE BUILDING
WASHINGTON DC 20510
(202) 224-6665
http://murkowski.senate.gov/webmail.html


Murray, Patty (D - WA)
173 RUSSELL SENATE OFFICE BUILDING
WASHINGTON DC 20510
(202) 224-2621
senator_murray@murray.senate.gov


# N

Nickles, Don (R - OK)
133 HART SENATE OFFICE BUILDING
WASHINGTON DC 20510
(202) 224-5754
senator@nickles.senate.gov


# R

Reed, Jack (D - RI)
320 HART SENATE OFFICE BUILDING
WASHINGTON DC 20510
(202) 224-4642
jack@reed.senate.gov

Reid, Harry  (D - NV)
528 HART SENATE OFFICE BUILDING
WASHINGTON DC 20510
(202) 224-3542
senator_reid@reid.senate.gov


Robb, Charles  (D - VA)
154 RUSSELL SENATE OFFICE BUILDING
WASHINGTON DC 20510
(202) 224-4024
senator@robb.senate.gov


Roberts, Pat  (R - KS)
302 HART SENATE OFFICE BUILDING
WASHINGTON DC 20510
(202) 224-4774
http://www.senate.gov/~roberts/email.htm


Rockefeller IV, John  (D - WV)
531 HART SENATE OFFICE BUILDING
WASHINGTON DC 20510
(202) 224-6472
senator@rockefeller.senate.gov


Roth Jr, William  (R - DE)
104 HART SENATE OFFICE BUILDING
WASHINGTON DC 20510
(202) 224-2441
comments@roth.senate.gov


# S


Santorum, Rick  (R - PA)
120 RUSSELL SENATE OFFICE BUILDING
WASHINGTON DC 20510
(202) 224-6324
http://www.senate.gov/~santorum/#email


Sarbanes, Paul  (D - MD)
309 HART SENATE OFFICE BUILDING
WASHINGTON DC 20510
(202) 224-4524
senator@sarbanes.senate.gov

Schumer, Charles (D - NY)
SH-313 DIRKSEN SENATE OFFICE BUILDING
WASHINGTON DC 20510
(202) 224-6542
senator@schumer.senate.gov

Sessions, Jeff (R - AL)
495 RUSSELL SENATE OFFICE BUILDING
WASHINGTON DC 20510
(202) 224-4124
senator@sessions.senate.gov

Shelby, Richard (R - AL)
110 HART SENATE OFFICE BUILDING
WASHINGTON DC 20510
(202) 224-5744
senator@shelby.senate.gov

Smith, Bob (I - NH)
307 DIRKSEN SENATE OFFICE BUILDING
WASHINGTON DC 20510
(202) 224-2841
opinion@smith.senate.gov

Smith, Gordon (R - OR)
404 RUSSELL SENATE OFFICE BUILDING
WASHINGTON DC 20510
(202) 224-3753
http://www.senate.gov/~gsmith/webform.html

Snowe, Olympia (R - ME)
250 RUSSELL SENATE OFFICE BUILDING
WASHINGTON DC 20510
(202) 224-5344
olympia@snowe.senate.gov

Specter, Arlen (R - PA)
711 HART SENATE OFFICE BUILDING
WASHINGTON DC 20510
(202) 224-4254
senator_specter@specter.senate.gov

Stevens, Ted  (R - AK)
522 HART SENATE OFFICE BUILDING
WASHINGTON DC 20510
(202) 224-3004
senator_stevens@stevens.senate.gov


# T


Thomas, Craig  (R - WY)
109 HART SENATE OFFICE BUILDING
WASHINGTON DC 20510
(202) 224-6441
http://www.senate.gov/~thomas/contact.html


Thompson, Fred  (R - TN)
523 DIRKSEN SENATE OFFICE BUILDING
WASHINGTON DC 20510
(202) 224-4944
senator_thompson@thompson.senate.gov


Thurmond, Strom  (R - SC)
217 RUSSELL SENATE OFFICE BUILDING
WASHINGTON DC 20510
(202) 224-5972
senator@thurmond.senate.gov


Torricelli, Robert  (D - NJ)
113 DIRKSEN SENATE OFFICE BUILDING
WASHINGTON DC 20510
(202) 224-3224
senator_torricelli@torricelli.senate.gov


# V


Voinovich, George  (R - OH)
317 HART SENATE OFFICE BUILDING
WASHINGTON DC 20510
(202) 224-3353
senator_voinovich@voinovich.senate.gov

# W

Warner, John  (R - VA)
225 RUSSELL SENATE OFFICE BUILDING
WASHINGTON DC 20510
(202) 224-2023
senator@warner.senate.gov


Wellstone, Paul  (D - MN)
136 HART SENATE OFFICE BUILDING
WASHINGTON DC 20510
(202) 224-5641
http://www.senate.gov/~wellstone/webform.html


Wyden, Ron  (D - OR)
516 HART SENATE OFFICE BUILDING
WASHINGTON DC 20510
(202) 224-5244
http://www.senate.gov/~wyden/mail.htm


Each individual member of the Senate decides how best to use Internet services. Please direct any questions about communication with your Senators to the specific office(s) in question using the following postal address format:

**For Member inquiries:**
Office of Senator (Name)
United States Senate
Washington, D.C. 20510


**For Committee inquiries:**
(Name of Committee)
United States Senate
Washington, D.C. 20510


You may also phone the United States Capitol switchboard at (202) 224-3121 and an operator will connect you directly with the Senator's Office.

Additional copies of this book may be ordered by contacting Rowland Books Unlimited, Inc. at the address listed below. Help get the word out, order one for a friend today.

**Rowland Books Unlimited Inc.**
**P.O. Box 189**
**40 S. Walnut St.**
**Chillicothe, Oh 45601**